Billy Haughton— The Master

Bill Heller

Bonus Books, Inc.
Chicago, IL

© 1999 Bonus Books, Inc.

All rights reserved

Except for appropriate use in critical reviews or works of scholarship, the reproduction or use of this work in any form or by any electronic, mechanical or other means now known or hereafter invented, including photocopying and recording, and in any information storage and retrieval system is forbidden without the written permission of the publisher.

02 01 00 99   4 3 2 1

Library of Congress Catalog Card Number: 99-23251

International Standard book Number: 1-56625-130-3

Bonus Books, Inc.
160 East Illinois Street
Chicago, Il 60611
www.bonus-books.com

Cover photo: Billy Haughton driving Green Speed by George Smallsreed. Courtesy of the United States Trotting Association

Cover design: Karen Sheets

Printed in the United States of America

Billy Haughton—
The Master

To Bill and Peter

Contents

Chapter 1	Billy's World	1
Chapter 2	The Fultonville Flash	13
Chapter 3	Dorothy	25
Chapter 4	Saratoga Nights	35
Chapter 5	The Dominator	43
Chapter 6	Bigger and Better	55
Chapter 7	The Yearling	65
Chapter 8	Another Billy	77
Chapter 9	Barefoot and Pregnant in Du Quoin	91
Chapter 10	Holley louyah—It's A Girl!	101
Chapter 11	Life in the Sixties	111
Chapter 12	Trouble At Home—And Good Times Too	121
Chapter 13	King of the Hambletonian	133
Chapter 14	A Litany of Champions	141
Chapter 15	Peter	155
Chapter 16	Burgomeister	185
Chapter 17	Cammie	193
Chapter 18	Tommy	203
Chapter 19	Nihilator—Like Father, Like Son	211
Chapter 20	Last Drive	219
Chapter 21	Carrying On	227

Acknowledgments

This is my ninth book, and I have never had so many people help me. I just hope I don't forget anyone. My apologies, if I do.

For openers, I thank Ebby Gerry and the Harness Racing Museum and Hall of Fame for the opportunity to write this book. And I thank my friend, Stan Bergstein, for contributing the foreword. If there is a more knowledgeable person on the planet about horse racing, I'd be shocked.

Dottie Haughton, a lady of unquestionable dignity, strength and class, opened up her entire life without hesitation. She not only spent countless hours doing interviews and helping me contact people, but also opened her home to me with her typical graciousness. I thank Billy Jr., Cammie, Holley, Tommy and Lynn Haughton for doing lengthy interviews. I was also a guest at Tommy and Lynn's house. All the Haughtons were consistent. None of them ducked a single question, no matter how personal or difficult.

Stanley and Jody Dancer were wonderful hosts, and I am especially grateful to Stanley for doing an interview in his Florida home with practically no warning. Trainer Doug Miller endured a lengthy interview which was extremely helpful in writing about both Billy and Peter. Jim Harrison, author of *The Care and Training of the Pacer and Trotter*, had valuable insights, as did Ben Steall, Ed Lohmeyer, Clarence Martin, Warren Harp, Clint Galbriath, Bill O'Donnell, John Campbell, Pat Troll, Buddy Gilmour and George Sholty, as well as Norma Campbell, Dr. Joe and Joan Bebry, Bert and Meg Anderson, Bill Moore, Max Hempt, Joe Caico, Murray Brown, Dick List, John "Doc" Steele, Dr. Bernard Brennan, Paul Brezinski and Bill Maddison.

My dear friend, Virginia O'Brien, the Director of the Saratoga Harness Hall of Fame, not only helped me research Billy's early career at Saratoga, but pored over dozens of yearbooks to help me. Ginny, you are the best! Also thanks to Saratoga Director of Public Relations Skip Carlson, a long-time friend, and his invaluable assistant, Millie Allen.

Another good friend and talented writer, Jay Leimbach, took considerable time to go through all of his memorabilia and send me tons of useful material on some of Billy's greatest horses as well as material about harness racing's history.

The entire publicity staff of the United States Trotting Association, especially David Carr, Ed Keys, and Ardith Carlton, were an immense help. Thanks also to Dean Hoffman and Nicole Kraft.

Gail Cunard's entire staff at the Harness Racing Museum, especially Donna Egan, helped in every way possible. So did Frank Drucker at Yonkers and Bob "Hollywood" Hayden at The Meadowlands.

My wife/editor Anna and my son, Bubba, were wonderful support as always, and I'd like to thank our dog, Belle Mont, too, for not eating the manuscript.

Joe Kyle, the excellent writer for *Horseman and*

Fair World, supplied extremely useful information about Billy's victories in the Hambletonian.

I drew a lot of material from hundreds of newspaper and magazine articles, and I gave credit to the writer every time there was a byline.

Thanks to Denise Schermerhorn at Cobleskill Ag & Tech; Marieta E. Crane of the Town of Glen and Jean O'Brien, who works in the guidance office of Fonda-Fultonville High School.

Finally, thanks to my friend/proofreader Yale Sussman.

Foreword

Every sport has its super heroes, larger-than-life figures who take on almost mythic proportions.

Baseball's Babe Ruth was the most enduring; basketball's Michael Jordan the most current.

Harness racing had its super hero, too. His name was Bill Haughton.

Putting it in a slightly different way, Bill Haughton was harness racing during the four decades in which he dominated it, as its most viable figure, most popular trainer-driver, most astonishing personality.

He first served notice of greatness in 1951, when he finished second to John Simpson in the sport's money-winning category.

The next year he burst to the top, and for eight straight years—from 1952 through 1959—he was harness racing's leading money-winning driver.

He won the title again in 1963, 1967 and 1968, giving him 12 money-winning crowns, and in all the years since only one driver—John Campbell—has been able to equal that accomplishment.

But that was only half of the story.

For six of those years—from 1953 through 1958—

Haughton also was the sport's top race-winning driver, making him the most dominant of all reinsmen in harness racing. And the most charismatic.

But it was not statistics or numbers that spelled out Bill Haughton's greatness. It was the quality of his life and his stature as a man. For harness racing, he was star, spokesman, superb Hall of Fame trainer and driver, inspiring father and family man, symbol of the very best the sport can produce. For hundreds, he was friend, adviser, counselor, authority and most of all gentleman, who, despite the busiest schedule in our business, would stop and talk—and more importantly listen—to all who needed his guidance, from wealthiest owner to newest groom.

In a day when few knights walk the earth, Bill Haughton was harness racing's shining knight, carrying our colors and his own higher and farther than all the rest with regal style and elegant grace. As much as this sport gave him, he gave back in full measure, and added to it a luster, an incandescent brightness, a wholesomeness and a symbolic presence that made all us proud just to know him, and happy just to be with him.

He had the innate and extraordinary ability to charm all in his chosen field, from the millionaires whose horses he trained and drove to the grooms who cared for them. And he was revered by all of them.

I was privileged to watch Bill Haughton, during that period, at the annual yearling auctions, and no one before or since could do what he would do. He had personally inspected almost every horse that interested him on the farms before the sale, and he not only knew their pedigrees as well as their confirmation, but could tell you about many of their forebearers that he had driven or remembered from the track.

He had marked every blemish and weakness, and every strength, in his sales catalogue, and he would buy those that he felt were priced right. That number would be in the dozens, and in reasonable price range (he was not a buyer of top priced horses, just good ones) and he did it whether he had an owner for them or not. Then, with the sale over, he would go to the bank of phones in the sales arena and call a dozen or more owners, telling each, "I bought a yearling for you today." And each would be thrilled, knowing the Master had looked after them. Not all of the yearlings became champions, of course, but many did, and the owners were happy either way to share the experience with a man whose knowledge and integrity were hallmarks of the game.

During those heady years, and ever afterwards until his tragic death in a driving accident on the final turn at Yonkers Raceway one wrenching night in 1986, he was simply Bill or Billy. There were a lot of other Williams around, but when one said "We asked Bill about that" or "Billy won another big one," everyone in harness racing knew who the speaker meant.

The double disaster that robbed harness racing of two of its most significant figures—Bill Haughton and, six years earlier, his son Peter, also in an accident, this time a car crash—deprived the sport of two of its shining stars. The fact that both are still etched deeply into the sport's psyche and sorely missed today provides insight into how important they were. The fact that a lengthy obituary and picture of Bill Haughton appeared in a major thoroughbred publication, *The Blood-Horse*, indicates the universal esteem in which he was held.

But to get a clearer picture of the height of their stature and the depth of their loss, and to learn more about the remarkable human being who rose from a rough hewn country kid who loved horses to a towering and polished figure who trained and drove and knew them better than anyone in the world, enjoy the story as told by one of America's foremost writers of horse racing.

Bill Haughton's story deserves to be told and preserved for all who knew him and for those who unfortunately never had that privilege, and no one is better equipped—or more talented—to tell it than Bill Heller.

—Stan Bergstein

Stan Bergstein is the Executive Vice-President of Harness Tracks of America

1

Billy's World

Billy Haughton had just won another stakes race, but this one was different.

It wasn't because he was back at Saratoga Harness, where he began his Hall of Fame career. It wasn't because his 3-year-old pacer, Trenton Time, had just won the $100,000 Battle of Saratoga, July 5, 1980. It was because the horse Trenton Time had beaten, the previously undefeated Niatross—widely regarded as one of the greatest pacers of all time—had lowered his left shoulder and tumbled over the hub rail after getting passed by Trenton Time in the stretch. This sent Clint Galbraith, his driver, trainer and co-owner, head first onto the infield. Niatross stood up immediately, but facing the opposite direction, with the sulky still attached. Galbraith had miraculously escaped physical injury.

All eyes were on Niatross and Galbraith. In eerie silence, Billy walked Trenton Time back from the winner's circle toward the paddock, then gave the reins to Trenton Time's trainer, Billy's son Cammie, so he could go and be with Galbraith, who was sitting by himself on the stairs outside the Racing Office. The two sat there quietly, as Billy comforted his still shaken friend.

"Billy felt almost as bad as I did because of what happened to the horse," Galbraith said 17 years later. "We were good friends. I think Billy was a friend to everybody."

Jim Harrison was the editor of the *Care and Training of the Pacer and Trotter*, a classic textbook about the sport with a different, great horseman each contributing one chapter. Except Billy Haughton, who wrote two.

"When I was doing the book, I worked with Stanley Dancer and Billy in Florida," Harrison said. "We'd work on the book several hours into the morning after they finished racing their horses that night at Pompano Park. When Stanley and I left the paddock, he would nod to people, smile and keep walking.

"You start out the paddock with Billy Haughton, and it would take an hour, because everybody would have a question for him about rigging a horse or something. I'd say, 'Come on, Bill,' and he'd say, 'Joe has a problem. Wait a minute.' I couldn't get him out of the paddock to write the damn book. Other horsemen would guard their secrets. Billy didn't care. Other horsemen didn't have time for you. Billy always had time for you. There were no bad people in Billy Haughton's world."

* * *

Dorothy Haughton, the first lady of harness racing, was fidgeting nervously. She was about to receive the "Billy Haughton Good Guy Award," named after her late husband, at the United States Harness Writers Association's Golden Anniversary Awards Dinner, April 20, 1997, at Saratoga Harness.

Her anxiety proved unfounded. She made her acceptance speech with typical class and dignity, and, afterwards, went out with her three grown sons, Billy Jr., Tommy and Cammie, to celebrate deep into the next morning.

What would harness racing be without the Haughtons? At one time, there were four of them driving and training horses together: Team Haughton, the Green Wave. For half a century, there has been at least one Haughton standing proudly on the backstretch in his green and white colors.

But the legacy Billy Haughton left wasn't limited to his brilliant horsemanship. And his impact can't be measured by the number of winners he drove and trained. "When Billy Haughton died, there was a void that could never be filled," said John Campbell, who has eclipsed Billy to become harness racing's all-time leader in earnings.

Other of Billy's records have been or may be passed, too, but they measure the accomplishments, not the man: four Hambletonians; five Little Brown Jugs, seven Messenger Stakes; 4,910 wins and $40,160,336 in earnings. The breadth of his career was such that arguably the two greatest horses he ever trained, Belle Acton and Nihilator, came 30 years apart.

At one time, Billy had a stable of some 200 horses, maybe the largest harness racing stable ever; and somehow managed to accommodate as many as 40 different owners simultaneously. "He had the most perfect personality for a horseman," Hall of Fame driver/trainer Stanley Dancer said. "He could get along with owners and people that nobody else could." Before the age of computers, Billy, with the help of his assistant for nearly 40 years, Al "Apples" Thomas, and Dottie or a bookkeeper, kept meticulous records of every horse's performance in each start, earnings, stakes payments and bills.

Billy's attention to detail was unwavering. "He

looked after every little thing," Dottie said. "He was a very conscientious horseman. He was always that way. The feeding program. The shoes. Everything. He was always in the blacksmith shop. Before he trained a horse, he'd walk to the front of the horse. He'd look up the bridle, down the bridle, down the front legs, then across the horse. Every single time. Maybe you didn't think he was looking, but he was, to make sure that the buckles were snapped in the bit, and that nothing was twisted, and that the blinders were on straight and not crooked. He'd also look at all four legs. Just a glance and he knew everything. It was amazing."

But Billy also had the wisdom to know he did not have all the answers. In a 1953 piece by New York City columnist Jimmy Powers, Billy was asked about tips for other horsemen. "The only tip I can give is that a man must expect to learn something every night. I know I do," he said. "If I live to be 100, I'll always learn something either in racing or training. Every experience and situation adds to your ability to meet new problems if you'll just let your brain work things out for you."

And if you're open to new ideas. "He would try anything with his horses, any new kind of equipment or if a guy came out selling a new product," said Eddie Lohmeyer, who drove for the Haughtons and was a close friend of Peter's. "Bill would always try something. If he tried 10 new things and one worked, he'd be one ahead of you."

Why was Billy great? He had God-given talent, a fierce love of all breeds of horses, and a constitution that defied credibility. He worked long days and frequently partied long nights, and was still the first one at the barn the next morning. "It didn't make any difference," said Ben Steall, who began his career as a groom under Billy before becoming one of his assistant trainers and a top driver himself. "He'd be .there at 5:30 the next morning. I saw him some nights not go to sleep."

Billy's close friend, driver/trainer George Sholty, said, "Billy could probably get along and work good with less sleep than anybody I knew."

Billy's lone concessions to reality were the catnaps that he'd take anywhere at anytime. He once fell asleep for a minute in the post parade at Roosevelt. "He was so tired that night," Dottie said. "He'd driven in another state that afternoon and driven all the way to Roosevelt. I saw his head drop down. The horse turned by himself and followed the other horses. And I saw him wake up. He knew it. He shook himself up. And he won the race, too. We laughed."

Billy's children weren't above having fun with their dad. "We'd be out to eat, and he'd catch a nap, maybe between an appetizer and the main course," Tommy said. "That's how tired he was. He'd eat and sleep 10 minutes and he'd be ready to roll all night. We'd always tell him that he called the waiter an asshole or something like that, and he'd say, 'No I didn't! No I didn't!' We'd always do that to him. And he'd believe it."

Other instances weren't funny. He nodded off driving a car many times, and somehow escaped injury. "He could fall asleep on a meat hook," Dottie said.

Yet Billy was so focused on his horses at the track that, after one night of racing at Yonkers, he left Dottie in the parking lot, not realizing his mistake until he got home. One morning he forgot that he had 3-year-old Billy Jr. with him at the track when he left town for another race. Apples brought Billy Jr. home. Many times, Billy forgot to eat, realizing late at night, "Jesus, I didn't even have a hot dog today."

Billy lived his life like he didn't want to miss a single second. "He never stopped," Dottie said. "No one knows how he did it. He was in perpetual motion. He was always like that. And it drove me nuts. We'd go to the farm and I'd look out the window, and there he'd go on cross country skis. I'd look out again, and there he'd go in a snowmobile. I'd look out again and he had the team hooked up to the sleigh. I used to say to him, 'Do you think you're going to die tomorrow? You've got to get all this done in two days?'"

Yet Billy always found time for others, no matter who they were. "He'd stop to talk to a groom longer than he'd talk to the president of the racetrack he'd meet in the very next step," Billy Haughton, Jr., said. "There was so much respect I had for my father as a human being."

Billy's neighbor and close friend for some 40 years. Dr. Joe Bebry, called Billy "the most unassuming individual on the face of the Earth."

Another long-time friend and client, Max Hempt of Hempt Farms, said, "Billy always had a good word for everybody, never critical. If Billy didn't like anyone, he wouldn't say it. I never heard him say a bad word about anyone."

Could Billy Haughton possibly have realized how deeply he touched so many people, even ones he hardly knew?

Whoever heard of a hometown testimonial dinner for a man who just turned 26 years old? Who gets a "Night" in his honor at a racetrack—in New York, no less, in front of thousands of adoring fans—when all the best years of his career are still ahead of him? Why would people take out ads in award journals saying "We still miss you Billy" two years after he's gone? What is it about a man that causes people to break down crying when they talk about him more than a decade after his death?

Mrs. Billy Herman, whose driver/trainer husband chose the same green and white colors to emulate Billy

Haughton, put it this way: "He seemed on a first-name basis with the world."

* * *

The letters, after Billy's death, came from everywhere, from people Dottie Haughton knew well and from people she had never met. They wrote to console her and her children, and in doing so, they painted a picture of her husband.

William E. Northern of Warsaw, Va., known as "The Coffee Man" because he operated a coffee service on the backstretch at Rosecroft Raceway in Maryland, wrote, "Very few people at the top of any profession will take time to talk to people they are not closely associated with. I think his willingness to talk to people such as myself is one of the reasons he was able to do so much for harness racing. We have lost a great leader and friend."

Mark and Joy Pierce, on vacation at the Monterey Plaza in Monterey, California, wrote "I will never forget being at Rockingham Park a few years ago with you and Bill. He was racing as a benefit for the track and the sport. Following the race I was with him as he left the jockeys [sic] room and met an elderly groom whom he had not seen in at least 15 years. Bill did not forget him and spoke with him for some time. Following that, he spent several minutes talking to a young boy and signing a program for him. In each case I could see it was a very special moment for the groom and the boy. They will never forget him and neither will we."

Mary Lou Dondarski, of Equine Portraiture in Tennent, N.J. wrote "Mr. Haughton touched so many of us and we were the better for it! From the $2 bettor to the moguls of the sport, you and he expressed a friendliness and dignity that cannot be forgotten."

Mike McCarthy wrote, "I feel compelled to write

this letter to try and explain what Billy meant to me and many people like me.

"Probably nobody will ever know all the lives that Billy Haughton touched. I'm sure you're hearing from most of those people now. I know he touched my life a great deal.

"A long, long time ago, I spent a few years working in the Haughton Stable. Billy touched me then and several times after that. No person with any sense at all would work in that stable for any length of time without beginning to feel like a real part of the "Green Wave." I know I sure did. He made you feel like a part of it. He made you feel important.

"I left your stable as a naive young man who thought he had a 'better offer.' That was and always will be the biggest mistake of my life. What better offer could a young man have than to learn from the master! Oh, to go back to those years and start all over again with the knowledge gained from our mistakes. I guess that's always been a timeless lament.

"Billy gave me so many things while I was there. Just as he gave so much to countless others. He was always so quick to share his knowledge, knowledge he worked so hard and sacrificed so much to gain. If you just paid attention around the barn, you couldn't go a day without learning something.

"The most important thing Billy shared, I think, was his love and respect for horses. This is the thing you should be most proud of. Of all the horses I saw him race, I never heard him say a bad word about any of them. No matter how bad they were. And, God knows, there were plenty of bad ones. As a matter of fact, I think I took care of most of them. He was a 'horseman' in the true sense. I really believe that, more than most people, he passed that love onto his horses through his hands. Both on the training track and on the racetrack.

He and his hands were so kind. I know that's what I loved most about him: his love and respect for the animal.

"Billy was also there for me after I left his stable. He was the determining factor in my getting appointed to officials' school and me getting employed as a paddock judge in Maryland. Billy ran a real one-sided ledger. He gave so much to so many, and had he lived to be 100 years old, we couldn't have even started to pay him back.

"I'm sure you are numb from people telling you how much he helped them. I have tears in my eyes now as I read back through this and resurrect all the memories I have of him. He was such a great man. Your lives as a family have been filled with glory for many years and equally stuffed with heart-wrenching tragedy. Please take comfort in knowing that, in whatever small way possible, many of us have shared these things with you. And then there's the memories. Who could ever forget Burgomeister at the Hambletonian? Or for me, that night at Pompano when Cammie won with Trenton Time in the stable's first start back after Peter's tragedy of so many years ago. Cammie came back to the winner's circle completely broken down and crying and so many of us stood in the grandstand crying just as hard. Be assured of this, and take the greatest amount of pride, because you are all a part. If harness racing goes on for millions of years to come, nobody will ever replace the name of Billy Haughton at the top."

Jim Harrison, in a letter to the Haughton family following Billy's death, shared a special moment he had had with Peter. "My only regret is that I never shared the story with Billy," he said. "I meant to so many times, but for one reason or another never did.

"Quite a few years ago at Delvin Miller's farm during Grand Circuit Week—perhaps the year that the

Adios statue was dedicated—Peter was sitting on a tack trunk in front of the Adios barn, and as I passed by, he asked me if I could spare a minute. I could of course, and he inquired as to whether I was familiar with the poem, 'The Dusty Old Jacket of Black.' You may have heard of it. Walter Palmer wrote it on the occasion of the death in a 1924 racing accident of another great and very popular horseman, Edward F. 'Pop' Geers. I did know the poem and darned if Peter and I didn't wind up sitting there on the trunk reciting it to one another. I never knew a young boy to get such pleasure out of a poem."

That poem was reprinted in the August, 1951, issue of *Hoof Beats*, the monthly harness racing magazine published by the United States Trotting Association. It read:

The Dusty Old Jacket Of Black

I have journeyed afar from the sunset so gold
And the mountains that reach toward the sky.
I've enjoyed the new friends and welcomed the old
As I watched the fleet trotters pass by.
But, Oh, there's a feeling I cannot explain
A sadness I cannot denote
'Way down in my heart there's a throb and a pain
For a black cap and a coat.

I see the contestants go rushing away
With a thrill that no sport can exceed.
The jackets of red and of green and of grey
Each showing in turn in the lead.
But though I may try, there's a mist in my eye
As the struggle begins at the track
For I can't find a trace of the furrowed old face
And a cap and a jacket of black.

Ah! I miss the colors that the Silent Man wore
And I miss the applause and the cheers
And his rugged old form as he turns at the score
And the honest endeavors of Geers.
The Trots have been thrilling and splendid and fast
But alas! There is something they Lack
For I miss the old master, the one who has passed
And his dusty old jacket of black.

—Walter Palmer

Harrison's letter continued, "Peter asked me about the meaning of the word 'endeavors.' I explained to him that Geers was known as a man of tremendous honesty and integrity who tried desperately to win every heat he ever raced and that 'endeavors' was used in the context of his life's work as an honest and ever-trying horseman. I asked him if he knew what I was trying to convey about Geers.

"I figure Peter was in the 10–12 age. His little face lit up like a 10-candle window at Christmas and he said, 'Oh, yes. I know. It means he was just like my dad.'"

2

The Fultonville Flash

Like his son Billy, who would dominate harness racing, William Francis Haughton dreamed of becoming a jockey, and actually rode thoroughbreds at county fairs. But his dreams evaporated when his father, an Irish contractor in Hornell, New York, learned that a rider at a nearby racetrack had been killed in an accident. He ordered his son to stop riding.

Regardless, William envisioned a career working with horses by becoming a veterinarian, and he took night school classes to do so. Then reality intruded. His family needed money. He found a job in a silk mill and later opened his own leather goods manufacturing plant in Fultonville, a village 40 miles west of Albany along the Mohawk River. He later owned a few horses and a beloved broodmare he once described as "almost part of the family." The broodmare produced several colts the Haughtons raised.

William's brother Cameron was a priest who died from a heart attack at the alter in church one Christmas Eve. Dottie and Billy would name one of their sons after him.

Billy's mother, Edith Greene, had horses in her background. Her brother traded carriage and saddle horses. But she didn't share a love of horses when, as a widow, she married William Francis Haughton, July 14, 1922.

William was intent on exposing his only child to horses, and he wasted little time doing so after William Robert Haughton's birth on Nov. 2, 1923, in Gloversville, site of the nearest hospital to Fultonville.

When Billy was one-year-old, his father took him to a cousin's farm in Cherry Valley near Utica, and gave him his first ride on a horse. A picture published with a story by Jim Harrison in the January 1954, edition of *Hoof Beats*, shows William sitting on a horse while cradling infant Billy.

Three years later, Billy and his dad were riding in a buggy when an automobile spooked their horse, who ran away. William eventually pulled the horse up, but Billy must have enjoyed that ride. He would spend most of the rest of his life driving horses.

Billy Haughton was raised in a large, three-story, green and cream Victorian house on River Street in Fultonvile flush on the banks of the Mohawk River and directly across from the Fonda Fairgrounds, accessible by a bridge over the river a stone's throw from his house. Their furniture was heavy oak Victorian, with adornments such as large lion's claws, in a living room featuring wallpaper with giant maroon feathers on a cream colored background. The pantry was a whole room full of pots and pans and dishes. There was an attic and a little garden outside.

William was a devout Catholic who enjoyed cigars and sherry, neither of which were condoned by his strict wife. Years later, Billy's dad would revel in solo visits to his son's house, where he was allowed to enjoy both pleasures. "Bill's mother ran the show," Dottie

Haughton said. "She was very dominating. Nobody had any choices."

That manifested itself at a young age with Billy, who was forced by his mother to take violin lessons.

"He used to take his violin to school in a paper sack so the kids wouldn't tease him," Dottie said. "He hated it. Hated it. That's what he told me. Real men don't play violins in Fultonville. Saxophone is one thing; a set of drums is another, but a violin?"

Billy Haughton, though, was all boy. He'd swallow worms and wrap snakes around his neck to scare girls. But, even before he was six years old, he found his greatest pleasure with horses. And he could see horses, thoroughbreds and standardbreds, race right across the river at the Fonda Fair. His dad would take him. They stayed after the races once or twice, and Billy saw the unerring work ethic of the grooms first-hand. Perhaps that's why, years later, he would always treat his own grooms with respect and appreciation.

Billy was five when his dad bought him a spotted black and white Shetland pony, Betty, and soon Billy was making pilgrimages to the Fair on her. Sometimes, he'd dress up as a cowboy. Then, at the age of 8, he hatched a better idea.

Betty had come equipped with a basket cart, and Billy decided to modify it. First, he ripped out the side seats in the cart, telling himself they weren't very "racy." They were replaced by a plain board laid over the top of the basket which Billy could sit on.

But where would he put his feet?

Billy went into his mother's pantry and removed a pair of shelf brackets, without telling her of course. Billy fastened the brackets, which were built at right angles, to the open front ends of the basket cart, effectively making them stirrups. He had literally transformed the cart into a sulky, which then allowed him to drive Betty up and down the streets of Fultonville.

After each foray, he would mimic the grooms he had studied by cooling Betty out. His mother, concerned Billy would use new sheets and fresh towels for horse blankets, supplied him with old rags and a couple of worn out sheets.

His father was certainly impressed, and always supportive. His mother, though, was anything but happy about Billy's obsession with horses. But, by the time Billy was in high school, it was inevitable, and eventually, she did come around.

Billy's dad bought him a bigger pony, Gypsy, and a second hand regulation sulky when Billy was nine or 10. Billy's pilgrimages to the fairgrounds became daily.

Around a silent, barren track after the Fair had left town, Billy drove Gypsy in race after race. Was it any different from an adolescent Michael Jordan shooting baskets by himself night after night in his driveway?

When the Fair returned the next summer, Billy began showing up at the blacksmith's shop every morning at 6 to learn about shoeing. Some days, he'd stay at the Fair until after dark, his unannounced apprenticeship interrupted only by an hour for lunch, one long day after another.

"Billy always had a pony that he kept right there in Fultonville in a little stall on the side of his garage," his boyhood and life-long friend Bill Moore said. "He used to ride the pony over to the Fairgrounds in the fall all the time. He used to try to get over there about every night."

Moore remembered Billy coming home on his pony late one night from the Fairgrounds. "He was in a hurry to get home," Moore said. "The pony slipped. He was going so fast with him that the pony's feet went out from under him. Bill was picking cobblestone out of his arse for quite a while."

Billy's daily excursions didn't sit well with his mother, who heard from friends, "You've got to keep that boy away from the Fairgrounds. You know there's a lot of people that drink over there." And, Moore said, they did.

Billy never got lost in alcohol more than any other teen-age boy does. Every once in a while, Bill Moore, who was tall for his age, Billy and maybe another pal would chip in their money, journey to Fonda, across the river from Fultonville, and buy a jug of Muscatelle wine they'd split.

Moore spent a lot more time with Billy ice skating every winter near the dairy farm where Moore lived on Russell Road.

Billy was close to his dad, and they wouldn't miss a Sunday in church. "One thing that helped Bill a lot was the undying faith that his father had in him that he would succeed," Moore said. "I think they were a very close family."

Billy's parents instilled in him a love of life, a personal code of honor, a willingness to help others and a tireless work ethic.

In the spring of 1938, Billy caught a break when Charlie Morril and his wife let Billy watch their daily preparations with the 10-horse stable they shipped to the Fairgrounds. One day they asked him if he'd like to rub a couple horses for experience. Billy leaped at the offer and soon was mucking out stalls, cooling out horses by walking them dozens of miles after workouts and races, and doing all of the thankless tasks a groom is asked to do—pro bono. His reward? The Morrils let him jog horses.

That summer, Billy jogged a trotter named Sir Dillon Volo in 2:20. When he learned that Sir Dillon Volo was for sale for $125, he tried to get his dad to buy the horse. His dad didn't have that amount of discretionary income, and Billy wisely didn't push for it.

Billy worked the summer of '38 on a farm, and returned to the Fairgrounds to work for the Morrils the next spring. One of their horses was a chestnut, free-legged pacer named Nailor, a son of Highland Scot owned by Dr. William F. Wyllie of nearby Gloversville.

Wyllie asked Billy if he'd like to train Nailor, and then some two weeks later sent him a second horse to train, Peter Voletta. Billy, working before and after school, was groom and trainer for both horses and was paid $7 a week. "I paid $3 for food, had $2 for pocket money and put the other $2 in the bank," Billy said. Billy learned a lot about splints by treating Peter Voletta, who had several.

When school ended, Wyllie asked Billy to take the horses on the New York State fair circuit with the stipulation that Wyllie would show up on race day and drive. At the age of 16, Billy was literally on his own.

"My first stop was at Altamont," Billy said years later. "I went over there with Nailor, and I was the only man on the grounds, and Nailor the only horse. It was the first time I'd been away from home and I was a little bit scared and frightened. But I threw myself down in the straw in the stall next to Nailor—I didn't have any cot—and went to sleep thinking how lucky I was."

Wyllie could never have imagined how lucky he was.

That summer, Billy paid close attention to Pete Losee, a top driver he tried to emulate.

Billy also rode thoroughbreds in several races at the Fonda Fair without winning one. When a horse in a race he was in broke his leg and had to be destroyed, Billy, who was getting too big to be a jockey anyway, soured on thoroughbreds. "They had the worst old horses in the world," Billy said in a TV interview. "And they had three harness races of three heats each. So there'd be nine heats of harness racing and then two thoroughbred races. And the purses were $75 up to $150. I really wanted to be a jockey, but I was too large. I had no chance."

So he turned his attention completely to harness racing.

By then, he'd reached a crossroads.

Harness racing was what he wanted, but it wasn't a last resort for him. Billy was mostly an A student in school and a good athlete, who played basketball for his high school team. He would choose his famous green and white colors to match his high school's and those of Vic Fleming, a driver Billy called "one of my idols as a kid."

But he'd gotten in the habit of skipping school to take care of his horses, and his mother and the high school principal tried to talk him into taking another direction. "The principal was a nice guy, but he had the wrong idea about horses," Billy said, "He thought I was wasting my time. So did my mom. The principal stressed that I ought to go out for baseball and basketball and other sports, in which I had shown some ability, but I finally managed to talk them down. That was the last time my mom tried to make me give up the game. I guess she sort of figured that I was in it for keeps. She was really fine about it after that."

In 1940, at the age of 16, Billy picked up two more horses, one for Wilbur Hall and a horse named Helen C. Billy's pay moved up to $15 a week.

Billy was on the fair circuit with the Wyllie stock in 1941, when, at the Vernon Fairgrounds (a half-mile predecessor to Vernon Downs in central New York State), Wyllie failed to show up to drive Nailor. Billy frantically searched the backstretch and finally found a last second substitute.

Later in the week, it happened again.

"The time came for a race and Dr. Wyllie had not shown up to drive his horse," Billy recounted. "Old Gil Whitmore was the presiding judge. I told him Dr. Wyllie was not available.

"'Give me $5 and drive him yourself,' Whitmore told me. The $5 was for my license to drive. I didn't have any colors and Doc was a six-footer. We managed to pin his sleeves up and take a tuck in the hat, and there I went in my first race.

"There were 14 or so in the field, and I scored in the third tier. We didn't get away until about the eighth score and I rushed out along the rail and found myself trailing the pole horse.

"I remember that I heard a horse coming as we went down the backside the first time and I pulled out. The fellow I moved in front of shouted something about 'those crazy kids,' but I didn't pay much attention. I was on top.

"Old Nailor held his own until they passed the three-quarter pole, and then, as I heard the others rushing up, I got a little scared and gave him his head. He made a big fat break and I finished fifth. I thought I had the heat won."

Dr. Wyllie arrived in time to drive Nailor to a third place finish in the second heat. That fall, Nailor bowed a tendon and was sold as a saddle horse. Billy didn't get another drive until the following year.

In 1941, Billy graduated high school and enrolled at Cobleskill State Agricultural College (now Ag & Tech), where he studied animal husbandry and graduated, May 20, 1943. He also landed a job at Saratoga Raceway in the summer of '42 as second trainer for Billy Muckle.

"Billy Muckle was a fine horseman," Billy said. "He never quite got to the Grand Circuit, but he was one of the old time drivers I learned the most from. It was more his management of his affairs that caused him not to be as great as he should have been. Because he really had an awful lot of ability with a horse. I saw him take horses from Vic Fleming and some other top Grand Circuit men, who didn't do well for them, and he did great with them. He was really a great horseman."

In the summer of '42, Billy trained Prologue Mac, a bad-acting gelding pacer owned by Harold Johannes of Johnstown, and Josedale Arrow for $30 a week. When Muckle got hurt that year, Billy took over and handled the whole stable for a while.

The stable was split up in the fall of 1942, and Billy took his horses to the fairs. At the Fonda Fair, Billy won his first race with Hollywood Arrow. From Fonda, the fair circuit moved on to Nassau, where Billy was involved in his first accident when he was thrown from the sulky. He escaped serious injury, though horses did roll over him.

Billy devoted full time to college in 1943, and didn't touch a horse. He tried enlisting in the Army, but was turned down because of a knee injury he'd suffered at Saratoga.

In 1944, 1945 and 1946, Billy split time training and working on a neighboring farm. His early record is hard to determine exactly because he was listed as Houghton as late as 1946.

On September 19, 1944, Billy won three heats of a $450 pace at Cobleskill with Prologue Mac in times of 2:16¾, 2:16¾ and 2:17½. Billy's name, however, was misspelled as `Houghton' in a summary of the race which appeared in the *Harness Horse* magazine. Two days later, he got his first 2:10 victory—a speed barrier then—behind Mighty Worthy, who won three heats of a $400 pace in 2:10, 2:08¼ and 2:09½. His name again was listed as Houghton.

Billy won four races at Saratoga with one second

and two thirds in 1944. On July 5, 1944, Haughton won a race with Josedale Lynn, a trotter owned by W. Cassaco of Gloversville, in 2:12½. On October 9, 1944, Billy drove Mighty Worthy to a fourth and a win in two heats of a $600 pace in times of 2:12 and 2:11.

In 1945 at Saratoga, he won two heats of a $300 pace with Hal Mix in 2:12 and 2:12¾. Then on July 2, he finished third with Desperado to Ringmaster in 2:12¾. His name, however, appeared in the following issue of Harness Horse spelled correctly. He won a $300 and $400 trot behind Desperado on July 12 and 18 in 2:12¾ and 2:22, respectively. On August 22nd, he won a $350 pace with Prologue Mac in 2:13.

There weren't many other highlights. Billy was anything but an immediate star driver and trainer. Rather he spent years learning everything he could about the game he loved so much, a rite of passage he administered unerringly to each of his sons who followed him into harness racing. There was no free ride to the top because their dad was Billy Haughton. Each of his sons spent three to four years learning the business from the absolute bottom up. If Billy had his way, it would be a regimen every would-be driver would follow. "When I tell people 'bottom,' I mean the very bottom," Billy said. "I mean learning to be a driver by walking hot horses after midnight, mucking out dirty stalls before dawn and performing a thousand and one other tedious and time-consuming tasks. I do not know a prominent driver who was not an expert with a rub rag long before he learned how to handle a whip. In my own organization, I make it a practice to promote from within, and such drivers as Al "Apples" Thomas, Clarence Martin, Irvin Roberts and Bill Vaughan were all good grooms long before they became good drivers. It's interesting, too, to observe that top trainers and drivers feel the same way when their own sons are involved. Johnny

Simpson, Jr., Warren Cameron and John Patterson, Jr.—in each case the father insisted that the son serve a lengthy apprenticeships in the shed row before being permitted to hold a line over a horse in a race. The late Fred Egan, one of the greatest horsemen who ever lived, told me he began working with horses when he was nine years old, but that he never had horses of his own until he was almost 35. He said it was the best thing that ever happened to him, because when he did start he knew what the business was all about."

Billy would, too. "He always knew what he was doing," said Pat Troll, who groomed for Billy and remains a groom for Tommy. "And he was nice to the caretakers."

One of Billy's early breaks was getting to know Dodger Griffith, a popular, older man who owned a little bar in a hotel on River Street in Fonda and trained harness horses at the Fonda Fairgrounds. "What really got Bill started was that Dodger Griffith had three or four horses he was training, and Dutch Huff, Dodger's trainer, went on a pretty good drunk," Moore said. "And I remember Bill telling me that Dodger was going to Saratoga and he said to Bill, 'Why don't we go over together? Let's put them all together and you train my horses.' That's what really got Bill started."

In 1946, Billy's stable increased to five. Joining Prologue Mac were Widow's Mite, a bay mare pacer owned by Dick "Listy" List of Amsterdam and Bill Ryan, Jr.; Connie's Pride, a 3-year-old pacing filly owned by Dr. William "Doc" Hesek of Johnstown; Thin Dime, a bay horse owned by Anthony Pluso and Joe DeSantis of Fonda, and Pat Dillon, whom Billy owned with Cliff Stanton.

Through early August 1946, only one of the five, Prologue Mac, showed a win at Saratoga. He'd won one of five starts. At that time, Widow's Mite was zero-for-six; Connie's Pride zero-for-four and Thin Dime zero-for-six. Neither Widow's Mite nor Connie Pride had finished in the money. Thin Dime was second once.

Billy waited until 1947 to open a public stable and was promptly the leading driver at the Saratoga fall meet. "I went to Saratoga with eight horses," he said. "The best ones could go 2:08. The others couldn't go in 2:12. And I got lucky and started winning some races."

He never stopped.

3

Dorothy

The first thing Dorothy Bischoff noticed about Billy Haughton was his hands. "He had strong hands, but he didn't have large hands," Dottie said.

Long before she held them, she held the reins of horses, thanks to her dad, Whitney, who supplemented an office job in Chappaqua, Westchester County, New York, by operating a riding stable, training horses and serving as a timer at nearby Yonkers Raceway. "The horsemanship, the love of animals, all came from him," Dottie said.

Whitney Bischoff's ancestors were German. His wife, Esther Linder's, roots were Swedish.

Dottie's maternal grandfather, Theodore Linder, was the head toolmaker at the General Electric plant in Dalton, Massachusetts. He helped develop the first plastic casing for high heels. Her grandmother, Bessie, kept a vegetable garden on their farm in Dalton, where they also kept cows. Both lived into their 90s. "My grandparents were wonderful," Dottie said. "I spent a lot of my childhood with them. Then they moved to Orlando, so I got to see them very often when Bill trained there at Ben White Raceway."

Esther was born in Bridgeport, Conn. When she was a baby, her family moved to Sweden, and when she was five, they moved back to the United States. She had one brother, Art. Esther came to Chappaqua as a visiting nurse, and met Whitney. They were married in 1925 in Chappaqua, where Esther would work many more years as a registered nurse.

Dottie was born during a blizzard Dec. 9, 1931, in nearby Mount Kisco. She had her first pony, Dear One, when she was 2½ years old, a gift from Ludwig Cramer, who stabled horses with Dottie's father. By the age of three years and eight months, Dottie, who was frequently called "Doll," was too small to sit in a jog cart. So she jogged her pony by standing up in a basket cart in the manner of a Roman gladiator in a chariot race. She used to pretend beet juice was liniment and use it on her dad's horses' legs underneath bandages. When the horse's bandages came out pink, it wasn't hard figuring out the culprit.

At the age of nine, she drove a horse in 2:10 on a half mile track. "That was a big accomplishment," she said. "That was good for any age. I trained horses. I rode them in shows. I rode jumpers. I really, really loved it."

Her dad, whom Dottie described as a good man with a bit of a temper, worked in the Town of Mt. Pleasant Comptroller's Office and then with the Department of Highways. He took Dottie with him when he went to Goshen, New York, former home of the Hambletonian from 1930–1942 and 1944–1956 and still the site of the Harness Racing Museum and Hall of Fame. He also took her to fairs when he raced at Orangeburg and Rhinebeck.

"We always went to the Hambletonian," Dottie said. "I went to every Hambletonian from 1931 until World

War II. One year (1935), Jimmy Wingfield, the groom, was cooling out Greyhound after he won. My father knew Jimmy and asked me if I wanted to sit on Greyhound's back. I wasn't even four years old."

Regardless, she said yes. "I also got a lock of hair from his mane and tail, but it got lost," Dottie said. "Many, many years later, I met Jimmy and he remembered that."

At Goshen Dottie got to sit in a jog cart with either of two talented drivers: Walter Cox and Henry Thomas. "I can remember when I was maybe 10, and I saw Dick Thomas, Henry Thomas' son," Dottie said. "He was a little older than I, and I made up my mind when I grew up I was going to marry Dick Thomas. We laugh about that all the time."

Dick Thomas followed his father into harness racing. Dottie would spend her life in harness racing, too.

Dottie, just like Billy Haughton, was an only child. But Dottie was also the only grandchild on both sides of her family, which meant she had no cousins.

Dottie's parents, who later divorced after Dottie married Billy, struggled through the Depression. "It was hard for everyone," Dottie said.

Like everyone else, they made do. It didn't rob them of special moments. One year on Christmas Eve, when Dottie was just old enough to question the veracity of Santa Claus, her dad sneaked up on the roof of their house and made footprints in the snow there, attributing them, of course, to reindeer. "It was so neat," Dottie said. "That made my mind up that there was a Santa."

Dottie has other fond Christmas memories of big parties thrown by her Aunt Dot, whom she's named after, and her Uncle Bert, who was a bank president in Pleasantville. "They had no children, and I was the apple of their eye," Dottie said. "Aunt Dot gave me my love of flowers. She taught me how to garden. And she taught me how to cook. She was a wonderful cook. She was very creative."

Every Memorial Day, the family went to the cemetery in Mount Kisco, where Dottie would pick lilacs and place them at the graves of her ancestors. One of them, her great, great uncle Abe Blauvelt, was an officer for the Union in the Civil War. There's a town near Nyack, New York, named for the Blauvelt family.

Other holidays were special for different reasons. The Fourth of July was traditionally spent at a picnic near Tarrytown, where the Bischoffs could watch a fireworks show over the Hudson River.

Dottie described her mom, who died at the age of 98 in August 1996, as a sweetheart. "Everybody adored her," Dottie said. "I loved her so much. I was always close to her. She was very sweet, but she was very old-fashioned. She didn't really understand when the boys started calling."

By then, Dottie's tomboyishness had grown into athleticism. She played basketball and field hockey and was so adept at lacrosse that she wound up teaching it as an instructor in a camp for two years in Vermont.

Dottie was a striking beauty, once called in *Sports Illustrated* as "perhaps the prettiest wife of a sports star in the country."

She had a "very big crush" on a boy, Roy Schaub, who would tempt fate by tossing pebbles at Dottie's window as late as 9:30 at night, so she'd come out on her little balcony. And she did. "I'd come out and pray that my mother didn't discover that," she said.

Dottie has always had a bit of the devil in her. One night in high school, Dottie sneaked outside, and, with a friend, Joyce Macklin, pushed Dottie's parents' car down the driveway to the road. They then drove to the soda shop in neighboring Pleasantville. Neither one had a driver's license. "Are you kidding? We thought we were hot stuff!,'' Dottie said. "We were gone about an hour, an hour and a half. They never found out."

Going to the Junior Prom was another matter. "My parents were very strict," Dottie said. "The boy who was taking me was in our living room, and they were discussing whether or not I could go in front of the boy. I was mortified. When I got home, we were lingering at the door. My mother started flashing the porch light on and off. I was so embarrassed, I thought I was going to die." The boy, Rusty Allen, was an Eagle Scout who used to take Dottie hunting and showed her how to use a shotgun. They are still friends today.

But the constant in Dottie's life was equine. "I always had a horse," she said.

The worst trouble Dottie got into during high school was when she rode her palomino, Suzy, around the Horace Greeley High School running track. "I didn't do it to wreck the track," she said. "A racetrack was a racetrack to me." Not to the principal, who called her in. "He said never do it again," she said. "I was terribly embarrassed."

Throughout her life, to this very day, she finds a pleasure in riding a horse that she can find nowhere else. "It's the greatest thing to ride," she said. "It still is. It's one of the best pleasures. You don't think of anything else in the world. You listen to the birds while you're in the woods. You talk to the horse. Communication with your horse is just incredible."

In less than a year, between her 12th and 13th birthdays, she experienced lows and highs with horses which are still vivid memories. When she was 12, she competed in a show at Lawrence Farms in Mount Kisco. The horse she was riding propped (stopped abruptly) to avoid jumping over a wooden barrier. "I went over his head and put my hands down to stop the fall and broke both my wrists," Dottie said. "I had to have casts on both of them. I was 12. It was terrible for a kid."

If her mother had her way, Dottie would never have climbed on a horse again. "She didn't want me to ride any more, but my dad did," Dottie said. "He said, 'You fall off, you get right back on.'"

Dottie did, without fear. "I've never been afraid of horses," she said. "Never."

The wrists healed quickly, and the following year, she enjoyed the thrill of a lifetime when her riding instructor in nearby Mamaroneck, Gordon Wright, entered Dottie in a show in Madison Square Garden. "He thought I was good enough," Dottie said. "I was scared, but I got a ribbon. I think I was second. There were about 20 kids in that class that day. My parents were there and my Aunt Dot and Uncle Bert."

She remembers riding with her father during World War II to sell some of their horses in Mount Kisco. "Because of gas rationing, a lot of people bought and drove horses," she said. My father sold quite a few horses that way. I can remember riding all the way to Mount Kisco. I'd just get on my horse and ride miles and miles and miles after school. I was always with horses."

She thought she could preserve that by becoming a veterinarian when she graduated high school. "That's what I really wanted to do," Dottie said. "But my mother talked me out of it."

Instead, she attended Manhattan Medical School, studying lab work and X-rays. "I really liked it, especially X-Rays," she said. She took a job at Northern Westchester Hospital in Mount Kisco on the day she graduated.

After dating him for two years, she became engaged to Malcomb "Pally" Enright from nearby Brewster, N.Y., who was in the Air Force and stationed in Texas. Her friends threw her a shower, and her future seemed set.

And then her dad invited Billy Haughton, a driver at

Yonkers who was already one of the top drivers in the country, home to have supper with the family one fall night in 1951.

"It wasn't meant to be a date," Dottie insists 48 years later. "It was just that he was such a nice person, and my dad invited him over to dinner. And he thought maybe I would like to meet Billy Haughton, the up and coming star at Yonkers, where my dad worked. With my horse background, that was certainly the reason. I know there was no other reason. He didn't fix me up on a date."

So, because it wasn't a date, after dinner, Dottie got into her own car to go back to the hospital, where she was living in a dorm, drove a couple blocks and noticed the gas tank was on "E." So she returned home, where Billy offered to drive her back.

On the way, Billy asked Dottie when her next day off was. She said Thursday, which was Columbus Day. Billy suggested she come down to Yonkers and he'd give her a horse to jog. Dottie thought that was great. "He had been going with a girl for eight years, Betty Olmstead, and she didn't care for horses at all," Dottie said.

But when Dottie showed up at the Haughton barn that morning, Billy was up on the track, training one of his horses. "He had told the boys that he had invited a girl down and to give me a really quiet, nice horse," Dottie said. "With him not there, they probably looked at each other and winked and gave me this horse that's afraid of everything. It was an October morning with the wind and tickets flying all around. When I got up on the racetrack and started him in front of the grandstand, he took off with me. And I mean took off."

Dottie did the only thing she could think of, steering the horse straight toward a fence. "When he got to the fence, he stopped himself," Dottie said. "Bill looked over and saw this and said, 'Oh, my God,' and came running over. He thought that was a great move. So right then, we were soulmates."

Then they had lunch at Howard Johnson's on Central Avenue in Yonkers. Billy asked Dottie if she wanted to go to a movie. "So I said, 'I guess so,' not thinking I was doing anything wrong," she said.

That night, after the movie, Billy, then 27, told 19-year-old Dottie that he'd soon be heading to Florida for the winter. Racetracks then, especially in the Northeast, weren't open 365 days a year and trainers would actually give their entire stable time off in a warm climate to prepare for a new season.

"He said, 'I really need someone to help me with the books,'" Dottie said. "And it ended up, 'How 'bout we get married?'"

Dottie was shocked. "'I can't believe you even said that,'" she replied. "'I'm engaged to someone else.' He didn't know that.

"And then he asked me all kinds of questions. And then he called the next day and the day after."

That Saturday night, Dottie went to the races at Yonkers with her mother. Bill was driving a horse that Dottie and her father had raised before selling him as a 2-year-old. The horse's name in the program was High Sir. "When I had him, his name was Melody," Dottie said. "It was just such a funny thing that none of us knew Bill when I raised this little baby foal, and here he ends up in Bill's stable."

Billy's persistence with Dottie paid off. They had lunch again. Dottie knew her life was changing.

Dottie called her fiance to break the bad news: "I called Texas and said, 'Pally, I'm sorry.' It was terrible, but I had made up my mind I was not going to write a letter to tell him. I was going to call. He was all right. He kept track of Bill's career. I heard that from friends."

The next week, Dottie told Bill she would marry

him. "My parents were absolutely delighted, because they adored him," Dottie said. "I knew it was the right thing. I really did."

On her wedding night, though, she had a single doubt: "I was just wondering the night we got married, was it really Bill I loved or the horses? Isn't that terrible? It happened so fast. Was it the horses that really got into my heart, or did I really love him? It was both. Absolutely. It was a great combination."

4

Saratoga Nights

Early in his career, Billy demonstrated a light touch with horses, the ability to gently communicate from the reins held in his hand to the bit in the horse's mouth. In *The Care and Training of the Trotter and Pacer*, published by the United States Trotting Association and used virtually as a textbook in the industry, Billy said: "In harness racing, natural ability in driving a horse can be translated primarily into 'light hands,' a talent peculiar to our sport. I believe great drivers are born and not made and that 'light hands' constitute the basic requirement. This has absolutely nothing to do with how big a man is or how much he weighs. I know little men who are heavy-handed and who will never make it to the top although they possess almost all the other skills. And I know one of the lightest touches of all belongs to Frank Safford, one of the heaviest men in our sport.

"To put it simply, heavy-handed men make hard-mouthed horses and horses with hard mouths cannot and do not respond quickly enough to the demands their drivers make on them in a race. Such a man driving such a horse can lose a fraction of a second of vital time three or four times in a race. When you figure that a full second corresponds roughly to five lengths in a horse race, and that almost half of all races contested are won or lost by a length or less, you can see how important it is to have light hands.

"I am too young to have seen him drive, but they tell me that Thomas W. Murphy had perhaps the lightest set of hands of them all, and that this accounted in large measure for his fantastic success. I can believe this because I know what a difference a light set of hands makes.

"One of the greatest I saw with light hands was the late Vic Fleming. He was in his prime when I was just a boy. I can see him yet racing at those upper New York State tracks in the late '30s, literally driving a horse with two fingers of each hand while they responded almost magically to his feather touch."

Billy got a great thrill when Thomas W. Murphy, who was known as "Wizard of the Reins," came to Saratoga 22 years after he retired to present a trophy at Saratoga to Albert K. Braim's Direct Vic after Billy drove him to a nose, wire-to-wire victory in 2:09⅕ over Cyril Hanover in the $2,000 Dan Patch Pace before a crowd of 5,417. Haughton, who won two earlier races that night, caught the catch drive after Direct Vic's regular driver, Aubrey Rodney, became ill. Billy later trained Laverne Hanover, the 1969 Little Brown Jug winner, for Tom Murphy, Thomas W. Murphy's son.

But it was Billy's drives behind Joe C. Abbe, a frequent winner at Saratoga, that impressed Dr. I. Ben "Doc" Ruben, a dentist in Charlton, in New York's Mohawk Valley, so much that he gave Billy $5,000 and told him to go to the 1947 Harrisburg (Pa.) Sale and buy a yearling. Billy bought one for $4,200 at the sale, and two years later, as a 3-year-old, Ankaway won nine of 16 starts at Saratoga and finished third in the second elimination—despite racing in a sulky with a damaged tire—and sixth in the final of the 1949 Little Brown Jug. Ankaway's accomplishments gave Billy instant credibility in selecting yearlings at sales, a skill he would hone his entire life as he became renown for judging yearlings. He literally wrote the book about selecting yearlings—well, the chapter of a book—in *The Care and Training of the Trotter and the Pacer*, as well as the chapter about driving.

By the end of 1947, Billy had several offers. He took a private job with Denny Woods and George Quiri of Canton and Amsterdam, N.Y. At that same Harrisburg Sale that year, they purchased six head for $5,000.

"Billy was a dynamic young man who attracted people because he was so successful," said veterinarian John "Doc" Steele, who is in his 53rd year in the business, though he now deals with show horses. Steele was a young veterinarian at Saratoga in the late '40s, and became Billy's vet, close friend, and, briefly, roommate. "In 1948, I was married, and we bought a house in Saratoga Springs," Steele said. "We had an extra room and Billy lived with us for one summer. It was a very close relationship. He was a very flamboyant young man who had talent to burn. He loved going out and having fun, but he was also a person who was first at the barn the next morning. I traveled with him some at night, and I couldn't keep up with him. He'd go on and I'd go to bed. Then he'd beat me to the barn in the morning."

Billy won a trotting race on opening night at Saratoga Harness in 1948 on Woods and Quiri's Willglow Jr. By then, he was also driving at Roosevelt Raceway, which opened on Long Island Sept. 2, 1940, and had quickly become one of the nation's premier tracks. Billy made his Roosevelt debut, Friday, May 21, 1948, driving Woods and Quiri's Fall Brook in the second race and finishing eighth. He was less than an immediate sensation on Long Island. Driving that spring meeting, run by the Old County Trotting Association, he had 23 drives with only two seconds and three thirds to show for it. That summer, he returned to Saratoga, before giving Roosevelt another shot.

On Friday, Oct. 1, 1948, in his 25th start at Roosevelt, he won his first race there in 2:07 behind Dewey Abbe, an aged bay gelding owned by O.K. Spur of Cambridge, N.Y., who returned $6.70 as the favorite.

At the end of '48, Woods and Quiri dissolved their partnership for personal reasons. Billy spent that winter in Aiken, South Carolina, with just six horses before returning to New York and opening a public stable again. He'd winter his horses in Aiken for three years before relocating his winter operations to Orlando, Florida.

"You can't beat Aiken either way," he explained to esteemed New York harness writer Lew Barasch, who would become Director of Public Relations for Roosevelt Raceway. "By the time we hit the northern climate, the weather has turned close to the temperature we were accustomed to down in Aiken. That means that our stock doesn't suffer from a wide difference in weather conditions. There'll be no horses going unsound or turning sore—not from the climate switch, at any rate."

In Aiken, Billy met Dr. Bernard Brennan, who would serve as Billy's veterinarian for the next quarter of a century. "I started to take care of the horses that he had at the time and we became very good friends," Brennan said. So good that Billy lived in a room adjacent to Brennan's home. "We spent many hours, not only professionally, but also as friends," Brennan said. "He had a wonderful ability to attract friends. He not only was very intelligent, but he was patient and willing to listen. He never looked for prestige in someone. He looked for the inner person. He'd stop and talk to grooms or presidents of racetracks. It made no difference to him, absolutely not."

And it never occurred to Billy not to share any information he knew about horses, even if he was talking to another stable's groom. "It was just his manner," Brennan said. "Other people, being as busy as they were with their schedules, would brush them off, but Billy would go into great detail. I'm sure a lot of the people Billy encouraged went on to become trainers. They broke the mold with Billy. There wasn't another one like him."

Billy had a profound influence on Brennan's career, too, encouraging him to give up his practice in South Carolina and relocate in New York, where Billy introduced him to many trainers. Brennan retired as a veterinarian in 1996, but his daughter, Nancy, one of 11 children, continues to practice equine medicine.

After campaigning a 12-horse stable at Roosevelt in the spring of 1949, Billy returned with an eight-horse stable for his last full summer at Saratoga. Billy won the overall 1949 Saratoga dash championship with 45 wins, all but two of them during the summer meet, to edge Aubrey Rodney by two. Tokyo Express, a 6-year-old pacer owned by John A. Zeyak and Joseph Donadio of Nassau, N.Y., went five-for-five at Saratoga that summer for Billy, who returned to Roosevelt in the fall. His other owners in 1949 were Colonel William C. Harris of Massapequa, Long Island, who had two pacers, Navy Hal and Harold Abbe, and three trotters, Carmel Boy, Reach Up and Statesman; Charles Doxsee of Islip, whose top horse was David Stone; Dr. Howard C. Johnson of Corinth; John Caputo and Anthony Finn of Ballston Spa; Georgie Quiri, William Huff of Hankins and the Saratoga Stable.

By the end of 1949, Billy realized he had to shift his base from Saratoga to Metropolitan New York to com-pete full-time at Roosevelt and Yonkers, which would open to harness racing the following year.

Billy had established a national presence in '49. He'd been the youngest driver (26) to race in the Hambletonian, but lost all chance when his horse, Crossbow, owned by Dunbar Bostwick, threw himself at the starting gate, according to a story in the *Harrisburg Evening News*. He also was the youngest driver in the Little Brown Jug, finishing third in an elimination with Ankaway.

Much of Billy's successful year was centered on his 7-year-old trotter Chris Spencer, who defeated the 1949 Champion Mare Proximity in the $20,000 David H. McConnell Memorial Mile and a Half Trot at Roosevelt in 3:08⅗ before 16,028 fans. Chris Spencer also won the $25,000 American Trotting Championship and the $10,000 Batavia Trot over Proximity and Hambletonian winner Demon Hanover. In the $50,000 2-mile stakes at Roosevelt, Chris Spencer was third to Demon Hanover and Proximity. Until Mal Burroughs won the 1997 Hambletonian with Malabar Man, Demon Hanover's driver, Harrison Hoyt, was the only amateur driver to ever win the Hambo. Hoyt thought enough of Billy to use him as a catch driver on his 2-year-old pacer Martin Vic. Billy won with him at Saratoga.

Before surrendering him to the world, the civic leaders of Fultonville decided to let everyone know how they felt about Billy, who had been dubbed "The Fultonville Flash." On Thursday, Nov. 3, 1949, more than 200 people—Fultonville's population was only 800—paid tribute to Billy at the Masonic Temple. Billy said that the dinner, sponsored by the Fultonville Community Club, meant more to him than any victory on the track. He'd turned 26 the day before.

On hand were his father, a thin man with glasses beaming with pride, and his mom; Fultonville Mayor

Peter Rossi, Town of Glen Supervisor Fred Lowe and Seeley Hodge, racing secretary of the Montgomery County Fair at Fonda. Miss Betty Wiswall, daughter of Saratoga Harness owner Frank Wiswall, was Billy's guest. At the time, she was a student at Smith College.

Billy was presented with a floral horseshoe made of gardenias from Saratoga Harness. He also got a leather suitcase as a gift from the Fultonville Community Club. Among the people he thanked for contributing to his success were owners Marshall McKay, Raymond Chase, Mr. and Mrs. Bill Cassaro, Dodger Griffith, Harold Joaniss, Bob Cobb and Dr. I. Ben Rubin.

Just 18 days after the testimonial dinner, Billy won the $50,000-added Golden West Trot at Hollywood Park behind Chris Spencer in a track record 2:33⅘ for the mile and a quarter, beating favored Rodney by a length and a quarter and paying $14.30 to win. "That was a big boost," Billy said years later. "That was the first $50,000 race I'd ever raced in. I don't think I'd ever raced for $10,000 before that." Billy was joined in the winner's circle by Fred Astaire, legendary race announcer Roy Shudt and Chris Spencer's owners, Mr. and Mrs. Dunbar Bostwick. Afterwards, Billy celebrated by dancing the night away with actress June Allyson and others at the Coconut Grove. "When we were driving together in California," his dear friend Delvin Miller said, "There weren't many places on the Sunset Strip that we missed."

Thanks to Chris Spencer's victory, Billy finished sixth in the country in earnings ($114,606) and ninth in races won (77) in 1949. But none of Billy Haughton's early success stories made as much impact on his career and his life as a single night of frustration at Saratoga. "Billy Muckle was a sharp old horseman," Billy said. "I remember that I had pretty rough going for a couple of weeks, and that I came back to the paddock one night uncertain as to whether I'd been in a horse race or rodeo (because of intimidating tactics by rival drivers). I was young and maybe a little headstrong, but definitely convinced that it was time to start dishing out a little of what I'd been taking, to prove that I was as game as the next fellow.

"I guess I expressed myself in no uncertain terms. Anyway, Billy heard me out without interrupting and then he put his arm around my shoulder and led me off to the side. 'Before you start doing things you'll be sorry for,' he said. 'I want to remind you that there's a big difference between being game and being foolish. I want you to remember how much the horse is worth, and how much the equipment you're using is worth, and how much your life is worth. But most of all, I want you to remember that there's another day coming.'"

It was advice Billy Haughton carried his entire life.

5

The Dominator

Billy Haughton's domination of harness racing as it began to enter its Golden Age in the 1950s and into the '60s was utterly remarkable.

From 1951 through 1968, he was first or second in the country in earnings 17 of 18 years, missing only in 1960. Eight of his 13 money winning titles came in a row, from 1952–59.

From '53–58, he was also the national leader in victories every single year.

Through 1998, only three other drivers in 53 years have ever led the country in both earnings and wins the same season: John Simpson, Sr., in 1951, Herve Filion seven times ('70–74 and '76–77) and Jack Moiseyev in 1993.

At Yonkers, Billy was nearly unbeatable. Yonkers opened in 1950 and Billy won every single driving title there in the '50s except in '56 when Stanley Dancer beat him. Billy's winning totals were 38 in 1950, then 43, 46, 52, 73 and 58 in 1955. He won with 54 in 1957, then had 65 and 77 wins the following two years.

Billy scored five four-win nights in the '50s at

Yonkers, three in the space of 14 days on April 27, 29 and May 10, 1954. He also won four on May 23, 1957, and on July 23, 1959. In 1963, he was third in wins (43), but first in winning percentage at 25.3.

Billy was less dominant at Roosevelt, finishing second by a single win to Stanley Dancer, 81–80, in 1955, fourth in '56, first in '57 (49 wins from 266 starts), third in '58, fourth in '60, 3rd in '62, third in '63, second in '64 and first in 1965 with 79 wins from 334 drives.

"There is only one reason Bill was great," Hall of Fame driver Bill O'Donnell said. "He was the best trainer and he was the best driver."

Is it any wonder Billy earned the nickname "The Master?" Or why he and his life-long friend Stanley Dancer, who won the money title four times and was second seven others, became known as "The Gold Dust Twins" in New York?

Harness racing was different in the '50s and '60s than it is today, so incredibly different.

Can you picture a racetrack without simulcasting, with win, place, show and a single Daily Double as the only betting options? Yet there are thousands of people jammed into Yonkers Raceway, just north of the Bronx in New York City, and Roosevelt Raceway on Long Island having the times of their lives.

No OTB. No simulcasting.

Imagine the best horses in each pacing and trotting division traveling and racing from track to track across the country week after week in the Grand Circuit, which offered the biggest stakes of the year and allowed fans all over the country to see the best horses. In person. "We traveled all over the country together," Ben Steall, one of Billy's assistant trainers, said. "We had a ball. Them were the fun days."

Billy Haughton, Jr. feels the same way. "The sport was great," he said. "My dad grew up in the golden years when it was at its pinnacle. And everybody worked on a handshake. We used to go and race like hell, but we'd all eat chicken out of the back of a station wagon afterwards. Beers, watermelon. The greatest times you'd ever want to have. Simple times, but great, because everybody got along. Do you know how easy it is to have a good time when everybody gets along?"

The horses got along better, too, in their careers. Back then, trainers gave their entire stable the winter off to get ready for the next season.

No winter racing.

It's a funny thing about having something available all the time. You never miss it.

It's no secret why the Little Brown Jug can draw 50,000 fans on Jug Day alone. It's because there is racing in Delaware, Ohio, for only one week a year.

It's why thoroughbreds racing year round at Belmont Park on Long Island and Aqueduct in Queens don't draw 5,000 from a market of millions some days, yet attract 20,000-plus a day at Saratoga in a city of 25,000 during its lone six weeks of racing.

Fans in New York used to miss harness racing.

Newspapers in New York used to write about it. *Sports Illustrated* used to write about it.

And the sport, with Billy and Stanley Dancer and the great ambassador of the sport, Delvin Miller, leading the way, prospered. In New York, it thrived. "Billy hit it at the right time and grew with it," veterinarian Doc Steele said.

Roosevelt Raceway's average nightly attendance topped 15,000 a night for 25 straight years from 1951 to 1975. It topped 20,000 from 1957 through '67—with a high of 26,042 in 1964 when more than 3.2 million fans attended the races: 3,229,243.

Yonkers, too, flourished. "Oh gosh, it was so crowded at the track," Dottie said. "It was the old Empire grandstand, a big white verandah. So many people there you could hardly find a seat. And the seats went all the way down into the first turn, just tiers and tiers of seats. It was amazing. It was great."

So was the racing. New York's two major tracks attracted the best horses and the best drivers and trainers in the country. One was Billy Haughton. Another was Stanley Dancer.

"I went to Roosevelt in '47, and Bill came in '48," Hall of Fame driver/trainer Stanley Dancer said in 1997. "We raced together in many, many races for a long, long time."

And they would dominate New York racing. "They called us 'The Gold Dust Twins,'" Dancer said. "One of us was usually in front, or the other one was. One owner after a race said, 'How can I win a race with the Gold Dust Twins in there? One takes care of the other.' It wasn't true. We both just had nine in (nine races) every night, and we were both good drivers. We were both aggressive, that's for sure. Before we started, they didn't do much hustling horses out of there (at the start). It was 'See how fast you can come home that last quarter.' We got a lot of horses, and we drove a lot of races. And we did very well. I think we both worked hard at it. Didn't take anything for granted."

They would share many special moments together. "When I won the Hambletonian in '83 with Duenna, there are so many things I will never forget," Dancer said. "The first one to congratulate me when I got out of the sulky was Billy Haughton. It was my fourth Hambletonian. He'd already won four. He was the first one there."

Clarence Martin is still involved in harness racing, more than 50 years after Billy gave him the chance of a lifetime: a job. "I was 17, 18 years old," Martin said.

A native of Lake Placid, N.Y., home twice to the

Winter Olympic Games in the majestic Adirondack Mountains, Martin had journeyed south to Saratoga Springs, hoping to make a career out of his passion: horses. "The main thing in my life was horses," he said. "I used to jog horses in Lake Placid. They had a little track out by the airport."

One night at Saratoga, Martin got to talking with Billy, a conversation which changed Martin's life. "He said, 'Why don't you come to work for me?'" Martin related. "It had to be '47. I was with him for 20 years. I ended up his main trainer for the Maryland-Delaware circuit. I'd get all the problem horses, the nasty ones. That's why my arms are 42 inches long."

Martin was also one of Billy's trainers charged with breaking yearlings in Florida every year. "There were hundreds of them sometimes," Martin said. "We had a barn with 120 horses and another barn with some more. Everybody had their own section. We'd train six horses in a set. When those horses went to the races, they were already used to it."

Martin preceded Billy's long-time assistant trainer, compatriot and close friend Al "Apples" Thomas. "I was with Bill probably longer than most of them," Martin said. "I was there before Apples. If you couldn't work for Bill Haughton, you couldn't work for anybody else. He never had a complaint. You were appreciated. You were part of the family. They were great people. I think they were the greatest people that ever lived. There are only two of us left, Dot and me, from the original stable. The last one, Billy Vaughan, died three weeks ago. He had cancer. They spread his ashes over Lake Okechobee, where his favorite fishing place was."

Martin, like so many others, was awed by Billy's horsemanship and driving abilities. "He was probably the best driver that ever lived," Martin said. "He was just gifted. He'd carry a dead horse from the three-quarter pole home like no one else could. I saw him at Yonkers one night. At the three-quarter pole, he was driving just a common filly, and she was as dead as a mackerel. And by the time they came out of the turn, he had her going again and won."

Billy wrote about it himself, in his chapter on driving in *Care and Training of the Pacer and Trotter*. He detailed his strategic decisions in a close race as his horse and another hooked up in mid-stretch:

"It is a battle between my horse and the one outside me. I have just gone to the whip. This is a horse that responds to whipping on the sulky shaft and I have the lines in the left hand, whip in the right and I am banging away at the shaft. He doesn't feel anything, but the noise of the whip against the shaft tells him it is time to do his very best, and he is trying.

"But he is tired. He had a tougher journey than the horse on the outside, and on paper he does not figure to be quite as good. Now we are in the last 50 yards and he is starting to fall apart on me.

"At this point, an amateur would threw the lines away, hit him a good clout with the whip and hope for the best. But this is where the professional does just the opposite.

"I feel my horse is going so I begin to lift him and work in rhythm with his action. As he strides forward and drops his head, I let the lines go forward with him, although they are still taut and he's still under my tight control. As he begins another stride and his head starts up, I am with him, lifting his head, playing gently on the lines asking for a little more; a little more than I have a right to ask for, a little more that he really has to give.

"But he is game and he gives me that little more. Now it is only forty feet to the wire, five horse and sulky lengths, one second on the watch. My moves are automatic and instinctive. My horse is completely out of gas

Billy Haughton with his pony, Betty. Billy made a sulky for her and drove her daily to the Fonda Fairgrounds across the Mohawk River from his house in Fultonville.

Billy Haughton, age 14, at the Fonda Fairgrounds in upstate New York. Billy was making 7 dollars a week as a groom.

The younger days of Hall-of-Famers Stanley Dancer, left and Billy Haughton at the Roosevelt Raceway in 1950. They were also known as "The Gold Dust Twins".

Billy with his outstanding filly Belle Acton. She was the 1955 2-Year-Old Pacer of the Year and 1958 Older Pacer of the Year.

Billy, Dottie, and Tommy in their den at home in Brookville, Long Island, after riding in 1964.

Peter, 9, and Billy in 1963 at Ben White Raceway in Orlando, FL.

Billy at Pompano Park, (FL), after driving his 2,500th winner in 1966.

Delvin Miller and Billy signing autographs at Roosevelt Raceway on a "Meet the Stars" night before the races that evening. HTA's Stan Bergstein (middle with glasses) is in the background.

Billy, after winning the first of his five Little Brown Jugs, with Laverne Hanover in Delaware, Ohio.

Billy driving one of his top pacers, Laverne Hanover. Owned by Tom Murphy, Laverne Hanover won 22 of 23 starts and finished his career with 61 wins, 11 seconds, and eight thirds in 98 starts.

Dottie Haughton winning an amateur driving race with Flo Kid at Roosevelt Raceway in 1964. Ebby Gerry, Jr., current President of the Harness Racing Museum and Hall of Fame, finishes second.

Billy with Armbro Omaha after winning the Little Brown Jug in 1974.

Billy and Keystone Pioneer after winning the Copenhagen Cup at Charlotteland Racetrack in Denmark, May 1977.

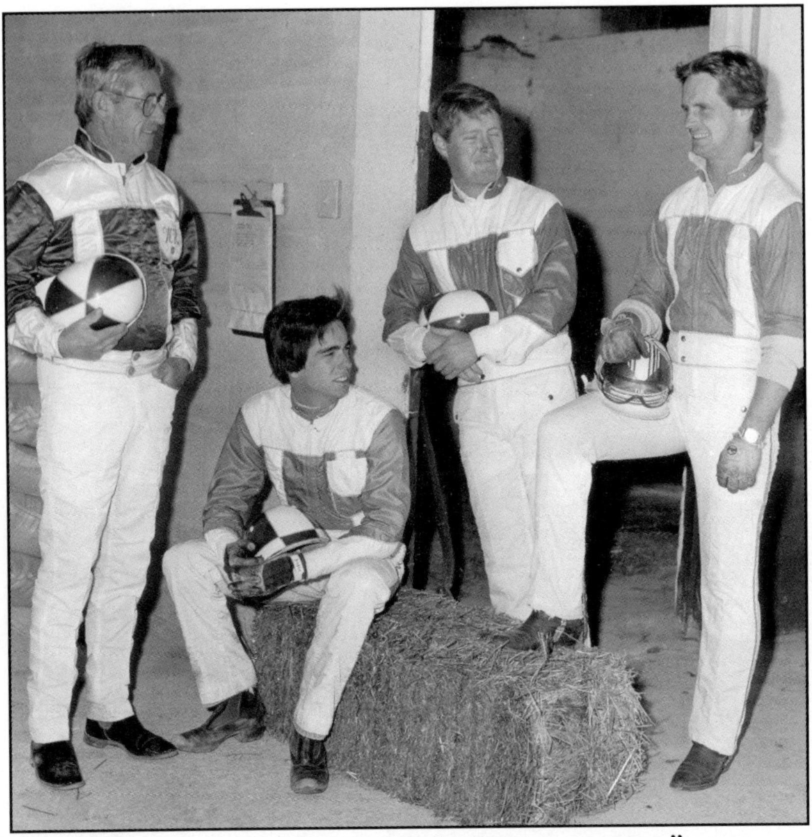

USTA photo by George Smallsreed

Billy, Cammie, Peter and Tommy—"The Great Green Wave"— at Pompano Park in 1978.

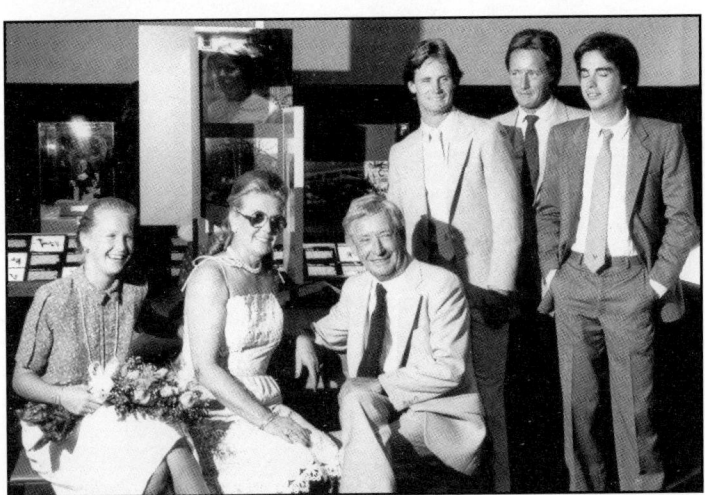

Holley, Dotttie, Billy, Tommy, Billy Jr. and Cammie at the Harness Racing Museum and Hall of Fame in Goshen, NY, for the dedication of the Peter D. Haughton Memorial Library Room and Peter D. Haughton Room of Immortals, July 1981.

Billy and Dottie study the yearling sales catalog at Blue Chip Farm in upstate New York. Billy was renowned for his expertise in judging yearlings. He would literally inspect every yearling at a sale.

Elgin Armstrong and Peter in the winner's circle after taking the Prix d'Eté with Armbro Omaha at Blue Bonnets in Montreal, Canada. Armbro Omaha was the 1974 3-Year-Old Pacer of the Year. This was Peter's first drive ever in a $100,000 stakes.

Peter winning the 1976 Kentucky Futurity with #1A Quick Pay, center. Billy is in the bike driving #1 Steve Lobell (rail), who was seeking the Trotting Triple Crown. On the outside is Soothsayer (#6) with Delvin Miller driving.

and I must carry him. I can do this. I know how. I have done it thousands of times before.

"He strides forward again, almost staggering. His head goes down and my hands go with him. When his head reaches its lowest point in what I know will be his final stride, I raise it back, gently yet firmly. I must show him that I am still with him, that I still have confidence in him and I must do it all with my hands. In that vital fraction of a second, I am literally carrying him past the wire.

"We cross the finish line and it is a tight one. So tight that I do not know whether I have won or lost . . . They post the winning number. It is mine. I am pleased. I have done my job well."

After splitting 1949 between Roosevelt in the spring, Saratoga in the summer and back to Roosevelt in the fall, Billy would have an exciting new venue to display his talent.

Yonkers Raceway, which had raced thoroughbreds for 35 years and been closed for seven, opened its new half-mile harness track on April 28, 1950. Before a crowd of 21,181, Billy won the first of two divisions of the Inaugural Pace with Colonel William C. Harris' Navy Hal, paying $7 to win.

Harris finished as the leading owner of the initial 19-night Yonkers meet, as Carmel Boy, then 8-years old, went four-for-four with earnings of $4,950. Reach Up had two wins and a second in four starts; Harold Abbe had two wins and a second in three starts, and Navy Hal had two wins, a second and a third in four starts.

But Billy's biggest victory at Yonkers in 1950 was with Chris Spencer, who won the $25,000 Gotham Trot. Chris Spencer also won the $25,000 Fort Miami at Toledo Raceway in Ohio and a pair of $5,000 Free-For-All trots at Roosevelt. Ankaway, Reach Up, Shady Hanover, Roy S., Mamscot, Propaganda, Hasty Pete,

Tryhussey, Flo Napoleon and Historian, who won a race at Goshen's mile-track in Orange County, N.Y. —the site of the Harness Racing Museum and Hall of Fame—all contributed to a breakthrough season for Billy, who also won the $5,000 Ash Grove Pace at Saratoga and the $10,000 Geers Stakes at Goshen pinch-hitting for his friend, Delvin Miller, on an outstanding 2-year-old pacer named Tar Heel. Billy, however, was not impressed with Tar Heel's offspring, initially. "We were at Rosecroft," Stanley Dancer said. "And Tar Heel and Star's Pride went to stud at about the same time. And the first two or three crops of Star's Pride were miserable to train. I said to Jim Harrison, 'Why don't you castrate that damn Star's Pride and save us trainers a lot of headaches?' And Billy says, 'While you're at it, why don't you castrate that damn Tar Heel? He does the same thing. You can't get them around the turns at all.'

"Well, they both went on to be great sires. A year later, one of the Star's Prides won a 2-year-old stakes and another one won the Hambletonian. I got the damnedest telegram from Harrison saying, 'They should be castrated?'"

By the end of 1950, Billy had amassed 86 victories and earnings of $181,881.20, ranking seventh and third nationally. John Simpson, Sr., and Del Miller finished 1-2 in victories with 111 and 108, respectively, and 2-1 in earnings: Simpson with $234,519 and Miller with $306,813.

Behind them, the Fultonville Flash was gaining momentum.

Billy, whose stable had grown to 33 horses by 1951, was unaware that his marital status would switch later that year, the year he met Dorothy Bischoff.

Their brief six-week courtship, ignited after Bill was invited home to dinner by Dottie's dad, included Dottie meeting Bill's parents in Fultonville. "There was no

Thruway then," Dottie said. "I went up to meet them before we got married. Bill's father wanted to be sure I was going to raise the children Catholic. It didn't bother me at all. I was Protestant. Believing in God was the main thing to me."

Dottie remembers their Victorian, three-story house right on the river, a little garden outside and the wallpaper inside that she still detests nearly 50 years later. "Ugghhh. That's what I remember the most," she said.

But she kept her opinion to herself at the time, and the visit with her future in-laws and Billy's Aunt Millie, who lived with his parents, rolled smoothly. "It went fine," Dottie said. "They liked me. I liked them. We had dinner at their house. Nobody went out to dinner in Fultonville. Are you kidding me? There weren't any restaurants. I don't think they ever went out to dinner anywhere. It was very nice, and we left the next morning because Bill had to drive that night at Yonkers."

Dottie got a kick out of Aunt Millie, who'd been crippled by childhood polio, but had not let the handicap deny her any enjoyment of life. "She was a character," Dottie said. "She weighed like 250 pounds and had a wonderful sense of humor. Bill's parents were so proper. Aunt Millie was just funny. I loved her."

Billy and Dottie were married on Saturday afternoon, Nov. 24, 1951 in St. John's and St. Mary's Catholic Church in Chappaqua. She wore a dusty pink brocade with bouffant skirt and hat and slippers to match, and carried a bouquet of white roses, carnations and chrysanthemums tied with white satin ribbons. Joyce Macklin, who'd helped Dottie hijack her parents' car to go to a soda shop years earlier, was the maid of honor. Carl Larsen of Buffalo, a second trainer for Billy, was best man. There was a reception afterwards for about 75 people at Dottie's parents' house.

They honeymooned in Bermuda, where Billy knew the Governor. "The Governor had horses, and he let us ride them," Dottie said. "We rode horseback miles and miles to the racetrack. They had harness races there. We had a wonderful time. The people were marvelous. We became lifetime friends with Sonny Holmes (who was the Director of Activities of the Elbow Beach Surf Club). We went back many times to visit."

They returned to Ben White Raceway in Orlando, Fla., where Billy wintered his stable, which had grown to more than 40 horses, for the first time. In the '60s, he shifted his winter stable to Pompano Park, which opened in south Florida, Feb. 4, 1964.

In Orlando that winter, Dottie first got to see the complete personality of a man she really did not know: "When you just meet someone, and six weeks later you get married, you really don't know him well. I really got to see how he was with other people and with the grooms and with the horses, and I started to really understand him as an individual. He was wonderful. He had a great sense of humor, and he was very, very kind. He never had a bad word for anyone. He'd speak to every groom every day and ask, 'How's your horse?' We had grooms that stayed with us for years and years. There was not a big turnover in our stable. It was wonderful to find out I made the right choice."

She was also pleased to find out that she had to rearrange her perspective on life. "When we got married, we stayed in a little apartment in Old Westbury [adjacent to Roosevelt Raceway on Long Island]," Dottie said. "It was in back of [Roosevelt owner] George Morton Levy's beautiful, huge Georgian home. It had a living room, a little bitty dining room, a kitchen and two little bitty bedrooms upstairs. I can remember standing there ironing in this little kitchen. And I figured that Bill had made $800 in like four days. And I put that iron down. And I said I may never iron again. I was laughing to myself, and I told him when he came home, and he laughed. He thought that was really funny. I had never really paid attention to money. Who cared, just as long as I could go to the grocery store? George Landers, who owned Belle Acton, had given me a new car, a convertible, as a gift. Wow! I didn't have a thing in the world to worry about. And all of a sudden, I didn't have to worry about ironing either."

Billy and Dottie Haughton at an awards dinner at Paradise Island in the Bahamas. *Sports Illustrated* once called her, "perhaps the prettiest wife of a sports star in the country".

6

Bigger and Bigger

By the end of 1951, Billy Haughton's stable had grown to 50 horses, requiring three assistant trainers: Clarence Martin, Al "Apples" Thomas and Bill "Bones" Vaughan. Ankaway and Harold Abbe, a pacer Billy switched to the trot, were two of his leading horses. Harold Abbe had seven wins and seven seconds, helping Billy finish second in the country in earnings ($220,916.28) behind John Simpson, Sr. ($333,136.25) Billy was first in the country in starts (694), third in wins (97)—Simpson and William N. McMillen were 1-2 with 118 and 98, respectively—and first in seconds (133) and thirds (91).

"Apples," who literally became a part of the Haughton family, was Alfred Wanstall Thomas of Ballston Spa, just a few furlongs south of Saratoga Springs. "He ate too much apple pie at the fair one time and got deathly sick, so the kids called him Apples after that," Dottie Haughton explained. "And it stuck. He came to work for Bill when Bill started at Saratoga. He was a very quiet, extremely meticulous person who had a good sense of humor and enjoyed the very simple things of life. He was the second trainer, then he ran the office in later years. He did all the shipping and all the entries at the different tracks and took care of all the books and did all the training schedules. He checked everything. Bill would tell Apples which horses he was going to train and which he was going to give the week off. And then Apples would go from there."

"My kids used to call him 'Uncle Al, the kiddies' pal.' When we went to Florida, he stayed at the house on Long Island. He and Geneva and Mary [two nannies] were there about every night, and they made sure that the children behaved."

In a fascinating two-part series on the Haughton operation in *Hoof Beats* in 1963, Mary Louise McGregor wrote of Apples:

"Most of the organizational details and records and charts are the responsibility of Al Thomas. For many years, Thomas worked quietly in the shadow of Haughton's ability. In the past few years, as the operation has expanded and as Haughton has been forced to be away from his headquarters more and more, Thomas has emerged as the top man, next in line to the boss. He's a plain-spoken, knowledgeable, hard-working 35-year-old (five years younger than Haughton) who does a competent job as understudy. In 1962, he won 42 races and over $100,000. Best of all, Thomas is a 'detail' man. He has set up most of the stable's system and he tends it like a clucking hen with a sizable brood. At this very moment, he can probably tell you the contents of Buxton Hanover's trunk, the size of Dark Sun's sulky, how fast they worked Duke Rodney on March 4, and where Haughton finished in the 1952 Bloomsburg Fair Stakes. The smoothness of this million-dollar operation is due largely to this profitable and natural alliance of Haughton's personal ability and Al Thomas' intuition. He seems to sense just what Haughton needs, wants and expects. It's a unique balance of unlike temperaments and personalities but the edges lock together like a jigsaw [puzzle] to produce the biggest, most successful stable operation in harness racing."

While the Haughton Stable would grow to number some 200 horses at its zenith—making it the largest horse racing operation in the world—Billy and Apples kept records on each one. "Apples was a big part of Billy's operation," driver Bill O'Donnell said.

Of course, this was long before the advent of computers. "No computers," Dot said. "Apples did it by hand and Bill did it in his head. If he were here today, he could tell you what kind of shoes and what kind of equipment every single horse he's ever had wore. It was amazing. In fact, you could probably mention a race, and he could probably tell you just how the race went, and who moved and where he moved. All in his head."

Apples worked for Billy the rest of Billy's life, then remained in the Haughton Stable working with Tommy. "He worked for Tommy until he went into a hospital in August, 1996," Dottie said. "Sadly, he died four days later." Tommy said, "It was almost like losing another member of the family."

The year 1952 was magical for Billy Haughton. He won his first Roosevelt driving title with 52 wins; the national money title by a lot with $311,728.45—James Jordan was second with $259,839.56—and was second nationally in wins with 110, 19 behind Levi Harner.

At the age of 29, he was the youngest driver to win the earnings title. But he never lost a deep ingrained respect for older drivers. "I'm no cocky driver who feels youth has an edge in this sport," he told columnist Jimmy Powers the following spring. "I duel with Henry Clukey. He's 65 and a grandfather four times. He's great. He keeps his youthful reflexes. That's important. There are other good rivals around—Henry Thomas,

65; Bi Shivley, 74; Ben White, 80; Fred Egan and Tom Berry in their 70s. Older men don't take foolish chances. They rely more on experience than daring."

Billy was never reluctant to draw from their experience. "The older horsemen almost had a hot stove league every day at the blacksmith's shop in the afternoons," Dr. Bernard Brennan, a veterinarian said. "Frank Ervin, who trained Bret Hanover, Sep Palin, who trained Greyhound, Jimmy Wingfield, Fred Egan, Harry Whitney, Ned Bower and Billy would hold conversations about any problems they were having with their horses. Billy was an eager participant and added a lot to that. There were times my own knowledge was enhanced. There was great camaraderie and sharing of knowledge. I think of those years as being foundation years for both Billy and myself."

Billy fashioned his first national earnings title with 41 different winners, led by Carmel Boy and Titanic, who each won six races. David Caudle, Dynamic Hal, Harold Abbe, Meadow Abbe and Stanton Hal won five apiece. Colby's Match, Ensign Melburn, Federal Hanover and Lonway each won four.

Billy's other winners were Ankaway, Autocrat, Belle Pointer, Bertram Hanover, Captain Carefree, Ceywey, Cheerful Hanover, Chris Spencer, Christie Hanover, Darn Flashy, Flo Napoleon, Hel Hague, Historian, Jetsam, Knight Boy, Mamscot, Maryland Hilly, Mighty Grattan, Miss Bobby Sox, Miss Mamie, Mynah Hanover, Navy Hal, Rapid Gallon, Reach Up, Royal Value, Tyler Hanover, Vivace Song and Wilmington's Star.

Maryland Hilly, owned by Mr. and Mrs. Carl J. Batter of Washington, D.C., and Billy were presented a trophy by New York Governor Thomas E. Dewey in front of the grandstand after winning the featured trot at the State Fairgrounds in Syracuse.

Another highlight came on Sept. 11, 1952, when Billy's 10-year-old gelding, Chris Spencer, came out of semi-retirement to win the Roosevelt Two-Mile Trot in 4:16⅗ before 24,450 fans. He'd been limited to racing in hometown fairs in '51 and '52 because of lameness, but recovered by swimming to win one more huge race for Billy.

Billy went to look at some colts at a sale at Delaware, Ohio, and was drafted to drive Wilmington's Star, a horse he'd never seen, when Harry Fitzpatrick fell ill. Billy won the first heat of the Little Brown Jug with him.

Life was grand, and Billy appreciated every minute of it. In that interview with Jimmy Powers, Billy said, "Last fall, with all the stars and a big moon hanging over the track, was the most beautiful sight ever. From the track, it's exciting: the sleek coats of the horses, the colors, the noise and the floodlights. From the stands, it's still more beautiful. I sat up there with my mouth open. Spring, summer or fall. It's a thrill. I wouldn't be in any other business. This is tops."

He was only just beginning.

Billy led the nation in wins and earnings in 1953. His 116 wins were nine more than Johnny Chapman in second, while his earnings of $374,527—the most by a driver in the history of the sport—clearly outdistanced his buddy Delvin Miller in second ($288,659).

Billy won the feature at opening night at Roosevelt with Tyler Hanover, who paid $52.50. He edged out another friend, Stanley Dancer, 52–50, to take the Yonkers dash title and was third in the Universal Drivers Rating System (with standards similar to a batting average in baseball) at .3546 behind Dancer (.362) and Hugh Bell (.3549).

By 1954, Billy's stable had grown to 69 horses, 49 pacers and 20 trotters, for an incredible number of different owners: 35. He had added Ted Cary to join Apples, Bones Vaughan and Clarence Martin as assistant trainers. Alan Crawford helped out on a visit as did Dottie's father, Whitney Bischoff. George Cochran, who also worked for Walter Gibbons, was the stable office manager.

Billy was charging owners $125 per month to train and $50 a month during the winter. He paid his grooms $80 a week during the racing season and $60 weekly in the off-season.

Billy won the opening race at Yonkers behind Mighty Jet ($5.40), who paced a mile in 2:07.3. After losing 11 straight, he won a race behind Florita ($4.80). Then Billy quickly posted three quadruple win nights. By May 11, he had an incredible record of 30 wins, 13 seconds and 17 thirds from 100 starts. On May 11, he won a Grand Circuit trot with Faber Hanover for a new owner, John Froehlich, a Long Island potato farmer in Hicksville who raced under the name Farmstead Acres, and a Grand Circuit pace with Piney Fingo, whom Dottie trained in Florida.

Dottie was not only adept at training horses, she was pretty good at driving them, too. She proved it in 1964, when she made her driving debut behind a horse named Ilo Kid in an amateur trot at Roosevelt Raceway. "He was one of the toughest trotters to get along with in the stable," Dottie said. "I went over and trained him for about three weeks before the race. Bill was so nervous he rode in the starting car the entire race. I was terribly nervous in the paddock. That was the first time I drove in front of a crowd. Billy wanted me to do it. I wanted to do it. As soon as they said 'Drivers up,' all the butterflies went away and I was just fine. I won the first heat. Then we came back in the second heat, and Norman Woolworth's horse stepped in my wheel and tore my tire out. But I just kept going. My horse got a little rough gaited in the last turn, but I had a hold of him and I won." For the effort, Dottie was presented with a silver bowl, a *Sports Illustrated* Award of Merit.

Billy was terribly proud of Dottie's horsemanship. "She has a better driving record than any of us," he said in a 1979 story in the *Hollywood (Fla.) Sun-Tattler* written by Barry Lepp. "She's had five races, winning three and taking second twice."

On August 12, 1954, Billy set a world record for a mile and a half, winning the $35,000 Nassau Pace with Hillsota in 3:04⅖ at Roosevelt.

Peter Delvin Haughton was born on Wednesday, Sept. 22, 1954, Little Brown Jug Day.

On November 29, Billy was named to the United States Trotting Association Board of Directors, a position he held until he died.

By year's end, he had won his second consecutive earnings title, a record $415,577.75, breaking his record from the year before, and also posted a record 153 wins, 24 more than Levi Harner's record.

The Haughton Stable's top earners in '54 were: Meadow Leo ($31,340.58), Quick Chief ($26,178.02), Arvilla Hanover ($24,108.64), Hillsota ($22,775), Piney Fingo ($18,775), Earl's Ensign ($18,076.85); David Caudle ($17,360), Buffalo Street ($16,475). Faber Hanover ($16,125), Counsel Pick ($15,475) and Bluett Hanover ($15,050).

Quick Chief, a son of Chief Abbedale Billy purchased as a yearling for John Froehlich, had nine wins and seven seconds in 18 starts as a 2-year-old, giving Billy his first divisional champion. The following year, Quick Chief gave Billy his first of five Little Brown Jugs in two minutes flat, beating, ironically, a horse named Dottie's Pick and 15 other rival 3-year-olds. Quick Chief went on to finish his sophomore campaign with 13 wins, three seconds and a third in 20 starts, earning $95,397 and 3-Year-Old Pacer of the Year honors. Quick Chief tailed off as a 4-year-old, winning only three of 22 starts. He won his lone start as a 5-year-old and retired with 26 wins, 11 seconds and five thirds in 61 career starts and earnings of $137,960.

Billy kept dominating through the '50s. He set two new records again leading the nation in earnings ($599,445.32) and wins (168) in '55 by huge margins. Joe O'Brien finished second to Billy in money won ($421,660.70), while Stanley Dancer was second in wins at 130.

Stanley got closer in '55, losing the dash title, 167–163, while Billy also won the money title with $572,945, well ahead of John Simpson Sr. ($455,301).

In '56, Billy and Simpson finished 1-2 in earnings again ($586,950 to $483,164), while Buddy Gilmour narrowly lost the dash title to Billy 156–152. Billy pulled a rare double in 1956, getting mentioned in two different stories in the same issue of *Sports Illustrated*. In *SI's* Scoreboard of Aug. 6, 1956, Billy, called "harness racing's busiest driver-trainer and three-time driving champion," was cited for "a unique triple" at Vernon Downs when he had three two-minute winners on the same Grand Circuit card: Duane Hanover in 1:58⅖ and 1:58⅗ to win the fourth leg of the $20,000 Empire State Pacing Classic, and his 3-year-old pacing filly superstar Belle Acton to tie a world record, taking the $5,968 Flora Temple Stake in 1:59.

A feature story written by Jeremiah Tax chronicled Billy's success for *SI* readers. "TAKE A GOOD LOOK at Billy Haughton, the sober, solid young man on the opposite page; there may never by another like him. At 32, he is the owner, manager, trainer and driver of the largest (98 trotters and pacers) and winningest public stable in harness racing history."

Tax wrote of Billy: "In a sport which has had somewhat more than its share of scandal and squabbles in recent years and which is still fighting a deep-rooted skepticism in metropolitan areas regarding its total purity, he has been a shining example of clean and colorful competition."

Tax was even more flattering to Dottie, who was pictured on the story's jump page holding the Little Brown Jug her husband won the year before with Quick Chief: "Since Ernie Vandeweghe quit basketball (Mrs. Vandeweghe is the former Miss America, Kay Hutchins) Dorothy Haughton may be the most beautiful wife of any athlete in the country."

Tax detailed Billy Haughton's daily regimen: "Haughton is up before 7 o'clock every morning. From 8 till past noon, he trains his horses at the track, tedious painstaking work with trotters and pacers which calls for patient attention to shoeing, balance, pace and gait, in addition to general conditioning. Most of the afternoon is taken up with the office routine of running a large stable: arranging for shipment of horses to tracks around the country and their stakes payments so they can race; the billing for feed, shoeing and harness; consultations with vets about ailing horses; the payroll for a staff of 38 grooms and five assistant trainers, and dozens of other chores. If he's lucky, Haughton gets a quick late lunch and change of clothes at home before he reports back to the track at 7 o'clock to start warming up his entries in that evening's races. With a stable his size, he usually drives in at least four races at the track where he is temporarily based. That brings him home about midnight."

Tax also detailed a typical Billy Haughton travel itinerary: "Monday afternoon he raced at the Kent & Sussex Fair in Harrington, Delaware; immediately afterwards he flew to Vernon Downs in upstate New York for stakes engagements that night. Tuesday afternoon, he was back at Harrington, and that night he raced at Roosevelt Raceway on Long Island. Wednesday afternoon and night he raced at Harrington and Roosevelt again. Thursday night he was back at Vernon. Friday and Saturday he raced at Roosevelt."

But what was Billy going to do at this point of his career? Slow down? No way. On or off the track. "Sometimes, if he'd been out with the guys after the races, he'd get home at 4 o'clock in the morning and get up at 6 or 6:15 just like nothing ever happened," Dottie said. "He could do it every night of the week if he wanted to."

Billy won both the dash and money title again in '57 (156 wins, four more than Buddy Gilmour; $586,950 to Simpson's $483,164) and '58, setting new records in wins (176, 21 ahead of Gilmour) and a whopping $816,659. Dancer was second at $454,881.

In its story about the 1957 leaders, *Hoof Beats* led with:

"Year after year after year after year, etc."

Though he finished second nationally in wins to Gilmour (165–57) in '59. Billy won his eighth consecutive money title ($711,435). The decade of the '50s belonged to him.

7

The Yearling

Billy Haughton earned the right to author the chapter on yearling section in the *Care and Training of the Pacer and Trotter*. Based on his exhausting regimen of examining each and every yearling before a sale, he experienced incredible success with many yearlings he purchased relatively cheaply. In doing so, he displayed unerring honesty with the owners he was bidding for, many of whom had given him carte blanche within a certain monetary range.

"I think he looked at more yearlings than any other person ever," noted breeder and long-time friend of the Haughtons, Max Hempt, said. "When he looked at a horse, he saw him inside and out. He could almost tell whether he was going to be a good tough race horse or if he was chicken hearted."

Billy didn't keep his observations to himself. He wrote in *Care and Training* that honesty with owners is "a policy I have and which I will always follow as long as I am in the horse business. I always tell my owners the absolute truth. I know there are other trainers who don't always lay it on the line with their owners. It is my opinion that this might work all right for a time, but that eventually it has got to catch up with you. Over the long run you and your owners are better off if you level with them and they level with you."

It wasn't empty rhetoric, rather a code of honor Billy lived by. "Everything was up front with Billy," Hempt said. "He was as honest as the day was long." That's why owners stayed with Billy. "When an owner went with him, he was with him for life," driver Bill O'Donnell said.

Bill Christine, the excellent turf writer for the *Los Angeles Times*, wrote about Billy and Delvin Miller at the 1969 Harrisburg (Pa.) Sale, where Billy would make a habit of staying an entire week, even when it meant missing the final week of the Yonkers' fall season. Many times, he stayed at Hempt's nearby farm. Hempt still owns horses with Tommy Haughton.

Christine wrote: "Bill and Delvin both fancied a filly. 'If you like her so much, I won't bid on her,'' Haughton told Miller. A little later, John Froehlich (one of Billy's biggest owners) asked Haughton if he'd do the bidding for him on the same filly. 'I can't,' Haughton said. "I've already promised Del that I'd stay away from her.' Del bought the filly, Delmonica Hanover, for $4,500. Froehlich bought another horse in the same sale, Spartan Hanover, for $90,000. After the sale, Miller offered Haughton a half interest in Delmonica Hanover. Haughton said, 'I can't accept that because I already told Froehlich that I couldn't help him get her.' A few years later (1974), Delmonica Hanover won the Roosevelt International Trot by a nose over Spartan Hanover."

Delmonica Hanover was one of the greatest trotting mares of all time and the 1974 Horse of the Year. But she was not the only great horse Billy literally handed away. In *Care and Training*, he told how he purchased a colt named Race Time at a sale for $19,000, without having a specific owner in mind. "I talked to several of my owners, pointing out that I liked him an awful lot, but that I was a little suspicious of his knees," Billy said. "For one reason or another, each of them turned him down and it looked as though I was going to be racing him myself. I didn't really mind that, although I must confess that I am not in the habit of buying $19,000 yearlings for my own account. The next morning, I ran into Ralph Baldwin, the Castleton Farm trainer. He asked me for whom I had bought the colt. I told him that as yet I didn't have an owner, and he mentioned that he didn't have a pacing colt in his string and might be interested in this one if we could work something out."

They did. A few days later, he gave Castleton an option on the colt for $25,000, and they bought him. Race Time went on to win $486,955. "The last time I saw him race, his knees were still holding up quite well," Billy noted dryly.

Of course, Billy had more successes than near misses, and he credited that to his intense preparation. "He didn't need to look at a yearling long," Murray Brown of historic Hanover Shoe Farms in Hanover, Pa., said. "He was the greatest horseman I've ever known and ever expect to know."

Billy purchased 50 to 60 yearlings annually at sales between August and November, usually in the range of $5,000 to $20,000, and shipped them south to either Aiken, S.C., or later to Orlando, Fla. That's where they would develop and join the rest of the Haughton Stable. Back then, tracks didn't operate 12 months a year, and horses actually got a good long break to wind down, be turned out and prepare for a new season in the spring.

Billy was a brilliant horseman, but also practical enough to realize that he should take every possible edge he could get in racing, especially since he was spending other people's money at a yearling sale. "Believe me, in buying yearlings you need all the edge you can get," he said. He felt he got a significant one by literally checking every single yearling at a sale, frequently scribbling copious notes on many of them, even some of the ones he wasn't overwhelmed with, and many times including a price range he thought was reasonable. "I know that if I continue to do my homework I am going to accomplish far more good than harm for myself and my owners," he said. "The one thing I know I can do by studying my lesson faithfully and preparing my homework carefully is to steer my owners away from yearlings, which, in my opinion, for reasons of conformation or pedigree or a combination of the two, have only a remote chance of making good. I have done this successfully enough for a sufficient number of years to have confidence in my ability in that respect."

He believed in that so much that one year he did it twice. "One year in the late '60s, Billy had looked at every yearling at Harrisburg, then had to race someone at Hollywood Park," Murray Brown said. "And he lost his catalogue with all his notes. He thought he may have lost it on the airplane. He offered a $1,000 reward, but it never showed up. So he did it again. He looked at every yearling again."

Among the many areas Billy judged in evaluating a yearling were: "the head, the width between eyes, eyes, ears, depth of chest, width between front legs, how he stands, not toeing out, foot angle of 47–48 degrees, white feet, no seedy feet, jowls, long neck, shoulder and heart girth, knees (critical), calf knees (avoid), angle of pastern which is a shock absorber, ankles, sesamoids, tendons, splints, curve of hock, curbs, even hips, tail, testicles down." Billy would have yearlings led up and down and note their disposition.

Eventually, in the early '70s, Billy began wearing glasses. "He used them to read the fine print in the track program," Dottie said. "He didn't wear them around the house. He had unbelievable vision."

Consummate horseman that he was, Billy took advantage of any information he thought was useful. In *Care and Training*, he wrote "Some years ago, I read that the late [thoroughbred trainer] Sunny Jim Fitzsimmons said he always wanted to be able to get four fingers between the jaws of any yearling he ever bought. He said that if he couldn't do that, they didn't have sufficient space there for proper air intake. I have been practicing this myself for a number of years now and I have found it to be generally true. I have marked this in my catalog for quite a few years, and in checking back, I haven't found a single horse that failed this 'finger test' that ever amounted to anything more than an ordinary raceway horse."

Billy felt he had another edge: the option of buying a yearling and keeping him. "My own buying range is a very broad one and I feel that I am better prepared if I have looked at every yearling," he said.

In doing that, and keeping his notes, he found as many as a "dozen times during a lengthy sale" instances when a yearling was being priced below what Billy thought he or she would bring. "This is where my practice of screening every yearling carefully comes in handy," he wrote in *Care and Training*. "I glance at my catalog markings and know immediately whether, in my own professional opinion, there is anything wrong with the colt. If there isn't; if he's one of those true 'sleepers' or 'overlays' that pop up every once in a while, I throw in a bid. I have acquired a number of darn good horses this way, horses I didn't intend to bid on but which I thought weren't bringing nearly the price their potential indicated. I am in a position to do this more readily than most trainers, because I have more owners than most (as many as 40 each year), and a number of them have given me virtual carte blanche in selecting one or more yearlings for them. I have another advantage, too, over many trainers. If I happen to buy a colt that for one reason or another none of my owners wants, I can pay for him myself and race him in my own name."

He didn't have that problem with Romulus Hanover, whom he bought for $35,000 for Froehlich at the 1965 Harrisburg Sale.

Billy had paid special attention to Romulus Hanover, because he was a full brother to Romeo Hanover, who was named the 1965 2-year-old Pacer of the Year after winning the $100,000 Lawrence B. Sheppard Pace and the $50,000 Fox Stakes. In 1966, the son of Dancer Hanover out of the Tar Heel mare Romola Hanover would become only the third 3-year-old pacer ever to win the pacing Triple Crown (the Cane Pace, Little Brown Jug and Messenger). Romeo Hanover would retire with a lifetime record of 36 wins, two seconds and four thirds from 44 starts and earnings of $658,505, not bad for a yearling sold for $8,500

"Because he was a full brother to Romeo Hanover, I had looked Romulus over very carefully before the sale and had given him high marks," Billy said.

In his sales catalog, Billy had written these notes:

Doesn't pace on lead
Very nice head
Looks more like thoroughbred
Great body
Hocks much better than Romeo
Right front foot slight dish
Pastern's long but sloped right
Should bring $50,000 or more

He didn't. "I thought Romulus would bring at least $50,000 and I remember saying to myself that I wouldn't have been surprised if he brought $60,000 or $70,000," he said. "I didn't have any owners who wanted to go that high so I forgot about him.

"But when Romulus entered the ring, he wasn't greeted by the frenzied bidding that I expected. I really didn't know why. Perhaps they thought Dancer Hanover and Romola Hanover couldn't do it twice in a row, or maybe they were concerned because his pasterns were a trifle long or because he had a slightly dished foot. But in my mind, Romulus was a far better individual than Romeo and I had already discounted the length of the pastern and the dished foot as minor faults that would not bother him.

"The bidding moved up to $25,000 at a fairly rapid clip but then it suddenly lagged. I couldn't believe my ears, but for all his pleading, [auctioneer] George Swineboard couldn't coax another bid from the crowd. At the last second, I threw up my hand and bid $27,000. He [the other bidder] went to $30,000; I bid $32,000. He went to $33,000 and I bid $35,000. That was how Romulus Hanover became the property of John Froehlich."

It was money well spent. As a 2-year-old in 1966, Romulus Hanover won a $10,136 division of the Arden Downs Stakes, the $14,323 Goshen Cup and a $22,314 division of the Hanover Colt Stakes. He did even better at 3, taking the $85,510 Adios and the $178,604 Messenger on the way to being named the 1967 3-year-old Pacer of the Year, winning 15 of 21 starts with two seconds and earnings of $277,636 for Froehlich's Farmstead Acres in Brookville, Long Island.

A year earlier, in the 1964 Lexington Sale, Billy found another multi-stakes winner for considerably less: $5,500. Billy was impressed with Carlisle, a trotting son of Hickory Pride, the first foal out of Good Note, a daughter of Phonograph.

Billy wrote these notes in the catalog:

> Leads good XXXX
> Nice round stroke
> Nice individual
> Could be a shade stouter
> Exceptionally sharp and alert
> I rubbed Rosemary [Phonograph's dam, whom
>   Billy had groomed]. Was good trotter
> Should bring $5,000–$8,000
> {Delvin and Mrs. Lloyds both like}

Delvin was Delvin Miller. Mrs. Margaret Lloyds was the wife of Lloyd Lloyds, one of Bill's owners. Billy bought the colt for Mr. and Mrs. Lloyds and Miller's wife, Mary Lib, for $5,500. Carlisle won the $18,600 E.H. Harriman Trophy and $13,150 Tompkins-Geers Stakes for 2-year-olds in 1965; the $87,180 Dexter Cup, $25,000 American National Stakes and $24,605 Hanover Colt Stakes in 1966 and the $89,580 American National Stakes Final in '67.

"Billy wasn't the kind of guy who went out and bought ten $100,000 horses," Clint Galbraith said. "He might buy one for $100,000, or he might buy one for $7,500. Billy didn't care what they cost. If he liked them, he bought them, and he made good horses out of them. He made a lot of good horses out of inexpensive yearlings."

Of all the yearlings Billy ever purchased, from his first big score with Ankaway, he never topped his purchase of Belle Acton for $1,600. "She was one of the greatest mares that ever lived," Billy said.

It's hard to dispute.

Belle Acton, a daughter of The Widower out of

Diane Scot by Scotland, was entered for auction at the 1954 yearling sale at Delaware, Ohio. "Belle Acton's by The Widower, and he was one of my favorite horses before I started to drive," Billy said in a story written by Henry King, Jr., in the December 1955, issue of *Hoof Beats*. "He had exceptional manners and he was a fast game pacer, too."

Billy liked the maternal family, too. "I'd heard a lot about Belle Acton's dam, Diane Scot," Billy said. "She was a good race mare who went around 2:04 on half-mile tracks. She'd had two pretty fair colts that I trained, The Kiltie and Dundee Lassie, and I kept thinking that Diane Scot might get a real good colt some day."

But Billy nearly missed that star. "To be perfectly honest, I wouldn't have gotten Belle Acton if there had been many more bids," he said. "I didn't want to go much over $2,000 for her, and I was lucky to get her."

One of his owners, George B. Landers, a contractor in Kittery, Maine, was even luckier. Billy bought Belle Acton for himself and then asked Landers if he'd be interested in buying her. Landers took the offer and didn't have to wait long to get his investment back.

Billy wintered the filly and the rest of his stable in Orlando, Fla., and she advanced so quickly that she won her debut, a matinee race there, on Feb. 19 of her 2-year-old season, in 2:31⅘ with Clarence Martin driving. Her next start was in Orlando, too, and she won another matinee race in 2:22⅘ with M. Teague on March 26.

Billy then gave his precocious filly five weeks off before entering her at Rosecroft Raceway, May 6, when she won a non-betting race by a neck in 2:08⅕ with Martin driving. Ten days later at Rosecroft, Apples Thomas was in the sulky, and Belle Acton won by a length and a quarter in 2:08⅘.

Billy then drove her in her pari-mutuel debut, May

20, when she won by three lengths in 2:08⅘ as the 9–10 favorite.

Belle Acton went on to post 15 wins, three seconds and two thirds in 21 starts, earning $40,299 in a remarkable juvenile campaign which culminated in her being named 2-Year-Old Pacer of the Year in 1955. From 1952, when the United States Harness Writers Association began making divisional awards, through 1967, when 2-year-old divisional awards were separated by sex, Belle Action was the lone filly to win that honor.

After winning at Laurel (now a thoroughbred track), Roosevelt, Vernon Downs and Goshen, Billy entered Belle Acton in the $14,400 Thruway Pace at Yonkers. Racing over a dull track, she won by a length and a half in 2:04⅕. "What made that race remarkable was that Belle Acton started from post seven that night and was parked out for a half mile before getting the lead," rival horseman Eddie Cobb said. "She brushed her last quarter in :29⅖ seconds over that kind of track, and that, let me tell you, was greatness."

She wasn't done, though Billy freshened her at Farmstead Acres in Brookville, Long Island, where she was turned out for two weeks before resuming racing.

In three heats of the Reading Futurity Sept. 16, she took on her Haughton stable-mate colt, Bachelor Hanover. Before the race, Belle Acton's owner, George Landers, and Bachelor Hanover's owner, Mrs. Hazel L. Rubin, flipped a coin to decide which of the two Billy would drive. Landers won, and Billy drove his filly, while Stanley Dancer handled Bachelor Hanover. Belle finished first, third and second in the three heats.

Eleven days later, the two Haughton stars hooked up again at Bloomsburg, and Billy drove her in two winning heats, setting a world record for 2-year-old filly pacers of a combined 4:11, 2:06 in the first heat and 2:05 in the second. Dancer again drove Bachelor Hanover.

Belle Acton had one start left in her brilliant 2-year-old season, the $14,200 Autumn Pace at Yonkers, again taking on colts including her stable-mate. Before the race, Mrs. Rubin pointed out to Billy that he'd driven the filly instead of her own colt in the previous two stakes. She asked him to drive her colt, and he complied, leaving Dancer in the sulky for Belle Acton's tour de force, a world record for 2-year-old fillies or colts on a half mile track when she paced in 2:02 ⅖, topping the existing 2:03 half-mile world record shared by Adios Boy and Haughton stable-mate Quick Chief.

In doing so, she defeated colts by 19 lengths, pacing her final half in :59⅗, incredible fractions then for a 2-year-old.

"I think Belle Acton is the greatest young pacer that ever lived," said Cobb, who finished second that night with Honest Jimmie, who himself held the world record for 2-year-old geldings on a half-mile track (2:05⅖). "We just couldn't keep up."

Hall of Famer John Simpson said, "Belle Acton's 2:02⅖ was the greatest colt [sic—2-year-old] performance I've ever seen on a half mile track. That's for sure."

In her dominating season, she'd finished out of the money just once, when she was "interfered with in tight quarters," according to King's story, and finished sixth.

When asked to compare his 2-year-old pacing stars, Belle Acton and Bachelor Hanover, who won the $26,578 Fox Stakes, Billy said, "Belle Acton has a faster record than Bachelor Hanover, but I'd rate them as pretty much of a toss-up right now. If really pressed for an answer, I'd have to lean toward Belle Acton, but Bachelor Hanover is a great fast colt. Bachelor beat Belle Acton two heats out of three in the Reading Futurity, but I realized afterwards I didn't have her too tightened up for that race. And Belle Acton beat him two heats at Bloomsburg."

They would meet again the following year in the initial running of the $71,500 Messenger Stakes at Roosevelt Raceway, and they finished 1-2, Belle Acton beating Bachelor Hanover. Billy drove Belle Acton, who finished her 3-year-old season with 19 wins, two seconds and a third in 24 starts, making $75,495 and time-trialing in 1:58⅗. In '57, she won 13 of 27 starts with four seconds, two thirds and earnings of $65,107.

In 1958, Belle Acton was named Pacer of the Year, the only mare so honored from 1952–66 before the award was divided by sex. That year, Belle Acton won $167,887, more than any pacer in the history of racing, topped only by the $186,101 earned by the trotter Scott Frost in 1955. She won 18 of 27 starts that year with five seconds and two thirds. Belle Acton posted one third in two starts in 1959, and was retired with a career record of 65 wins, 14 seconds and eight thirds in 101 starts and $353,062 in earnings.

Forty years later, Dancer would still say that Belle Acton was the greatest horse Billy ever trained.

8

Another Billy

In 1952, as he ascended to the top of his profession, Billy Haughton had more than horses to occupy his head. Dottie was pregnant.

On Oct. 28, 1952, Dottie and her mom were in Connecticut visiting friends, when Dottie's water broke. Dottie had her mother drive her to Yonkers, where Billy was racing that night. They arrived there after the fifth race.

Dottie sent word to the paddock that her water had broken, and a messenger returned to ask Dottie if Bill should scratch his horse in the upcoming seventh race. "I said, 'No, no. Let him race the horse. I'll wait,'" Dottie replied.

She waited. Then Bill drove her back to their new home in Massapequa on the south shore of Long Island so Dottie could shower and get her things. Then they drove to Mercy Hill Hospital in Rockville Center, Long Island, 22 miles away, where Dottie completed a torturous labor. "I was in hard labor for 48 hours," she said. "Oh my God, it was horrible."

It got worse. Dottie broke into a fever. She actually

gave birth in the hall the night of Oct. 30, and the nurses wouldn't let her see her new-born, first child because of the fever.

Billy was racing that night at Yonkers. The hospital called the patrol judge, who yelled down to Billy in the post parade for the third race, "You got a boy, Bill!" Bill finished third in the race with Colby's Match, then won the fifth with a 12–1 longshot, Captain Carefree, and raced to the hospital with Apples. They got to see the baby before Dottie did.

The Haughtons named their son William Harris Haughton after Billy and his stable's biggest owner, Colonel William C. Harris, in Massapequa. And Billy's stable kept on winning, which encouraged even more owners to join in, as his stable grew to become the biggest in the world.

Those weren't the only numbers increasing for him. His family size kept growing, too, forcing the Haughtons to relocate on Long Island from their apartment in Old Westbury to a starter home in Massapequa in 1952 to a new, larger house which Dottie helped design in Brookville on the north shore in '55, and then into a huge, 22-room house in Oyster Bay, six miles northwest of Brookville in the early '60s.

By then, the Haughtons were a family of seven. Following Billy Jr.'s birth on Oct. 30, 1952, Peter was born Sept. 22, 1954. Dottie lost two babies before Tommy was born Feb. 27, 1957. After again losing a baby, Dottie gave birth to Cammie, Feb. 6, 1960, and finally, to a girl. Holley was born Jan. 31, 1961.

What was it like growing up a Haughton?

It was nothing like "Leave It To Beaver," rather a frequently frantic household with people buzzing in and out at all hours. Dad was literally out every evening and many times on the road for days at a time.

Television was a foreign world to Billy Haughton.

"He never got a chance to ever watch anything on television," Dottie said. "When did he have time? He just didn't. He was always rushing and going, and his eye would find something on TV and he'd say, 'Whoaaaa. Call the judges and tell them I'll be late.' He'd pause in the kitchen on his way out and notice Donald Duck or the Roadrunner in a cartoon. He'd stay glued to the television and say, 'Sweetie, call the paddock and tell them I'll be right there. I'm on my way.' I'd always call the paddock for him. I thought it was pretty neat. We used to laugh all the time about it."

Morning schedules depended on the demands placed on Billy.

"I saw my dad work seven days a week," Billy Jr. said. "I remember him leaving the house at 6 in the morning, getting home in the afternoon to make phone calls 3 to 4; taking an hour nap and coming home midnight [after the races]. "He was a workaholic. And he loved what he did. In a way, I'm glad what happened to him [his fatal accident] happened to him at a racetrack, doing what he loved. I just wish I was closer to him. You don't realize what you have until it's gone."

He understood his father's absence from their house. He didn't like it, but he also didn't resent it. "No, it was expected," Billy Jr. said. "It just came with the territory. It was his job."

Billy Jr. would take a job with his dad, but unlike his three younger brothers, it was in his dad's office, not in the Haughton Stable at Roosevelt Raceway in Westbury, Long Island. Roosevelt Raceway is gone, but not forgotten. "I have so many memories from there," Billy Jr. said. "I remember him and my mom leading me from one barn to the other in a cowboy hat and a cowboy suit. I was about 3 years old. I've seen a photo of it. I can remember the old cars and the old people, the old times."

Some memories were more pleasant than others. "I remember when I was a kid at the barn, and there was a terrible fire," he said. "I remember a great old trotter named Mary Duke got killed in that fire. It was a thing I had nightmares about for a long time. Something like that really sticks with you. Innocent horses. They don't know what to do. The problem is that a lot of times they run back into the barn after they are led out."

That's because they seek a safe haven, and mistakenly conclude that it must be in their homes: the stalls in the barn that's on fire.

Billy Jr. never found a haven on the backstretch, instead carving a related career selling horsemen's insurance. "I had dreams of being a catch driver when I was a kid," he said. "That would be nice, just to get on the good horses and drive in a race. Oh, the thrill! The thought of it was great, but you can't do just that."

Not if your dad was Billy Haughton. Giving any of his kids an easy career path was never even considered. "You've got to come up through the ranks, like anyone else," Billy Jr. said.

And that was a problem for him, as far back as Billy Jr. can remember. "We had ponies when we were really young," Billy Jr. said. "But I just never got along with them. Peter always did. I fell off a lot. When I was walking a horse, a little thing like that, I could stay on. I could post (when the horse trotted) okay. But once we got on the trail, if a horse shied from a squirrel moving or something, I'd always end up on the ground hurt. Pop would say. 'Get back up on him. Show him who's boss.'

"'Pop, do me a favor this time. You get back up on him and show him who's boss. I'm walking home.' I remember one day I must have walked three miles home. I did not want to get up on that horse again.

"I remember my mom telling us that she got such a

bad concussion when she fell off a horse. She almost got killed one time riding horseback. I'm thinking, 'Hey, I'm not doing too good as it is now. Do I want to chance this much longer?'

"So I grew up to get on my mini bike and go kart and ride away. I liked that. It was easy. I didn't fall off a lot. I just didn't like the horses that much.

"I saw my dad and my brother give it a hundred percent and love it. And I couldn't give 50 percent and like it. I loved what they were doing. I'd look in the paper for their results. I liked going to the races. I liked watching them. But I didn't like being there and mucking out the stalls and grooming and have to fight with the bits and the big heavy horses and getting struck any second. Or to worry about that. I just didn't like it that much."

Billy Jr., who was called "Boogie" as a kid, would find his haven on a golf course, starting when he was eight. He became good enough to captain his golf team at prep school all four years he was there. "My dad started me in golf when I was eight, and I could hit it right away," Billy Jr. said. "I played with old guys and I could hit the ball in the hole from the green and they'd be amazed. I'd say, 'Wow, everybody thinks I'm pretty good.' I liked that. I thought that was pretty cool. So I played golf and I loved it."

Almost as much as he loved getting into trouble. Or so it seemed. When he was four or five, he filled his mom's new Cadillac's gas tank with sand. "We told her it was gas," he said. Another time, he stuck a coke bottle in the exhaust pipe, causing an explosion which severed an artery in his mother's arm. "No wonder we got a beating," he said. One time, he poured nail polish over his head and went screaming to his mother yelling that he'd split his head. Earlier, he and the kid next door,

Johnny Ritter, sunk the Ritter family's boat by drilling holes in it.

His parents decided to send Billy Jr. to St. Francis Prep in York, Pennsylvania, when he was 14. "I didn't like it, but I respected it," Billy Jr. said. "My dad was never around. He was always out racing and traveling here and there. I was there from '67 to '70, so I missed a lot of the golden years of my dad, his ultimate pride. But I used to get the Daily News sent to me at school. I could read the results in the paper. I always liked looking at that. I remember being very proud of my dad. I wasn't really happy at the time going to prep school. I don't think any of the kids that were there were happy. They thought it was a prison term."

In some respects it was. St. Francis was a strict Catholic school where students wore coat and tie; were required to eat all the food on their plates, and endured detention, spankings and beatings with a paddle. "All of those kids would have been tearing up the school if there wasn't that type of discipline, because a lot of the kids were real tough," Billy Jr. said.

At St. Francis, Billy Jr. discovered he did not have football or smoking in his future, though he tried both. In his ninth grade year, at 4-foot-11 and 98 pounds, he joined the football team, playing junior varsity as a quarterback and linebacker. "I used to get my head handed to me," he said. "We scrimmaged the varsity, and they had a 6-foot, 195-pound senior that was from Jackson, Mississippi. He was a big, black muscular running back who ran the 100 in about 11 seconds flat with pads on.

"We had to scrimmage, so I played linebacker on defense against him. And one day, he came through the line and I went to hit him, and it felt like he ripped my arms out of my sockets. He kind of stuck to my chest and face. And I laid there for a few minutes trying to figure out where I was. And then I got up, and I took my shoulder pads and my helmet off and I went to work for the Yearbook, because you could listen to the Mets games on the radio and smoke cigarettes. And I had just started to smoke."

Incredibly, this hardened prep school allowed kids to smoke if they were 13 or older and brought a note from their parents. "My friends were all starting, and I smoked," he said. "And I remember, the first couple of times I inhaled, I turned green. I thought I was going to die. I went to my bunk and lay there for hours writhing in pain and then persisted to smoke another couple of years, and I gave it up. My body was screaming very loudly: 'You idiot!'"

Billy Jr. survived St. Francis, and became editor of the Yearbook, and, then, at the young age of 17, attended Wake Forest. "I made a mistake," he said. "I should have taken a year or two off to figure out what I wanted to do. I was too young to go to college. The college was great and my grades were decent. I was okay in school. But I didn't even try out for the golf team because I had just fallen in love. And they had such a great golf team. Lanny Wadkins was in the my class and a couple other great players."

Billy Jr. spent two years at Wake Forest before transferring to New York Institute of Technology, right near Roosevelt Raceway. He went to college part-time for three years to earn a B.A. in marketing, while also returning to harness racing by working in his dad's trailer. "I analyzed feed costs; I did billing, and I called owners to tell them when their horses were in and the results," he said.

Previously, when he was 16, he had worked at Yonkers part time, pinning up the photo finishes in the grandstand. It was an intimidating experience for him. "Here I am, 16 years old, being escorted by a security officer to hang a photo finish," he said. "And, man, every time it was real close, a nose, I didn't want to hang that picture. Because there was always somebody yelling, 'They moved the wire,' or 'They changed the angle.'"

It's been a pet peeve of Billy Jr. for a long time: "So many people I talk to say, 'Oh, they hold them back. You see them all the time, they're leaning back.'

"Well, that's a driver trying to give lift to the sulky, to lift the arches to help the horse coming through the lane. And they see it as a guy sitting back and holding the horse. They lose a few bets and they get a twisted picture of what a person's like, just because of a poor performance on behalf of an animal. I regret that about the sport. Sure you get bad apples in every sport."

But he said he never heard that about his dad. "I'm just so impressed, that with the business being the nature it is, that somebody didn't say, 'Oh, that son of a bitch,'" or 'Oh, did he stiff me one night,'" Billy Jr. said.

"I never heard bad things about him, and that's what amazed me. As far as race fixing, he was probably on the farthest end of the spectrum away from that. He didn't even gamble on the sport. He never bet on harness racing. It was just a thing he had about it. He didn't have the time, for one thing. And he made enough money where he didn't have to worry about it. Occasionally, when he owned a thoroughbred, he'd go over with a couple of my guys and Peter, my brother, and they'd maybe throw $10 on a horse they had running that day. And I don't even know why they did that. Because if they had to bet an exacta, they wouldn't have known how."

But his dad did lose money at the track. Billy Haughton had a tough time saying, "No."

"My dad always had some money in his pocket in case somebody needed it," Billy Jr. said. "He used to have a guy named Thin Dime Murphy. He was about 90-years old up at Vernon Downs. Old-timer. Loved horses. Was always a good groom. And he'd come around, and he didn't have much money. And my dad would always give him a few dollars. A lot of the guys would help the grooms out just because they didn't have any pension plan or any kind of health benefits or a decent place to live. He was a groom, maybe at one time for my dad, probably at one time for everybody. Any of the grooms, if they were short that week, he'd help them because a groom isn't a high paying position. Pop wasn't a guy that wanted to be known as a rich guy, and he didn't flaunt what he had, but he would always give to others.'"

Dottie knew: "I'll bet he was owed a couple hundred thousand dollars when he died, money he just handed out to people through the years. When they'd come to give it back, he'd say, 'That's okay; don't worry about it."

That wasn't the only way Bill Haughton lost money. "He got taken a lot, because he was easy," Billy Jr. said. "He was soft. Somebody would talk him into something. He'd go, 'Okay, okay.' And then the next thing you know, one of the accountants embezzled him out of $125,000. Some other guy he loaned $10,000 to never showed up, and this one and that one. God, if you ever made up a list of what he probably gave out . . .

"But it never changed him. He never said, 'That son of a bitch.'"

He did once: to Billy Jr. when he was 20 and living at home. And, despite Billy Jr.'s litany of other childhood crimes, this one time he was innocent.

Billy's car had shot brakes. He left it in the driveway with the keys on the front hall table. And one day, he and Dottie went out in her car.

When they came home, his car was gone. The keys

were, too. "We didn't know if somebody had stolen it or what," Dottie said. "So we're blaming poor Billy. Billy had nothing to do with it, but we were sure it was Billy. Billy was always getting into something."

The culprit, though, was Tommy, then 15, who had never driven before. He and a couple friends had taken a joy ride through several hundred acres of Schiff's Estate (mostly woods, riding trails and fields owned by thoroughbred horse owner John Schiff). They went down a hill. The brakes failed and they smacked into a tree, ruining the radiator.

Billy Jr. then walked in the front door.

"I said, 'Hi, Dad,'" Billy Jr. recounted.

"He said, 'You son of a bitch.'"

Tommy heard that and took off, while Billy Jr. attempted to convince his father that, at least this time anyway, he wasn't the villain. "I didn't blame him for being mad, but he had the wrong guy," Billy Jr. said.

Tommy, meanwhile, disappeared for two days, leaving a note that he was sorry for what he had done and that he thought it was better if he ran away.

Dottie panicked. "Nobody had seen Tommy," she said. "We were wild. We were frantic. So I ran downtown to all his friends' houses and begged them: if they know where he is, tell us. We don't care if he's been bad. Just please tell us."

Unknown to his parents, Tommy was hiding on the roof of their neighbor's barn. "Watching everything," Dottie said. "Scared to death to come down. Finally, the neighbors noticed him up there and called us and said, 'Don't worry. He's here.' By that time, they had coaxed him down and talked to him. Can you imagine? Poor Tommy."

Tommy? How about innocent Billy Jr.?

Tommy's punishment? "Nothing," Dottie said. "We were so happy that he was okay. Everybody does something like that once in his lifetime. As long as it's a good lesson, that was all the punishment he needed. The way he had felt for all that time and staying all night long on that roof was punishment enough."

Billy Jr.'s credibility with his parents wasn't helped by a Halloween years earlier when, at the age of 11, a little girl and her father showed up at the Haughton's house. "He had smooshed an egg on her head," Dottie said. "There were broken eggs on this little girl's head. And the father came to the door with the child. Hadn't even wiped the eggs out of the kid's face. The yolks were in her eyes. And there she was crying in her little Halloween outfit.

"He said two words: 'Your son.'"

Billy Jr. hid in the woods with his friends, gradually working up the courage to go home. "My dad said to me, 'Come here,'" Billy Jr. said. "I said, 'Oh, boy.' He says to me, 'Listen, I'm not really as mad at you about doing it as much as I want to know that you're going to tell me the truth about what happened.'"

Billy Jr. denied it.

Bad choice. Off goes Billy's belt. "He tells me, 'This is hurting me more than it's hurting you,'" Billy Jr. said. "About three times he hit me with that belt, whack, whack, whack, and finally I said, 'Pop, I've got to be an idiot. I don't know why I didn't tell you in the first place. I'm lying. I'm sorry, I'm sorry. I'm sorry.' And he stopped hitting me."

Such displays of anger were few and far between for Billy Haughton, in his house or at the track. "He was so unusual in the fact that he never got too high or too low," Billy Jr. said. "He was always on an even keel. He was a very happy person. I think the whole key to life is enjoying what you do. And he did."

Tommy and Cammie seemed headed in opposite directions growing up. Tommy was interested in sports, especially football, not horses. Cammie wanted to join his father at the track.

"I didn't really care at all about horses," Tommy said. "The biggest thing that kept me away was that my dad was working so hard as I was growing up. He was gone in the morning before we'd go to school. And he might be home a little bit in the afternoon before he'd go to the races at night. I didn't see much of him. I didn't resent it. I just thought I would maybe like to do something different."

He wasn't completely adverse to horses. When he was 10, he'd sneak out at the crack of dawn on Sunday mornings to tail along after fox hunts nearby. He even jumped fences until his parents found out. That ended that.

Tommy was a quarterback in football and played basketball and track and field. He also boxed when he was 14. "I played a sport every season," he said. "I was good in all of them." He was good enough in football to be named a high school All-American.

But he might never have learned to kick a football without the help of his mother, still a devout Green Bay Packers fan. "She was always in love with the Green Bay Packers," Tommy said. "She'd come out there and play with us, throwing it around and kicking it around."

Dottie remembers the day Tommy came home from school and said, "Mom, Coach says I've got to kick. I tried. I'm not very good."

No problem. "I said, 'Wait a minute. I've got [Green Bay kicker] Don Chandler's book here. Let's look and see," Dottie said.

Dottie corralled Holley and Cammie and headed outside. Holley and Cammie were sent to the paddock to catch the football or chase it. Dottie was the holder.

"I went through the whole thing," Dottie said. "How many steps you take. Follow through. We did that for about an hour that afternoon. The next day, he goes to practice, and the coach says, 'Jesus, Tommy, where the hell did you ever learn to kick like that?' He said, 'My mom.'"

Tommy kept improving in football—eventually he'd get a scholarship to East Stroudsburg University in Pennsylvania—and his dad tried making every high school game that his schedule allowed, sometimes flying on the redeye from California if it meant he could get home in time. "He would do that for his kids," Tommy said.

Cammie grew up with one thing on his mind. "Horses, horses, horses," he said. "I didn't want to sit in the classroom. I wanted to run to the barn. I wanted to run over to Roosevelt Raceway all the time. I used to go put on Carmine Abbatiello's red silks and say, 'My dad's going to beat you tonight, buddy.' Carmine would laugh."

Nobody laughed when Cammie announced he was going to quit school. "He just didn't want to go anymore," Dottie said. "He stopped school early and went to work for Bill. We didn't have a choice. He was going to run away."

He did, but it was with his dad on the Grand Circuit as a groom. "We went out west to Springfield, Illinois, Indianapolis and Du Quoin," Cammie said. "You'd take care of your horses in the morning and hit the midway in the afternoon. Riding out there in the truck with all the other grooms was unbelievable. The talks, the hay flying. That was some life. That was the best part of my life, being a groom for my dad."

9

Barefoot and Pregnant in Du Quoin

Billy Haughton won four Hambletonians in seven years, but it took him a long time to get the first one with Christopher T in 1974. Up to that point, more than a few people kept asking Billy when he was going to end this "jinx," so he figured he needed all the help he could get and asked Dottie to come with him every year. In fact, when Christopher T won the Hambo, Billy told Dottie, "Sweetie, I finally won one. You don't ever have to come back to Du Quoin."

That's because he left her:

Barefoot and pregnant in Du Quoin

Dottie was some seven months pregnant when Billy again asked her to come to the 1957 Hambletonian, which was then held at the state fairgrounds in Du Quoin, Ill., before moving to The Meadowlands in 1981. Billy was scheduled to drive his talented filly Flicka Frost against colts in the trotting classic.

Dottie agreed to go. This was their game plan: she would meet him at Roosevelt Raceway the night before the Hambletonian after Billy drove in his last race that night; Apples would drive them to the airport; they would fly to Washington, D.C.; make a connection to St. Louis, the nearest major airport, and make the three-hour drive to Du Quoin.

The itinerary began unraveling right at the start. At Idlewild (now JFK) Airport, they learned their flight was delayed. This didn't bode well for their connection from Washington, D.C., to St. Louis.

Dottie narrated:

"We got into Washington around midnight or 12:30. All the coffee shops were closed. We leaned against each other on this hard bench, as my feet were swelling outside of my shoes. The Hambletonian is the next day. At 7:30 the next morning, we had to fly from Washington to Chicago, then Chicago to St. Louis. We chartered a plane to Carbondale. Get to Carbondale 20 miles from Du Quoin. There were no cars available to rent, and there were no taxis."

The solution? Stick your thumb out. The Haughtons caught a ride with a farmer in a pick-up truck, who took them to Du Quoin.

"He let us off on the opposite side of where our barn was," Dottie said. "We both jumped out, and Bill said, 'You take your time. I'm going to run.' So he took off running. I got the bags to Frank Ervin's barn [the first one she saw]. I gave them to someone and they locked them up in the feed room.

"I started walking. It was about 106 degrees. I had to take off my shoes because my blisters popped and were bleeding. The dust was like talcum powder, so dry. I was in such a mess with no sleep and I couldn't find a seat anywhere.

"They were frying fish at a stand near the paddock. There was a seat, and I was sitting there, and I heard them starting to call the race [the Hambletonian]. Bill had gotten there in time. And Flicka Frost was in front at the three-quarters pole. And the announcer said,

'Oops. She made a break.' I started to cry. All these people were looking at me and they didn't know what to make of me. I was crying and crying. That was the crowning blow."

It wasn't.

After the day's races were over, Dottie journeyed to the barn. Billy wanted to check on Flicka Frost one last time.

That's when Billy said, "Jesus Christ, I forgot to get us a room!"

Dottie took a good long look at Flicka Frost, who appeared quite comfortable on her bed of straw. "I just wanted to lay down next to Flicka Frost," Dottie said.

She didn't. Using his considerable influence, Billy was able to get hold of a motel room which was so bad that two of Hall of Famer Joe O'Brien's owners had vacated it. "No air conditioning; torn screens," Dottie said. "It looked fine to me."

* * *

There are countless road tales from Billy Haughton's career.

"I don't think we ever walked to an airplane, I really don't," Dottie said. "It was always running through the terminal and praying that they hadn't pulled the ladder up or closed the gates. We missed planes a couple of times. It made him very upset. We jumped in the car and drove."

Stanley Dancer made many trips with Billy, some by airplane and some by car. Though they had more than one frightening air flight, Stanley was never more scared than he was with Billy behind the steering wheel at the end of a night. "I always worried that he'd die in his car," Stanley said. "He was picking me up one night in Florida, maybe 15 years ago. He had two or three owners with him, and they'd been out. I said, 'You want me to drive, Bill?'

"He said, 'No, no, I'm fine.'

"I don't think we'd gone two miles and he dozed right off. I said, 'Whoa, I'm going to drive.'

"To him, it was just a catnap. He'd fall asleep with ease. Many times I'd have to wake him up in the drivers' room. Maybe he'd skip one race when he wasn't driving, and there he was sound asleep."

Once Billy was asleep, he was tough to rouse. "Back when they had piston airplanes, we were going to Buffalo or Batavia out of La Guardia Airport," Stanley said. "Gee whiz, it was thunder and lightning and the plane was rocking all over and he's sound asleep with his head against the window. I seen these nuns with their rosary beads. I'm not Catholic, and I don't know a lot about it, but, man, they're working those things. And I woke him up. I said, 'Billy, we're going to crash! We're going down! Look!'

"He looks and says, 'Ah, it's a little thunder storm.'

"I point to the nuns and say, 'Look!'"

"He says, 'Naaah, they're just praying. It's nothing.'

"He went back to sleep."

* * *

There were other near-misses for Billy and Peter, too. Billy and Peter were riding in Herve Filion's private helicopter one night. "They took off for The Meadowlands from a little helicopter pad in Mineola (Long Island)," Dottie said. "I watched them go up and drove away. The next thing I know, Bill was on the phone. The engine had seized. Some jerk put in the wrong fuel. They had to land on the top of a building."

They lived to talk about it. Another time, Billy and Peter took a private plane from Long Island to the small airport near Monticello Raceway. The landing left a lot to be desired. "They went off the end of the runway, down over the embankment and tore the wing off the plane," Dottie said. "But they went ahead and raced that night. They sent another plane for them to come back to Long Island. I would have walked home."

Another time, Peter's plane lost all its electrical power and was forced to make an emergency landing without lights or a radio at an Air Force base in New Jersey. His plane was greeted by troops carrying machine guns. Peter didn't care. He got out of the plane, bent over and literally kissed the ground.

* * *

Stanley Dancer could neither sleep as easily as Bill nor party as long.

"Many, many times we flew to California to race together," Stanley said. "Billy could out-party me. I did my share of it, but he was tough. We were both USTA Directors. Gosh, we'd have meetings and go to dinner and go out. I'd party out, but he'd keep on going. He had great stamina."

Years later, John Campbell, who was good friends with Peter Haughton, would travel with Billy and reach the same conclusion. "We rode on the same plane a lot of times," Campbell said. "He was an amazing man. His stamina and enthusiasm was just incredible. He just loved doing what he was doing. You never caught him out of sorts or being irritable. He could be on the go a lot and it didn't matter."

Bill O'Donnell marveled at Haughton's constitution, too. "Boy, did he ever have fun," O'Donnell said. "He only required three or four hours of sleep a night. I can only do it two or three days, and then I have to crash. I have no idea how he did it. No idea. We were at Rosecroft (Maryland) for the Breeders Crown. He went to a party and had a few drinks. He was pretty blitzed.

He could go to sleep anywhere, and he'd wake up completely sober."

Billy Haughton would go anywhere and do just about anything to promote the sport of harness racing he loved so dearly. "We drove elephants against each other at Pompano," Stanley Dancer said. "I won one race, Bill won one and we had a dead heat. It didn't bother him, but I got hit by a trunk." Billy also drove camels and zebras in publicity stunts. Anything to help harness racing.

And when a racetrack official asked if he could make an out-of-town appearance, he did, if his schedule permitted it. Dottie can remember only one planned appearance Billy had to cancel. "We were supposed to fly to New Zealand, and one of our top horses had gotten lame," Dottie said. "We were at the farm in New Hampshire. He said, 'I just can't go.' He called New Zealand and made his apologies. And they were so disappointed. That was the only time I could ever remember him not making it to a track."

Billy and Dottie appeared at just about every annual United States Harness Writers Awards Dinner and every annual Hall of Fame Day in Goshen, N.Y., when new inductees are feted.

"One year at Vero Beach, we were racing back home on one of our boats to make the Harness Writers Dinner and the water pump went," Dottie said. "He was so upset because we were going to miss the Dinner. He would go every year. And every year he went to the Hall of Fame, unless he had some big race that Sunday. Always. It's a great honor to be in the Hall of Fame. The least thing you can do is to show up on Hall of Fame Day. Delvin Miller always did. He just kept on giving. There aren't too many like him. I wish there were. If more people in this world, not just athletes, gave a little more than what they expected to get, what a good world we'd live in."

Billy and Delvin competed in the Mickey Mantle Sports Festival in Sorrento, Florida, February 1–2, 1958, playing golf to raise money for the Damon Runyon Cancer Fund and Hodgkins Disease Fund. Billy also did fundraisers for muscular dystrophy and once developed a sulky for handicapped people.

Peter Haughton, just like his dad, promoted the sport, too. At the age of 23, he went up to Foxboro Raceway in Massachusetts on opening night, Dec. 1, 1977, for a five race competition against local driving star John Hogan.

In 1982, the Saratoga Chapter of the U.S. Harness Writers Association had a bold plan: to create a local Hall of Fame. Through an incredible amount of work by Saratoga Harness announcer George Miller—a disciple of Roy Shudt who also became a legend at Saratoga—the idea actually took shape. A fund-raising dinner was a prerequisite, and in a blatant attempt to attract the most number of people, letters went out to two very famous horsemen and their wives, asking them if they could interrupt their schedules to attend a Hall of Fame kickoff dinner at Saratoga Harness on a Sunday night. Both Billy and Dottie Haughton and Glen and Paula Garnsey made the time; attended the dinner; insisted on paying their own way there; insisted on paying for tickets, and turned the dinner into a huge success. And both couples had a great time doing it, square dancing and partying the night away. The Saratoga Hall of Fame remains an outstanding regional museum under the guidance of Virginia O'Brien, the former denmother of the Saratoga pressbox, guide for children's backstretch tours, and first woman member of the Saratoga Chapter of the Harness Writers Association.

* * *

As popular as Billy was at Saratoga, he was also a big hit at Prince Edward Island in Canada after making an appearance at Charlottetown Driving Park on August 12, 1968, as part of Old Home Week and the Provincial Exhibition. A banner headline in *The Charlottetown, Prince Edward Island Guardian* read:

Haughton Tells Crowd
He Likes This Country

The story read: "'I like your country and wish I could stay longer to see more of it,' Haughton told a crowd at the opening ceremonies. 'I think it is a real honor to be able to have won a few more races than Joe O'Brien from the Island, and it was good to watch racing in the place from which so many good drivers have come, like James 'Roach' MacGregor and Earl Avery.'"

* * *

Stan Bergstein, Executive Vice President of Harness Tracks of America and a life-long friend of the whole Haughton family, told this story about Billy:

On a winter trip to Canada, where he was asked to speak at a horsemen's dinner, Billy made quite an impression on Hall of Famer Ron Walpes' son, Randy, an aspiring driver. Upon hearing that Randy wanted to be a driver, Billy pulled his whip out of his traveling bag, autographed the handle and presented it to Randy to use in his first race for luck. Randy used it once, then hung it on a wall. At the dinner, Randy said to his dad, "Can you imagine Mr. Haughton coming all this way up from Florida to talk at this time of year?" Ron agreed on Bill's special qualities, and then, with his usual delightful needle, said to his son, "He's something special all right, but how about your old man?" Ron's son turned to him and said, "You're great Dad, but you're no Mr. Haughton."

Billy with 2½ year-old Holley at the Ben White Raceway training track in 1963.

10

Holley louyah— It's A Girl!

Dottie Haughton always wanted a daughter. In her eighth and final pregnancy, she got her wish. She was ecstatic when Holley Haughton was born, Jan. 31, 1961. "After wanting a girl, all I ever wanted, she was so special," Dottie said. "Doctor Rozier was happier than anybody. He felt proud, like he'd finally given me a little girl. It was wonderful, just wonderful, but I never had time to spoil her." Dottie paused and laughed, "Because of all the rotten little boys."

Holley, though, held her own in the Haughton hierarchy. "She handled herself just fine with those boys," Dottie said. "They used to shoot her in the butt with BBs and she'd get on the garden tractor and run them over. She was just as tough. And she could run faster than a couple of them."

Holley, of course, spent part of her childhood as a tomboy. "How could I not be?" she asked. "I grew up with four brothers. Of course it was a little tough for me with all the brothers. I tried to keep up with all of them."

Yet while she played with her brothers and their friends, she also admired her mother's femininity and class. "I always idolized my mother as being so much of a lady," Holley said. "I had to keep that. I enjoyed being like a lady, too, getting dressed up and doing all the lady things. So I had a little bit of both."

She developed a love of horses and an interest in photography, at one point converting the wine cellar in the basement of their house into a darkroom.

With her father away much of the time, and Dottie intermittently accompanying him, Holley, like her brothers, had other adults in their lives: Geneva Stubbs, a housekeeper from Aberdine, North Carolina, who worked for the Haughtons for 19 years (1962–81), and Mary Tatum, a nanny who worked for the Haughtons in the '70s and remains friends with Holley and Dottie to this day, and, of course, Apples.

"He was there for us," Holley said. "If we missed the bus, he was there to take us to school. He lived with us in Oyster Bay when my mother had her stroke and was paralyzed.

"Mary was like a nanny. Geneva did a lot of the cooking and the cleaning and the laundry, and Mary helped, too, with that, and with our homework to make sure everything got done. I have to say they were very good about making us do certain things around the house, too, learning responsibilities. A lot of it came from them. They were there, a very big part of our lives."

Horses were, too. There's a picture in the June 1963, issue of *Hoof Beats* of Billy Haughton jogging a horse in Florida with Holley in his lap helping her daddy hold on to the reins. Holley wasn't even 2½ years old. Holley began showing horses when she was 3½. "I wasn't really as fond of going to the track as I was being around the horses we had at home," she said. "I mean I really enjoyed the riding horses."

The one she loved the most was In The Light. "He

was one of the thoroughbreds mom and dad had," she said. "He wasn't doing that good, and they brought him home for the summer along with Stout Fellow, another retired thoroughbred that Peter used to ride all the time. Peter even shod him a couple of times. We used to try to ride as much as we could together."

The Haughtons owned dozens of thoroughbreds, and Billy seriously considered training them after he retired from harness racing. Hall of Fame jockey Ron Turcotte, rider of the immortal Secretariat, was one of the Haughtons' neighbors in Oyster Bay.

"In The Light was a chestnut and he kind of reminded me of Secreteriat," Holley said. "It was around the time Secretariat was very popular. I really enjoyed In The Light coming home for the summer. He was 3 at the time, and I was in the sixth grade. That was a challenge for me to work him. There was a big estate back behind the house (Schiff's Estate) and we used to ride through the woods. And there was this big hill. My dad used to say, 'We've got to build his legs up and get him to the races.'"

Holley endeavored to do just that. "There was—and still is—a very big water tower on the Schiff Estate," she said. "It was like a big landmark. And there was a big briar patch behind the tower. In The Light and I were out one afternoon by ourselves, and I didn't know it, but they were re-surfacing or re-finishing that water tower. We went up into the woods, and we got right by the water tower, and they fired up one of the huge sanders that they used to refinish it. And he went crazy. He reared up and backed in. And we got all tangled up in the briar patch. It was a little scary."

Holley rushed home on In The Light. Billy was home from Roosevelt that afternoon. "And I was trying to tell him about this," Holley said. "To me, it was very important. The horse had been cut up, and I really needed to know what things to do. I was telling him the story and he nodded out on me."

Catnap. Holley had to wait. "He needed that rest," she said.

Holley had to settle for a quick word with her dad later, before he rushed out of the house to return to the track.

In The Light recovered and returned to the races.

"He came home for two summers then went back to the track," Holley said. "I didn't know they had put him in a claiming race. And it was mud and pouring rain. And he hated the mud. He got so mad that he won the race, but he had been claimed, and I never saw him again."

It wasn't Holley's lone heartbreak with one of her horses. The Haughtons named a pacing filly Holley By Golly, one of the four horses 16-year-old Peter had on the road when he toured the Pennsylvania fair circuit in 1970 to gain experience.

Unfortunately, she broke down in a race at Allentown and had to be euthanized. Peter called Holley with the bad news. "That was a very tough time for me," Holley said. "First of all, having a horse named after you is kind of an honor. I'll never forget the day I got the call." The pain in her voice still resonates nearly 30 years later.

More frequently, there were happier times, and times she got in trouble, too.

"I really have to say, because of the way I was raised, I never did anything really bad," she said. "I always had in the back of my mind my mother and father reminding us about respect, and about how hard they worked for us, and to remember right from wrong. Even when I went out with friends, I didn't want to really get into trouble. I was always the one who tended to want to go home."

Almost always.

Holley was 14 when she said good night to her mother, went upstairs to her room, and then sneaked out with some of her friends.

Dottie and Apples were in the house that night, and Dottie found out Holley wasn't in her room at 10 p.m.. "I was so upset," Dottie said. "I went into Apples' room and I said, 'She is not in her room. She is not in this house.' I waited and waited and waited and waited."

Holley got back at 2 in the morning and was horrified to see the light on in her room. She told her friends, "Oh my God, I'm in big trouble."

She decided to sneak up the back stairway, where she could hear Dottie and Apples talking about her. Holley heard something else. "I had on these thick dungaree jeans, and when you walked, they'd go swishhh, swishhh," she said. So she took them off. Coming up the stairs, she heard Dottie say to Apples, "Go to bed and I'll deal with her in the morning."

Holley darted into Geneva's bathroom in the hallway, ditched her pants, skulked back to her room and turned on the light.

There was Dottie sitting on her bed.

"So I turned off the light," Holley said.

Dottie yelled, "Turn that light on and get over here! And where are your pants?"

Holley was punished, but not as much as her parents thought. "My punishment was that I didn't get to see my friends for the summer, and I had to go to our farm in New Hampshire and work," she said. "But little did they know, it really wasn't that much punishment for me, because I really did love the farm. That was when we had the cows, and my Morgan, Charlie, was just two at the time. I hated to leave my friends, but I enjoyed the farm."

Twenty-five years later, she and her two children, Peter and Jake, relocated from South Florida to Pioneer Farm, in Newfields, New Hampshire, which Dottie and Bill had purchased in 1976 with the earnings from the best horse Dottie ever owned, World Champion Keystone Pioneer. Dottie currently splits her year between Pioneer Farm and Florida.

"I bred her dam, Passing Speed," Dottie said. "Keystone Pioneer was in a sale, but we bought her back for $12,500. But Bill didn't tell me for two weeks that I had a partner. He sold half of her. One of our owners, Arnold Bachner, wanted to give half of the horse to his estranged wife to try to win her back. He asked Bill if he could buy half the filly. As usual, Bill could not say no."

Keystone Pioneer was an incredible trotting mare who won several stakes as a 3-year-old filly in 1975, all with Dick DeSantis driving: a $10,320 division of the Arden Downs Stakes; the $59,567 Hambletonian Oaks and the $19,475 Kentucky Futurity Filly Division. That season she was fifth in the Haughton Stable in earnings, making $110,791. After '75, Billy or Peter usually drove her. In 1977, she was fourth in the stable, making $235,683 and helping Peter post a three-for-three driving night. On a sloppy track at Yonkers in the fall, Peter, who had started out the Yonkers meet zero-for-seven, had three drives and won them all with Gypsy Flyer, Keystone Pioneer and Superchick. Keystone Pioneer returned two years later to win the 1979 $35,000 Titan Cup at Goshen with Billy driving. She finished her career as a 6-year-old in 1980 with total earnings of $1,071,927 from a career record of 64 wins, 32 seconds and 19 thirds in 162 starts. She was the first American bred and owned trotting filly to ever win a million dollars and was inducted into the Harness Racing Museum and Hall of Fame in 1998.

Dottie's desire to buy a farm in New England started with her increasing displeasure at the number of stable help and their friends using the Haughton house in Oyster Bay, Long Island, as a second home. "The grooms used to call it 'The Country Club,'" Dottie said. "It wasn't really our place where we could relax any more. The grooms stayed in the guest rooms when the horses they cared for were turned out in one of our paddocks adjacent to the house. I cooked for them and did their wash. I got to the point where I just needed time with Bill. I didn't need to look out at the pool, and there he is talking to owners and there are three girls from Sweden laying there in their bikinis that the grooms had invited. They didn't need to be listening to everything he said on the phone. So I said to him, 'Let's go to Vermont and buy a little farm somewhere.' I always wanted a farm. Well, he thought that was a great idea."

Billy called Bill Rosenberg, the founder of Dunkin' Donuts and one of Bill's owners. The Rosenbergs, who lived in New Hampshire, were also good friends with the Haughtons.

Billy and Dottie flew into Boston, rented a car and stopped by the Rosenbergs. "By the time we got there, he already had a real estate guy there waiting to show us around New Hampshire," Dottie said. "We looked and looked all day, and finally this place was sitting there and was exactly what I wanted. It was a little rundown, and a bunch of hippies lived in it, but I could just see the possibilities. So that's the place I bought in '76 with the money that Keystone Pioneer won. We'd all stay there on weekends and holidays. We loved the farm.

"Peter joked, 'We're the only family that the parents ran away from home and left the kids behind.'"

After driving at Roosevelt Raceway on Saturday nights, Billy would routinely catch the last flight to

Boston out of LaGuardia Airport. "It left at midnight," Dottie said. "I'd drive from the farm to Boston and pick him up at one in the morning. We'd get back at 2 a.m. He usually could stay until Monday."

The original house on Pioneer Farm was built in 1697, its wooden floors milled right on the property. The Haughtons have added two wings onto the 12-room main house. There's a guest house—originally a spring house with a well—two huge barns, run-in sheds in the paddocks for the horses, and five fields ranging from one to five acres.

In New Hampshire, Dottie could pursue other interests. One was growing vegetables and fruits and making preserves and entering them annually in the New Hampshire State Fair, where she has won 36 first prizes. She might not have always had the best produce, but nobody had cleaner vegetables. Dottie is fastidious to a high degree, so much that she'd get down on her hands and knees and clean her carrots with a toothbrush to show in competition. "It's worse than you can imagine," Dottie said of her obsession. "I'm just a neatness freak."

She's also a flower enthusiast. After becoming one of the youngest members of the Syosset Garden Club on Long Island, becoming its president four years later, and winning a record number of competitions, she decided she wanted to become a judge in flower shows. "And that took five years of courses," she said. "That took up a lot of my time, but I enjoyed every minute of it."

She has more free time in New Hampshire to pursue her passion for gardening thanks to Marino DiMambro, who's been taking care of Pioneer Farm for 20 years and counting. Like so many others, Marino became close to Peter. "He was the nicest guy you ever met," Marino said. "He never said 'I'm better than you.'"

None of the Haughtons said that. To them, everyone was family. Every Christmas, Billy would hook big sleigh bells on the horses and he and Dottie would take friends and neighbors for sleigh rides through the woods, singing along with Frank Sinatra Christmas tapes. "Then we'd stop at our cabin in the woods, sit by the woodstove and have hot cocoa," Dottie said. "It was so much fun."

Pioneer Farm became the home of one of Billy and Dottie's favorite horses, Dr. Dewars, named for the elder Haughtons' favorite brand of Scotch. Dottie, who bred Dr. Dewars, the first horse Peter drove in a race, explained: "Sometimes, Bill would be away from home for a week when the kids were little. The minute he walked in, if they had been bad, I'd go, 'Oh, you've got to talk to this one! Or you've got to spank that one!' And he'd just say, 'Come on sweetie, let's have a little Dr. Dewars. It'll calm you right down.' And, before you knew it, it wasn't the end of the world."

Dottie brought Dr. Dewars out of retirement to race at the Rochester Fair in New Hampshire, entrusting him to Warren Harp, a New England horseman who became close to the Haughtons. "I knew Billy since 1949 or 1950," Harp said. "I remember one night at Rockingham Park. He had raced Bret's Star there. We came out of the locker room and we were taking Bill and Dottie back to the airport, and we were late. Dottie kept saying, 'Come on Bill; come on Bill.' And a boy came out, he was 12 or 13. And he asked Bill a question. I bet Bill talked to him 20 minutes to half an hour. He didn't care if he missed the plane. He always had time for everybody. It didn't make a difference who you were."

Ben Steall, an assistant to Billy for many years, saw it happen all the time. "Bill knew everybody," he said. "It didn't matter what groom it was. He knew them by their first name and he'd talk to them just like he talked to anybody."

But Billy did more than just talk. Nobody knows

that better than Harp, who got in an accident at Scarborough Downs in Portland, Maine, and broke his ankle. "It was on the 11 o'clock news," Harp said. "Well, the next morning, it was raining and miserable. He and Dot showed up at my farm at about 8 o'clock. This man jogged every horse I had, eight or 10 horses. Dottie was helping my wife, Joan, clean stalls. How many people of the stature of Billy Haughton would do this for anyone? We had lunch. He said, 'Warren, you have two nice horses. You should get rid of the others.' And he was right."

Billy and Dottie never got rid of Dr. Dewars. He lived on Pioneer Farm to the age of 29 when he slipped on ice and broke his hip. "He was still king of the hill," Dottie said. "I'd bring him in and hook him up to a carriage and you'd think he was in the second race at Roosevelt. His ears would perk up and he'd stand there like a young horse. He just loved to be hooked up and driven. He was a joy his whole life."

11

Life in the Sixties

By 1963, the Haughton Stable was clearly the most successful and biggest harness racing operation in the world. At the age of 40, Billy Haughton had no midlife crisis. He was too busy.

In her fascinating two part series in *Hoof Beats*, Mary Louise McGregor detailed the intricate operations of the Haughton Stable as it wintered at Ben White Raceway in Orlando, Florida.

Billy had 122 horses with him that winter and 70 people on the stable payroll, including full-time assistant trainers Al "Apples" Thomas, Bill "Bones" Vaughan, Joe Greene, Irvin Roberts and Rudy Robinet. Jim Siver worked for the Haughton Stable in the winter only. Mrs. Jan Bell was Haughton's personal secretary and receptionist, and Apples' wife Billie was the stable bookkeeper and "indispensable" office manager.

But much of the stable's operations were accessible only by speaking with Billy himself. "I don't write much down, but I keep it all up here," Haughton told McGregor, pointing to his forehead. "I guess I depend mostly on my trainers, and I expect them to keep the grooms on their toes. I like to bring my second trainers up from the grooms' ranks. There's less dissension that way and most of them make it if they just get a chance."

The Haughton Stable was housed in a huge, renovated building that was formerly the headquarters for the Florida Livestock Exposition and once had an arena for showing cattle. Billy also used an 18-stall barn on the other side of the track.

"At one time we had over 200 horses, which was the biggest racing stable in the world," Dottie said. "We usually had 160 in Florida, maybe another 20 at Brandywine (a track in Delaware) and one year we even had to send some to the South Florida Training Center (near Pompano Park) with one of the trainers because we didn't have enough room."

And one year, they almost didn't make it back from Florida. "One time, we hadn't gotten paid by a few owners that had a lot of horses with us, and we were getting ready to ship north," Dottie said. "When you ship in boxcars, you have to have the money. Bill said, "I don't know if I can make the payment.'

"I said, 'Wait a minute.' I went and got my bankbook and there was enough money. He was so proud of that. He said, 'Where did you get this money?' I said, "Out of your pocket all these years.' He never missed a $10 or $20. I put it in a bank account. I must have stolen $20,000 from him," she laughed.

Dottie has fond memories of winters in Orlando. "We'd take the whole stable down in a big train in boxcars," she said. "They'd go from Yonkers and pull up right on the side of Ben White Raceway. And out they'd come. We had a big Quanset barn. It was like an airplane hangar. The aged horses would be turned out for about three months. They'd get a nice vacation. Then you'd get them ready and you'd break your babies."

The horsemen there held weekly parties and

dances on Friday or Saturday nights, many times at the Haughtons' house on a lake. "Everybody would get together," Dottie said. "After curfew at midnight, the bands from town would come to the house, and we'd have live music. It was great. We had so much fun in those days."

She remembers her Peter being a Marshall for matinee races. "He had a little pony," she said. "He was about seven or eight."

Dottie remembers many of the antics of Delvin Miller, who'd show off by eating glass or fishbones in front of people. "All those terrible things to shock people," Dottie laughed.

One afternoon he shocked himself. He wanted to throw a firecracker dud on the track near the fence where some of the owners watched their horses from the parking lot. "Someone replaced his dud with a real one," Dottie said. "And Delvin threw this lit firecracker out on the track to scare everybody. The damn thing went off. The horses reared up, and one owner hit the gas pedal when she heard the explosion and went through the fence and right across the track. Nobody got hurt, but cars got wrecked and the horses were, oh my God, scared."

But life in Florida wasn't all parties and pranks. Trainers in the Haughton Stable were required to check in daily at 6:45 a.m. to ensure that everyone else was on duty. If someone was missing, his pay was docked and another man was asked to work a double shift so no horse missed a scheduled work.

Work schedules were posted on Sundays with seven horses listed in sets, which usually numbered three 2-year-old horses, two green horses and two aged horses, allowing Billy a chance to drive different horses.

Trainers picked up yellow slips each morning listing their horses, sets and approximate times they were to train their horses in. At the end of the morning, the actual times were written in with brief comments about any problems, allowing Apples to keep a progress report on each horse.

Apples then routinely rotated sets. McGregor explained: "For instance, the first set on Monday will work as the second set on Thursday. No man pulls the last set each time, nor does he get the early session every time."

Horses began working at 8 or 8:30 each morning, except on Sundays. Billy was usually there by 6 to personally train the problem horses. "He was a real good horsemen and a hard worker," breeder Max Hempt said. "He trained all the trouble horses. He'd be out at six in the morning with them. Maybe their gait was wrong or there was something else wrong. He wouldn't let a second trainer take care it. Then at 8, he would start training his regular horses."

Breeder Murray Brown of Hanover Shoe Farms said, "If I was a horse, I'd want to be in one of his mutt (trouble horses) classes. Just getting hands-on attention from the Master would be unbelievable."

Seton Hanover, owned by John Froehlich, received as much attention as any horse Billy ever trained.

"He was a grand looking colt that Apples said was horrible from Day One," Brown said. "He didn't even know how to pace and he tore up equipment."

Stanley Dancer remembers Seton Hanover intimately: "Apples had him and he couldn't get him on the pace. He was by Dancer Hanover, and they were all pretty tough to get pacing. They brought him down to Florida so Billy could go with him. He went with him every day. And he got to be a pretty good pacer."

One day, he was better than good when he upset Dancer's champion pacer, Albatross.

Billy made a practice of bringing his horses around

to racing condition slowly. "I don't believe in going fast early with my colts," he said. "I don't feel that they're really up to it so early. I like to drop them a little each week and do it gradually."

Accordingly, before horses begin turning for training miles in the winter, they jogged a maximum of five miles daily. Horses jog clockwise for easy exercise, but train fast miles and race counter-clockwise. Once they started turning, horses jogged two miles after a work day and three miles every other day. When they returned to race, horses usually warmed up with slow miles, a first trip in 2:30 and a second trip in 2:25. Many other trainers worked their horses faster.

Feeding in Florida was scheduled at 6 a.m., 11:45 a.m. and 4:45 p.m. All grooms were required to return to the stable by 4:15. "Prices don't mean a thing when we're buying feed," Apples said. Billy had heavy clover hay shipped by tractor-trailer from Ohio to Florida and sweet-smelling straw shipped from Tennessee. Billy bought triple-cleaned oats, bran, sweet feed and Stamm, a food supplement, from the Pillsbury Company in Orlando, and also gave his horses a liquid supplement, Livitol, which was supplied by his veterinarian, Dr. Bernard Brennan.

Billy used straw, rather than sawdust, for horses' bedding. "It's drier, not much more expensive, and it's an expense the owners should be willing to pay," he said.

Two trainers remained on duty in the afternoon doing odd jobs, including taking care of equipment. One trainer remained on duty on Sundays, from 7 a.m. to noon and from 3 p.m. to 6 p.m. A night watchman worked from 9 p.m. to 6 a.m. and had six check-in stations. He also had the authority to fire any employee who got out of hand.

Billy used plastic hobbles for most of his pacers and changed them every year. Harnesses were traded in every two years. "We never buy anything outright," Apples said. "We always try to make trades when we need equipment." One interesting innovation Billy tried was using thoroughbred blinkers. Apples explained, "We find that these hoods fit a horse better than a closed bridle, and besides we can turn the blinker cups any way we choose."

Shoeing was handled by Wilmer "Bud" Benner, a long-time Haughton employee.

McGregor said Billy paid "the top going rate for caretakers," and also gave grooms a paddock fee at the races. Two grooms were required to paddock every horse that raced.

"Most of our men stay with us," Apples said. "If you can't work for Haughton, you can't work for anyone."

But Billy's popularity wasn't confined to his employees. On May 20, 1963, he was honored by the United States Trotting Association at Roosevelt Raceway for becoming the first driver in harness racing history to win 2,000 races. During the 22-minute trackside ceremony in the winner's circle before the first race, Billy received a slew of gifts including King's Park, a thoroughbred hunter, from Roosevelt Raceway; a saddle, bridle and other riding equipment from Stanley Dancer, George Sholty and the other Roosevelt horsemen; a watch from his employees; Tiffany sterling silver service and cabinet from his owners, including Mrs. William C. Harris, whose late husband Colonel William C. Harris was Billy's first big owner; Steubenville glassware from Harness Tracks of America; antique silver goblets from the Standardbred Owners Association, and a gold pen and pencil set from the United States Harness Writers Association.

But there was one present left for Billy, Dottie, 10-year-old Billy Jr; Peter (8), Tommy (6), Cammie (3) and

Holley (2): the reaction of the more than 20,000 fans at Roosevelt. After the ceremony, the Haughtons were scheduled for a reception at the Raceway's Director's Lounge. To get there, they had to trasverse the huge apron in front of the grandstand. As they made their way, Billy was stopped repeatedly by fans wishing to shake his hand. When he stopped to sign one autograph, there were suddenly dozens. It took Billy 20 minutes to make a one-minute walk as he kept signing autographs and thanking fans. Only when the announcer said, "They're off" for the first race, did the crowd finally thin out.

Billy Haughton Jr. will never forget that evening. "It was like Babe Ruth Night or Hank Aaron Night," he said, the wonder still in his voice 35 years later. "They gave him a horse, a beautiful leather saddle. They gave him silverware, all kinds of things. And the crowd . . . the crowd was packed around us as far deep as you could see right up to the fence yelling and clapping."

In a profile of Billy in *Sports Illustrated* the following June, entitled "An Emperor in Harness," Mark Kram wrote of that night: "The official program was perfunctory, heavy with superlatives, gifts and so forth, but it remained for the fans to raise the evening to a point beyond the pedestrian. In a rare display of affection, they swarmed around him at the end of the presentations. He signed autographs, a scene that might have moved some veteran horseplayers to blush.

"'You know,' says his wife, 'We thought about it a long time before we decided to bring the children that night. We were worried about how the people would react. They even booed Adios Butler the night he was retired, and when Eddie Arcaro retired, the thoroughbred crowd booed him. The way they acted toward Billy was really a surprise. It was one of the finest moments in his career.'"

The *SI* profile called Haughton's harness empire "an almost flawless combination of human and horse that ranks as one of the finest single achievements in American sports." Dottie was referred to as "a wife who always looks as if she just stepped out of Town & Country," and Kram revealed Haughton's exhausting schedule, his deep love of harness racing and his interest in thoroughbreds which sometimes bordered on obsession.

In the *SI* article, Dottie said, "The house could be burning down, but Bill wouldn't know it unless the Daily Racing Form started to burn."

Privately, she'd tell him, "Boy it was a good thing we had our family before you found that Racing Form."

It might have led to a second career. "He thought when he retired and the boys took over the stable, sort of as a sidelight, he'd like to have a couple thoroughbreds and train them," Dottie said. "He always loved the thoroughbreds, so it was just a natural thing. He just thought he could do that job."

Dottie estimated they owned some 100 thoroughbreds through the years, mostly claimers, but a few allowance horses and a couple who competed in stakes. One was Spring Sun, who won a stakes at Pimlico. Another, Lady DeGrasse, won three straight races at Sunshine Park one winter. Billy and Dottie had less success with Lord Rip, a converted saddle horse Billy bought for $500. He was barred at Sunshine Park. "The officials at Sunshine Park told Bill Owen, my trainer there, that Lord Rip would not be permitted to race again," Billy told Louis Effrat in a story in the Sunday *New York Times*, April 10, 1960. "Any horse that reaches 5, has made eight starts and is still a maiden is automatically ruled off our track, they informed Owen."

Billy and Dottie regularly frequented Belmont and Aqueduct on Long Island. In Oyster Bay, they were neighbors of Secretariat's jockey, Ronnie Turcotte, and his family. Billy knew thoroughbred trainers John Nerud, Leroy Jolley, Horatio Luro and Ed Neloy, who trained the Haughtons' thoroughbreds in New York.

But Billy's love of horses wasn't limited to two breeds. In 1960, he had two riding horses, Duncan, a 12-year-old gray gelding hunter, and Peter Campbell II, an 8-year-old black gelding open jumper, who was a gift from Norman Woolworth. Considering that Stanley Dancer trained for Woolworth, Woolworth's gift to Billy speaks loudly of the camaraderie among rival horsemen and owners. "Riding those two horses relaxed me more than sleeping, even though they move along at a pretty good clip," Billy said.

Draft horses did not, but Billy and Dottie not only owned them, but won ribbons and trophies in pulling contests with them throughout New England. "He and Dottie just thoroughly enjoyed it," John Cashman, president of Castleton Farm, said. "It was always the horse, Billy's relaxation. He was a tremendously competitive human being, whether it was fishing or owning a thoroughbred or driving trotters and pacers."

The Haughtons' ability with draft horses was highlighted in a story in the *Rockingham County Gazette and Bordertown News*, July 26, 1978, Exeter Edition. "If you went to a competition every week and won, you'd still wouldn't earn enough to feed one horse, never mind the team," Dottie told reporter Bradford Dutton. "We feed them three times a day, a total of 24 quarts of grain, as well as hay and a protein supplement: alfalfa cubes. These horses pull better for you when they receive a lot of attention and care. In the months before and during the competitive season, we exercise them daily to build endurance."

Dwight Sharp was a part-owner. Pat Neal drove the Haughton team in competition. A team of ten 2,500-

pound draft horses could pull close to 50,000 pounds of weight a distance of six feet. "We had the No. 1 team in New Hampshire, and it was No. 2 in all of New England," Dottie said.

But the breed which intrigued Billy the most was the thoroughbred. In that 1964 *Sports Illustrated* article, Billy explained why he read the Racing Form religiously: "The accent is on human interest. No twin doubles or betting. They give you a different look at racing. If they can't say anything good, they don't say it. I wish we had a publication like it. It would certainly help the image of trotting quite a bit."

He did all he could every single night, which is why more than 20,000 fans at Roosevelt that night were asking for autographs instead of screaming obscenities. The $2 bettor and the sport's biggest bettors shared the belief that every single time Billy took the race track, he relentlessly pursued a single objective: to win. And he did his damnedest to make that happen, very rarely making mistakes along the way. "I was watching him closely, as I always do, because even Billy can fall into a driving pattern, and someone who is watching can detect it," Apples said in the *SI* story. "Well, anyway, there were something like 130 races in which he didn't make a mistake. Not one mistake in driving. It was a great exhibition."

Billy didn't usually get mad when other drivers made a mistake. But after competing against a careless young driver in a stakes at Brandywine one night, Billy couldn't help himself. "Just how in the hell did you get your license anyway?" Billy demanded. The youngster replied, "You signed for me, Mr. Haughton."

Stanley Dancer, who was there that night, still laughs at the memory. "Billy just shook his head and walked away," Stanley said. "I used to sign many of the applications, too."

12

Trouble At Home—
And Good Times Too

In 1966, Dottie Haughton had a lot on her mind. It almost killed her.

As if raising five children with her husband frequently away from their 22-room house in Oyster Bay wasn't demanding enough, Dottie took on an added responsibility. Billy had just fired his bookkeeper, and asked Dottie to help out. At the time, the stable had some 160 horses. "Bill brought home the old books, and I had all the stakes payments and all the billing," Dottie said. "He moved everything home, and that was the only way we could do it until he found somebody else. And I think I had so much pressure that the artery in my neck kinked and there was a blockage or something."

On a routine day, she had lunch with Billy and their accountant. "We came back to the house and I said, 'Just let me lay down for a couple of minutes,'" Dottie said. She went to the bedroom and laid down, which she rarely did during the afternoon.

Billy was scheduled to drive that night at Monticello Raceway, a 2½-hour drive upstate from Long Island. "I was going to go to Monticello with him that night so he wouldn't fall asleep at the wheel," Dottie said.

Dottie woke up and wanted to go to the bathroom. "I couldn't make myself walk around the bed," she said. "I was going towards the windows. I didn't have any control of where I was going. It was scary, very scary."

Billy called his neighbor and doctor, Joe Bebry, and asked him to meet Dottie at the hospital. Billy had his secretary take her there, and headed to Monticello alone to honor his commitment to drive there.

The little Dottie remembers from the hospital that day wasn't good: "I can remember getting into Administration, and them asking my name. And I knew my name, but I couldn't tell them. It was the most frustrating thing. It was so horrible that this answer was inside of you and you could not tell them."

Dottie, at the young age of 34, had suffered a stroke. Her entire right side was paralyzed. Doctors feared that she would never walk again.

She stayed in the hospital for almost a week, and then was flown to Houston to see Dr. Michael DeBakey, the famed cardiologist. "They did two procedures on a Saturday, and it accidentally collapsed my lungs," Dottie said. "Then they had to re-inflate them, which was extremely painful. Bill was so distraught seeing me in so much pain, that I begged him to leave Texas and go back to work, which he did. My mother came from Florida to stay with me. I was in terrible shape. It was a mess when I came home. I came back in worse shape than when I went."

Her five children were scared, none more than 5-year-old Holley: "I remember a lot of times praying at the side of my bed at night, 'Please keep this family together.' If it helped or not, I don't know. I believe in God to an extent, but we're not a real religious family. My dad was Catholic. We'd go to church Christmas Eve and Easter when he was home. He was the one who would take us. We did do Sunday school and catechism. But I know there were many, many times that I would kneel down at my bed at night to pray that my mother would walk, because she was paralyzed for quite a while (eight months). A lot of that time I have put out of my mind because it scared me."

Tommy, then 9, would sit on the floor in the hallway and watch Dottie in the mirror. "If I needed to go to the bathroom, he was right there," Dottie said. "And he'd sit there and sit there and watch me. He was a pretty special little boy."

Dottie recovered. She regained the use of her entire right side. "They said there was a very good chance she may never walk again," Holley said. "But as you can see to this day, she's a fighter, and I think that's what helped her get through it."

Dottie figured she was almost through it when Bill dropped a bombshell before walking out the door one morning. "I was just getting so I could drag my leg up the stairs," Dottie said. "And Bill announced as he was going away to race,

'Oh, by the way, Mother and Auntie are coming tomorrow by ambulance to live with us.'

'Come back here! What are you talking about?'"

When asked 30 years later if she wanted to kill her husband at that point, she said, "Sure I did."

Dottie's greatest character flaw is the same one she saw in her husband: she just couldn't say no. "I didn't have any choice," she said. "What was I going to do? It was family."

Dottie got a concession from Billy to hold off for three more days. She rented a hospital bed with supporting sides for Aunt Millie, who had been crippled by polio as a youngster and was obese.

Billy's mom required immediate stomach surgery

for a blockage, and Dr. Bebry, who would perform the operation, instructed her to make her will. "She was in bad shape when she arrived," Dottie said. "She couldn't even keep water down."

But the surgery proved successful and Billy's mother recovered. She lived there eight years before passing away.

Dottie got another houseguest, when her aunt Dorothy, who was an alcoholic, moved in. "So we had to lock up all the liquor," she said. "I figured I was feeding 14 people a day. I was running a nursing home without a license."

Billy's mom preferred keeping to herself upstairs, where she and Aunt Millie lived in a wing of the immense house. "They stayed there in their little wing, because Aunt Millie couldn't walk and Bill's mother didn't want to come downstairs," Dottie said. "I had a kitchen put in upstairs. She decided she was going to make her own tea. She had a television and a beautiful corner room with windows overlooking the driveway and a fireplace in the bedroom. She wanted to be in her own room. I don't know if the kids and all the noise made her nervous. The kids always went in to visit her. Bill would go see her when he could, and I would, too. She was very happy to do what she was doing. We made her come down for Christmas. Thank God, I didn't have to be there every minute. They had everything there, so there was no reason for me to be there. And when I got better from the stroke, I was out and about."

Dottie did have help in Geneva and Mary. "We kind of had a routine between Mary and Geneva," Holley said. "With all of us, my aunt and my grandmother and everything going on, and my dad in and out traveling, we all had our own duty. There were things that we had to do. I give Mary and Geneva and Apples a lot of credit for teaching us that things had to get done. We all had to clear off the table at night. There were a lot of us that had to eat in that house. And with groceries. When my mother pulled up with a carload of groceries, we all had to help unload them. So it didn't really seem to be that hectic because we had a good routine going."

She and her brothers had already gotten used to one routine: that their famous dad was out of the house a lot. And that fame carried consequences.

"I admired him very much, because I saw how hard he worked and how giving he was to all of us," Holley said. "He missed being around us just as much as we missed being around him. And whenever it was feasible for us to be there with him, we were there. No matter what he had to do to get us there.

"I saw what he came from. Neither of his parents were as successful as he was. And everything he made, he gave to us, which was a lot to be remembered and cherished. It was more than most people got. And he made it all on his own out there. I always idolized him for that. Plus he loved everything he did. When I describe my father, the biggest thing I have to say is he loved life and making the people around him happy. And remembering people."

Holley had a couple of friends over and introduced them to Billy one day. "Then maybe three or four years later, they came over, and he remembered their names," Holley said. "It totally amazed them. They said, 'I can't believe your dad remembered my name.' They were so impressed. He always made me very proud of him. Always, no matter what he did."

Dottie tried explaining to her kids the role of the media in their father's life. "My mother was really good about always talking to us and trying to teach us about the media, about how he had to be interviewed, and that we had to understand," Holley said. "These were things we had to understand because my dad was so successful."

But one incident caught everyone by surprise. "I had to have been in the fourth grade, and somebody had left a threatening letter on my dad's car at Roosevelt," Holley said. "There had been some threats to other drivers. And the police had to come to our house in Oyster Bay one night. And it really frightened me. The next couple of days, somebody drove us to school, rather than letting us go by ourselves. That's when it really struck me that he was famous." Billy nailed the windows shut so nobody could open them from the outside. Nothing happened.

Fame had other trappings. Billy Haughton was a highly successful man who was out of town a lot and loved to socialize. Out of town, other women were part of those nights. Dottie said, "They were out there. It goes with the territory."

Holley said, "As far as rumors and stories about other women, we all knew deep down in our hearts that my mother was his woman. He idolized her, and she was very, very supportive and always there for him. He put her up on a pedestal, and he made us all know that she was the most important thing in his life."

But once again, Dottie was almost taken out of his life. Just two years after her first stroke, Dottie had another. Dottie was accompanying Billy to Monticello Raceway. This time she made it there, but when they got to the track, Dottie didn't feel well. "I said, 'Let me just sit in the car here because I don't feel real good,'" she recalled.

Billy left to warm up his horse, and by the time he returned to the car, Dottie knew something serious was wrong again. She remembers sitting between two people in the car riding to a hospital. "I was sitting in the front seat, and I was bouncing off both of them," Dottie said. "I didn't have the balance to sit there. I was so embarrassed. I was just falling all over them."

Dottie wound up at Columbia Presbyterian Hospital in Manhattan. She stayed there for two months, did physical therapy and recovered. "It wasn't nearly as bad as the first one," she said.

* * *

There were plenty of good times in the Haughton household. And downright silly ones.

Billy thought he had a great housewarming gift for Dottie when they moved into their 22-room house in Oyster Bay. At least that's what he told her when he called one September night, 1964, from the Lexington Horse Sales. "I thought that he'd been to Laffayette Gallery (a gift store in Lexington) and bought me a beautiful new piece of furniture," Dottie said.

Close. He'd bought her two oxen from Elgin Armstrong of Canada.

"Evidently, he'd gotten into the Scotch pretty good," Dottie said.

By the time the oxen arrived, Billy had gone to Florida to start training his colts.

"They arrived in early December, these two huge oxen with great big horns and brass tips on their horns," Dottie said.

Dottie wasn't the only one who wasn't thrilled with the beasts. "I had a thoroughbred in the barn that I'd ride," Dottie said. "I loved him dearly. And he was so terrified of the oxen."

The oxen, however, made a great impression at the Haughton's New Year's Eve party at their new house. "Bill and George Sholty and Jimmy Cruise decided they were going to bring the oxen into the house, my brand-new gorgeous house," Dottie said. "That's what they said to me. I told them there is absolutely no way they're coming near the front door."

The three musketeers had to settle for circling the oxen around the driveway. Then Billy returned to Florida leaving Dottie with her new pets. She named them Line and Bright, paraded them through the neighborhood and quickly lost her patience. "By the middle of January, I had had it with the oxen," Dottie said. "I tried taking care of them and feeding them, and they each ate over a bale of hay a day. It was just terrible. It wasn't bad enough to have to feed all the kids and take care of the house. I had to take care of these oxen besides. It was just ridiculous."

Dottie called Billy in Florida and laid down the law. Billy arranged for their departure to his buddy Delvin Miller's Meadowcroft Farm in Pennsylvania. Only he wasn't exactly sure what day someone would show up to take them.

So one morning, Dottie, wearing a white winter coat, went into nearby Garden City to shop at Saks Fifth Avenue. "They were having a big sale," she said. When she got home, she was delighted to see a huge truck in her driveway.

Dottie said, "A guy came running out of the truck up to the car and said, 'I can't get these oxen out. I don't know what to do with them.'"

Dottie did: "I said, 'Don't worry, I'll get them in the truck.' I didn't even think about changing my clothes. I wanted them out of there. So I went to the barn, and drove them out, and I got them on the truck. After I get the second one tied in, I walked between them, and one of them did their business. And it splashed all over the front of my coat and on my face. I was so embarrassed I though I was absolutely going to die, after I had done this wonderful job of getting those two on the truck. The truck driver was trying to hide his laughter, and I was in tears. They lived a long life over at Delvin Miller's farm."

Dottie wasn't above having fun at Bill's expense.

To clean the pool at their house in Oyster Bay, Dottie or Billy used an electric vacuum. "The damn thing never worked," Dottie said. "One day, Bill comes home all dressed up from somewhere, and the first thing he sees is that thing stuck again. I saw him leaning over the pool trying to fix it. I don't know what made me do it."

Dottie pushed Billy in the pool, ran upstairs laughing and locked the door. "I still feel good I did it," she said. "He was ready to kill me, but he was laughing, too."

At their house in south Florida—which they bought in 1966 when Bill started racing horses every winter at Pompano Park in Pompano Beach just north of Fort Lauderdale—Bill didn't wear anything to bed one Saturday night. The next morning, Bill leaned out his front door to grab the newspaper. "And the devil made me do it again," Dottie laughed. "I locked the door. Here he was outside, stark naked on Sunday morning, screaming 'Let me in!' I was laughing so hard."

Another time in Pompano, Stanley Dancer had a party at his home. "It was sort of a loud, pretty wild party," Dottie said. "Everybody was drinking. And those were the days when everybody streaked. Somebody dared Bill and the next thing I know, 'Oh, my God!' Through the living room comes Billy Haughton streaking. All he had on was his sneakers. I never saw anybody run so fast in my life."

Nobody would ever accuse Billy Haughton of not enjoying life, even when he was ordered not to. When Billy was 58, he had a cataract in one eye and underwent eye surgery in Miami that winter. "The doctor said, 'I don't want you to do anything for a week,'" Dottie related.

So they went up to their farm in New Hampshire, where Billy went skiing while hooked up to a horse Dottie was riding in front of him. "I was riding the horse through the woods as fast as we could go, and he was skiing behind me," Dottie said. He and Dottie also snowmobiled some 50 miles every day. Good thing he was taking it easy.

"He always liked speed," his New Hampshire neighbor, Bert Anderson, said. Bert and his wife, Meg, have lived in New Hampshire since 1947. Bert, who ran a shop that made hydraulic and wheelchair lifts, quickly hit it off with Billy, as did Meg with Dottie.

"We got to like them very much," Bert said. "You couldn't ask for a better man. He was one hell of a nice guy, never got mad at anybody. He liked to be outdoors on the go all the time."

Bert introduced him to snowmobiles. "That's how he started," Bert said. "I had them, and he liked them. We were out one night, and a big storm had finished. We were going like a bat out of hell, three of us. He hit a clump of grass and he and the snowmobile went flying up through the air, and he landed on this bush. I was scared he got hurt. I said, 'Are you hurt?' He said, 'No, but I can't see.'"

There was a reason. His glasses were covered with snow. Bert couldn't keep from laughing as Billy did just what he would do with a horse. He got right back on and took off again.

Bert remembers seeing Billy skiing behind a horse Dottie was riding. "It was the first time I ever saw it," Bert said. "He was skiing behind Dottie hollering, 'Faster, faster.'"

Back in the '60s, Billy would drive his Austin-Healey 3000 sports car at speeds up to 120 miles per hour after he cut a deal with Paul O'Shea, a three-time national sports car racing champion. Billy taught

O'Shea how to train standardbreds and O'Shea showed Billy car racing.

Billy would frequently water ski at high speeds in Florida, and though he was often pictured with a cigarette in his mouth—he quit cold turkey one year—he took care of his body well enough to play in pick-up basketball games into his 40s. "Even though he was small (5-foot-9), he was good," Dottie said. His weight varied little from 155 to 165 pounds.

"He was very active," Dottie said. "He did exercises and he took care of himself. He didn't go overboard with big desserts."

He did, however, have midnight snacks. Make that midnight dinners. At home. With friends. After he woke up Dottie.

"He'd just bring people home for dinner, absolutely unannounced, at midnight or at one o'clock in the morning," Dottie said. "Many nights, I got up when he brought someone home from Roosevelt after the last race and made linguini with white clam sauce at one o'clock in the morning. Many nights. And it was fun. He'd wake me up and very gently tell me who was there. And I'd say, 'Did you eat?'"

Dottie didn't consider other options. "It never entered my mind," she said. "People bitch and complain today. That's the way it was then. And it was fun, too."

Other nights, when there were no unannounced late dinner guests, Billy would also wake Dottie when he got home from the track. They'd share a drink and discuss how his horses raced that night. That's about the only chance they got to share quiet moments together.

What was it like living with Billy Haughton? Dottie said, "It was exciting and exhausting, but it was never dull."

13

King of the Hambletonian

Billy Haughton's domination of harness racing was missing one jewel: the biggest one. From his first drive behind Crossbow in the 1949 Hambletonian, he had been zero-for-15 in the sport's most prestigious race. "It didn't bug Bill a lot, but that's all he read about: that it had eluded him all these years," Dottie said.

Well, it had: for 25 years. Billy was close, finishing third in 1959 with Circo to Frank Ervin's Diller Hanover; third in '64 with Speedy Count to John Simpson, Sr.'s Ayres, and third in '67 with Keystone Pride behind Del Cameron's winner, Speedy Streak.

Christopher T, a son of Ayres owned by John K. Thro, a pharmacist in Mankato, Minnesota, hardly seemed the candidate to end the drought in 1974, though he was bred by Thro and his partner, Don Millar, to be a top trotter. Christopher T's dam was none other than Flicka Frost, the filly who had been guilty of not sharing her bed of straw with Dottie and then made up for it by producing her first Hambletonian winner, Timothy T, in 1970.

Billy didn't expect Christopher T to match the feat. He'd won five of 17 starts as a 2-year-old, and wasn't doing much better at 3. "All along, I thought Golden Sovereign was the best (3-year-old trotter)," Billy said. "Christopher T hadn't done well all year, mainly because of injuries. He ran such a bad race in Indianapolis (in the Horseman Futurity). I was in third position all the way, never left the fence, and he finished seventh. And I said to Mr. Thro after the race, I'd leave it (starting in the Hambletonian) up to him. He said, 'Well, we've come this far. We might as well go all the way.'

"And that's the only reason. Had I been paying the starting fee and it was my horse, I doubt very much if I would have started him."

But he did, drawing two inside the outside post in a field of 11 in the second elimination as 22 3-year-old trotters went to post over a track dulled by two days of rain. Billy made two changes on Christopher T before the Hambletonian. He took off most of his shoe weight and warmed him up faster than usual, hoping it would make a difference.

Stanley Dancer's Nevele Diamond won the first elimination by four lengths in 2:00⅗, beating Keystone Gabriel, who was second with Billy driving, and Journalist, who was fourth with Peter.

The second elimination was vintage Billy Haughton. He made at least six crucial decisions that translated into Christopher T's victory over Golden Sovereign and three other top 3-year-olds: Anvil, Stock Split and Sing Away Herbert.

First, Billy left with Christopher T. He felt he had to because of the poor post position. "My intention was to just try and get a good position," he said.

Second, he made a commitment to make the front instead of looking for a tuck.

Third, once he made the lead by the first quarter in

:29⅖, he let Stock Split, moving up outside of him, to take the lead. "My horse hadn't been [racing] good and I didn't feel I could use him too hard [to park out Stock Split] and have any chance at all," he said.

Fourth, by the half in :59, Golden Sovereign had made the front, leaving Stock Split second on the rail and Christopher T behind him in third. When Sing Away Herbert moved up first over on the outside, Billy had to make a quick decision: follow him second over on the outside or stay in and risk getting boxed. Billy stayed in. "I almost came out to follow him, but I was afraid to do it because my horse just hadn't been that good," he said.

Fifth, heading into the stretch, Golden Sovereign held the lead over Stock Split, who was poised to go outside Golden Sovereign, as Sing Away Herbert began to tire on the outside. Billy ducked inside with Christopher T, only to have Stock Split veer back inside, cutting that lane off.

Sixth, in an instant, Billy gathered Christopher T and veered him sharply to the outside around all three horses in front of him just as Anvil stormed up to join them in deep stretch. "I started through along the rail, and then Stock Split came right back over and shut me off," Billy said. "I came out the other way around Sing Away Herbert and almost got shut off by Anvil, who was on the outside."

Billy, however, had the strongest horse. "Once he got loose, he had plenty left," Billy said. Christopher T won in 1:59⅘.

To win the Hambletonian then, a horse had to win two heats on the same day.

In the third heat, Stanley drew the rail with Nevele Diamond, leaving Billy the two post. Anvil led early, then was passed by Nevele Diamond through a quarter in :28⅖ and a half in :58⅗. Sing Away Herbert moved first over and this time Billy followed him. "This time I did because I was a little braver, because my horse had raced so well the first time," Billy said.

Sing Away Herbert cleared the lead by the three-quarters, but Christopher T had dead aim and roared past to win in 1:58⅗ and give Billy his first Hambletonian. "I moved him out and he just trotted free," Billy said.

Billy couldn't have been happier. "I can't believe it," he said afterwards. "I'm as stunned as I am happy. I didn't expect him to win today. In fact, I thought Golden Sovereign was tons the best. This has to be my most satisfying victory."

Christopher T didn't give him many more, finishing his 3-year-old season with four victories in 23 starts. But Billy had him peaked at the right time.

Once he'd won his first Hambletonian, Billy didn't stop. He won the 1976 Hambletonian with Steve Lobell and the '77 running with Horse of the Year Green Speed.

Steve Lobell's victory nearly cost the horse his life. And that was after he finished 14th in the first heat.

Owned by partners Dick Herman and Murray Seigel of Mill Island Stable of Brooklyn, N.Y., Steve Lobell, a son of Speedy Count who won just two of nine starts as a 2-year-old, was hoping to duplicate his win in the Yonkers Trot and take a shot at the Trotting Triple Crown.

In the first heat, Steve Lobell lost a shoe at the three-eighths and finished 14th. Zoot Suit, a son of 1968 Hambletonian winner and World Champion Nevele Pride, was the surprise winner in 1:58⅕ for Vernon Dancer. Peter was fourth with Quick Pay, while Vernon's brother Stanley was last in the massive field of 18 with Nevele Thunder, who had been syndicated for $1.5 million. In the second heat, Nevele Thunder would suffer a fractured bone in his left front let leg and be vanned off.

Steve Lobell won the second heat, tying Super Bowl's 1:56⅖ world record for 3-year-old trotters. Joe O'Brien's outstanding filly Armbro Regina, who was 17th in the first heat, came from 18th at the quarter to finish second in the second heat. Quick Pay was third for Peter.

Any hope Billy had of ending the Hambletonian in the third heat vanished when Steve Lobell hit a hard spot on the track and began pacing, which made him crossfire and cut his left front leg. Armbro Regina edged Zoot Suit and Quick Pay in a three-horse photo finish in 1:56⅗, equaling Japa's world record for fillies.

That set up a fourth heat between the three winners on a humid day with the temperature in the '80s. Billy called the judges to scratch his colt because of his cuts, but the judges informed Billy that scratching Steve Lobell from the final would make his owners forfeit third place money. The owners decided to let Billy race him. "We figured we could take a ride around the racetrack with the hope we might be able to beat the other two down the stretch," Billy said.

It didn't seem likely as O'Brien hustled Armbro Regina to the lead, Zoot Suit sat in second and Steve Lobell third through crawling early fractions of :30⅗, 1:02⅘ and 1:34⅘. "I didn't think I could beat O'Brien once he got to the front end and slowed it up," Billy said.

But with a crowd of some 14,000, including Illinois Governor Dan Walker, and a live national TV audience on CBS watching, Steve Lobell got the job done anyway, roaring home in :27⅘ to win by half a length over the filly, who was second but disqualified to third for interfering with Zoot Suit in the stretch.

Then things got ugly.

Steve Lobell collapsed in his stall from dehydration after the race. According to Bob Hackett's story in *The Horsemen and Fair World*, as many as 10 people were used to keep Steve Lobell standing as he was being iced, rubbed and given fluids by Dr. Tom Dunkin. Steve Lobell's groom, Anders Norlander, did much of the work.

"It was very hot that day," Dottie said, "We put ice on his head to cool him down. He was ready to collapse."

After he stabilized, Billy and Dottie went to the traditional post-race party at the home of Grand Circuit President Bill Hayes, who ran the Hambletonian with his family. Billy was not in good spirits. "He was angry," Dottie said. "He said, 'For all you people that think that heats are great, I've got a horse over there who's dying.'"

Steve Lobell didn't die. He was better the next morning. But he would be denied the Trotting Triple Crown by Quick Pay and Peter Haughton. Steve Lobell concluded his 3-year-old season with 10 wins, five seconds and three thirds in 28 starts and earnings of $357,005.

Compared to '76, the 1977 Hambletonian was a breeze for Billy, who made it three Hambos in four years with his Horse of the Year Green Speed in identical world record heats of 1:55⅗.

Green Speed, a son of Speedy Rodney out of the Hickory Pride mare Peridot, was named by Dottie, but owned by Beverly Lloyds, second wife of Lloyd Lloyds, who bred the colt. Though Peridot's first foal, Peridot Pride, won $117,000, Lloyd Lloyds consigned Green Speed to the Harrisburg Sale. Before the sale, Billy got his first look at the colt, loved him, and finally convinced Lloyds to buy him back out of the sale at the last minute. Lloyds then gave Green Speed to Beverly as a gift.

At 2, Green Speed won eight of 15 starts with three thirds and $99,781 in earnings.

At 3, coming off a victory in the Yonkers Trot, Green Speed was joined in the Hambletonian by Peter's Cold Comfort, and they were the heavy favorites as a Haughton Stable entry in a field of 16 with six trotters starting from the second tier.

Leaving from the nine post, Billy committed early to the lead and raced Green Speed three wide to the half, where he was a parked out fourth. Green Speed swept to the lead by the three-quarters in 1:27⅕ and held off fast-closing Texas by a length in a world record for 3-year-olds, tying the all-age world record. Cold Comfort broke and finished last.

"It was a hell of a mile," Billy said after the first heat.

Winning the first heat made the second one easy as Green Speed left from the rail. Billy sat third behind Reprise and Native Straight through a :28⅕ opening quarter before rushing to the top and taking control of the race. Green Speed hit the half in :57⅗, the three-quarters in 1:27⅕ and the mile in an identical 1:55⅗ with Texas a length and a half back in second. Cold Comfort challenged at the top of the stretch, but weakened to fourth.

"I always thought Green Speed was a terrific trotter, and today he proved it," Billy said.

Green Speed could have made his case even stronger by winning the Kentucky Futurity to sweep the Trotting Triple Crown, but Billy didn't keep him eligible for the stakes. "I sure wish we kept him eligible to the Triple Crown," Billy said. "We missed the Kentucky Futurity payment. It was just my fault. At the time, I didn't believe he would turn out to be so good."

He stayed that good, taking 16 of his 21 starts at 3, and 13 of 20 starts at 4. For his career, he had 37 wins, four seconds and six thirds in 56 starts and $953,013 in earnings.

14

A Litany of Champions

Quick Chief and Belle Acton, the 2-Year-Old Pacer of the Year in 1954 and '55, respectively, began a string of outstanding horses and divisional champions that would populate the Haughton Stable for more than four decades.

In the intervening 31 years between Quick Chief and Nihilator, the 1985 Horse of the Year, were 1977 Horse of the Year Green Speed, 1968 Pacing Triple Crown winner and two-time champion Rum Customer, two-time Canadian Horse of the Year and champion Handle With Care, two-time champions Laverne Hanover, Keystone Pioneer and Final Score, and divisional champions Trader Horn, Duke Rodney, Flamboyant, Romulus Hanover, Meadow Elva, Christopher T, Armbro Omaha, Keystone Model, Steve Lobell, Doublemint, McKinzie Almahurst and Naughty But Nice.

In 1974 alone, the Haughton Stable won 87 major stakes: 37 by 2-year-olds, 40 by 3-year-olds and 10 by older horses. In one night of racing at Liberty Bell in

Philadelphia in 1966, Billy won all six Grand Circuit races, earning $157,037.

Billy's other major stakes winners in the '50s were Arvilla Hanover, Bachelor Hanover, Charming Barbara, Galophone and Jan Hanover.

His major stakes winners in the '60s included Bergen Hanover, Berry Hill, Bit O' Sugar, Buxton Hanover, Carlisle, Chapel Chief, Cupid's Arrow, Gay Frost, Hickory Hill, Ideal Rodney, Incorporator, Keystone Brian, Keystone Pride, Maneros Pride, Meadow Paige (who won the 1967 Cane Pace), Mr. Pride, My Opinion, Nardins Byrd, Nardins Gayblade, Next Knight, Race Time Boy, Smart Rodney, Speedy Count, Stand By, That's Great, Thorpe Marge, Torpedo and Vicar Hanover.

In the decade of the '60s, Billy finished third in earnings in 1960, then second twice, first, second, first, second, first twice and third in 1969. His highest win total ever came in 1965 when he posted 222 wins from 910 starts, finishing a distant second to Bob Farrington (310). Billy's two highest UDR percentages also came in the '60s, .409 in 1966 and .416 in 1968, the year he was inducted into the Harness Racing Museum and Hall of Fame.

His major stakes winners in the '70s included A.C.'s Orion, Angel's Flight, Armbro Norma, Arica, Ata Connie, Best Of Donut, Bret's Champ, Bret's Star, Broadcaster B, Chappaqua Hanover, Cher Hanover, Cold Comfort, Counts Pride, Crash, Delvin Hanover, Dunnigan Lobell, Falcon Almahurst, Fanny Hall, Farmstead's Fame, Future Fame, Gil Hanover, Glasgow, Haygood, Hazel Hanover, Henson Hanover, High Score, JJ's Metro, Journalist, Keystone Gabriel, Keystone Signal, Keystone Smartie, Lightning Strikes, Lord Hanover, Meadow Grant, Meadow Wilma, Modest Yankee, National Byrd, Pagan Princess, Pammy Lobell, Puppet,

Quick Pay, Race Time Boy, Racing Bretta, Rosemary, Scandalize, Seedling Herbert, Silent Majority, Sonata Hill, Spartan Almahurst, Spartan Hanover, Spearmint, Storm Damage, Surefire Hanover, Surfer Scott, Sweet Edie, Wellwood Hanover, Windshield Wiper, Wishmaker and Worthy Master.

When Billy finished third in earnings in 1970, it was the 22nd straight year that he finished in the top three. Billy was sixth in earnings in '71, then fifth, seventh, second, seventh, sixth, 10th and eighth in 1978, the 31st consecutive year he finished in the Top Ten. He missed in '79, then was ninth, 10th and eighth in 1982, when he recorded his highest earnings ever, $2,534,181.

His other major stakes winners in the first 5½ years of the '80s included Audobon Hanover, Better Heather, Big Band Sound, Burgomeister, Caressable, Chairmanoftheboard, Coleman Lobell, First Attraction, Inside Joke, Kading, Keystone Flamingo, Keystone Signal, Nut House, Robin Almahurst, Season Champion, Silky Cedar, Southern Style, Traveling Salesman, Valentina and Worthy Bowl.

Those are ONLY the horses he drove to win MAJOR stakes, not all his winning stakes drives. It does not include all the other stakes winners he trained who were driven by either one of his sons, an assistant trainer in the Haughton Stable or one of the dozens of catch drivers he used around North America. As a trainer, the list of Billy Haughton's stakes winners is endless.

Other than that, Billy didn't have much impact.

It seemed whenever a Haughton horse stepped out of the spotlight, there were two or three stable-mates fighting to take his place.

Trader Horn, a remarkably durable trotter, won 44 of 107 races from 1956–59, before going zero-for-12 in 1960.

No problem. Duke Rodney stepped in and had a sensational five seasons from 1960–64, winning 40 of 109 starts and over $600,000. He raced in '65 and '66, but won just one of 13 starts.

By then, Billy had a full quintet of superstars. The trotting mare Flamboyant won 27 of 54 starts from '66 to '68, with 10 seconds, five thirds and $449,802 in the bank. Meadow Elva, a pacing mare, won 40 of 113 starts from 1966 to 1970 with 24 seconds, 17 thirds and $356,071 in earnings. Bill bought Meadow Elva at a sale for $6,500," Dottie said. "She went on to be a world's champion. So we put it in a private trust for the kids. Peter liked her very much when he was a kid."

Laverne Hanover, owned by Tom Murphy (the former driver's son), was a son of Tar Heel who won 22 of 23 starts with one third in 1968, earning $180,864. As a 3-year-old, he won 21 of 28 starts and $290,668. He won 10 of 29 starts as a 4-year-old, including a victory in the $100,000 Hollywood Classic, with seven seconds and two thirds and earnings of $218,758. He won eight of 18 starts at 5, earning $178,180. In his remarkable career, Laverne Hanover won 61 of 98 starts with 11 seconds, eight thirds and $868,557 in earnings.

By the time Laverne Hanover slowed down a bit, Romulus Hanover and Rum Customer had burst onto the scene. Romulus Hanover won 31 of 49 starts from 1966 to '69 with four seconds, two thirds and earnings of $485,000. Among his victories were the $14,323 Goshen Cup in '66 and the $178,064 Messenger Stakes in '67.

Rum Customer won the 1968 Pacing Triple Crown, taking the Little Brown Jug in 1:59⅗, the Adios in 1:59⅘ and the Messenger in 2:01⅕. He won the Jug despite a viral infection which kept him sidelined for 19 days, forcing him to miss the Jug Preview.

Rum Customer was bred by Mr. and Mrs. R.C. Larkin and originally owned by Lloyd Lloyds' Kenni-

Tommy Haughton, after becoming the youngest driver to win the Hambletonian with Speed Bowl in 1982, with Dottie, Holley, and Billy.

Herve Filion, Delvin Miller, Yankees' pitching great and harness horse owner Whitey Ford, Stanley Dancer and Billy Haughton.

One of the last pictures taken of Billy in May 1986, at Roosevelt Raceway.

Pioneer Farm in New Hampshire. Dottie's owned the farm for over twenty years. She calls it "my favorite place" and spends half her year there.

Billy Jr. and Tommy on Christmas Eve, 1998, at Tommy and Lynn's house in Parkland, Florida.

Dottie and Billie with Dr. Dewars in New Hampshire. The trotter won his first start, which was also Peter Haughton's first drive ever.

Billy, Cammie and Tommy after Billy won the 1981 $1,760,000 Woodrow Wilson Pace at The Meadowlands with McKinzie Almahurst, subsequently named the 2-Year-Old Pacer of the Year.

worth Farms. Louis and Connie Mancuso became co-owners when Lloyds traded part ownership in Rum Customer for an airplane owned by Louis Mancuso, who was Billy's personal pilot.

As a 4-year-old, Rum Customer won 12 of 27 starts, with six seconds and four thirds and earnings of $182,331 in 1969.

Laverne Hanover edged Rum Customer, who won 10 of 32 starts and $211,455 in 1970, to be the No. 1 earner in the Haughton Stable that year. Two-year-old trotter A.C.'s Orion had seven wins, including the $25,000 Scotland Trot Classic, and nine seconds in 16 starts, making $107,507. Pridewood, a 4-year-old trotter, made $95,835 thanks to a victory in the Realization Trot at Roosevelt Raceway. Keystone Aaron, a 3-year-old pacer, won 13 of 31 starts and $91,462. Fanny Hall, a 3-year-old filly pacer, made $87,071. Other top earners were 3-year-old trotter Gil Hanover ($85,525), 2-year-old pacer Seton Hanover ($77,291), 3-year-old filly trotter Tammie Hill ($69,983), who won the $38,571 Lady Suffolk Trot at Roosevelt; 3-year-old filly pacer Lana Hill ($66,015) and a trio of 2-year-old filly trotters: Sonata Hill ($53,610), Real Cool ($40,603) and Blue Nile ($30,437).

That year at Yonkers, Billy's 37 wins in 172 starts gave him a 21.5 win percentage, No. 1 among all drivers with a minimum of 150 starts. He also had 38 seconds and 23 thirds.

Rum Customer nipped Laverne Hanover for bragging rights in the Haughton Stable in 1971, earning $195,673 to Laverne Hanover's $178,180. Rum Customer, then 6, became harness racing's fourth millionaire and won in 1:58⅗ at Hollywood Park. Laverne Hanover's highlights included a win in the $100,000 Martin Tannabaum International at Yonkers. Other major earners were: Carbine Hanover ($112,481);

A.C.'s Orion ($76,471), Marshmallow ($74,356), Real Cool ($73,045), Armbro Lament ($66,420), Flush ($61,872), Gert Barmin ($60,000), Pammy Lobell ($50,254), Cap d'Antibes ($37,606) and Lord Hanover ($36,661).

Rum Customer won 52 of 140 career starts with 27 seconds and 25 thirds and $1,001,548 in earnings. He died on October 18, 1995, at the age of 30 after standing stud in New Zealand.

In September of 1972, Billy picked up Silent Majority, a top 3-year-old, when Montreal owner Irving Liverman decided to change trainers. "He wanted to take Silent Majority away from Stanley Dancer, and he wanted Bill to take him," Dottie said. "Bill called Stanley and said, 'I'm not going to take this horse.' Stanley said, 'If you don't take him, someone else is going to get him.'"

So Billy took Silent Majority, and the son of Henry T. Adios continued a fantastic 3-year-old season, winning eight straight races, including the $154,733 Messenger at Roosevelt and the $106,500 L.K. Shapiro at Hollywood Park. He made $304,169 for the year, $172,966 with Billy.

Billy had another top 3-year-old pacer in Cory. The son of Bret Hanover won in 1:56⅗, ended Strike Out's seven-race win streak and earned $183,731. Spartan Hanover, an $80,000 yearling, won four races and $149,481 despite battling Stanley Dancer's Triple Crown winner Super Bowl all year long. Pammy Lobell ($92,127), Sonata Hill ($78,493), Redmond Land ($73,250), Gert Barmin ($65,200), Flush ($63,000), Racing Sailor ($54,856), Carbine Hanover ($51,450) and Magnus Apollo ($50,775) all topped $50,000 in earnings.

If Belle Acton wasn't Billy's greatest filly, Handle With Care certainly was. The daughter of Meadow

Skipper, out of Lady Emily by Hillsota, was owned by Irving Liverman. She was a perfect 17-for-17 as a 2-year-old in 1973, making $141,169. As a 3-year-old in 1974, she won 19 of 24 starts with three seconds and a third and earnings of $226,278.

As a 4-year-old, she took on the best pacing colts in North America week after week. Her winning percentage dipped—she won nine of her first 18 starts that year—but her prestige certainly did not. She had a spectacular burst of speed, never more evident than on the night of June 14, 1975, at Yonkers. Competing in the $100,000, 1¼-mile International Pace, she went off at 4–1. Billy drove her that week from the four post and she was sixth at the half and seventh as the field entered the backstretch for the final time. Billy tipped her out wide and she accelerated past the entire field in an amazing single sweep, making the lead by the turn and rolling to a two length win in 2:30⅕. She had just brushed past a field of the best pacers in the world as if they were standing still.

Armbro Omaha, who won just two of 17 starts as a 2-year-old, bounced back to become the 1974 3-Year-Old Pacer of the Year, winning the $104,350 Adios, the $132,638 Little Brown Jug, the Prix d'Eté and the $151,043 Messenger Stakes. He led the country in earnings with $357,146 thanks to 11 wins, nine seconds and two thirds in 32 starts. He was third in the Cane Pace behind Boyden Hanover and stable-mate Bret's Star, a race which cost him the Pacing Triple Crown.

Handle With Care made $248,409 in 1975, slightly less than Haughton stable-mate Bret's Champ ($259,548). Competing against a sensational 3-year-old crop that included Silk Stockings, Nero and Seatrain, Bret's Champ had nine wins, six seconds and eight thirds for owners Joe Caico and Rodney and Edward Andrews. The trio were also partners on Bret's Star.

"At the time, they were the fastest brothers in the history of the sport," said Caico, a real estate dealer who recruited Billy to be his trainer in 1972. "He was the best guy in the business, and I met him at the Liberty Bell Sale and told him I'd like to give him some horses."

Caico, who still owns horses with Tommy, has never regretted the decision. He and the Andrews had another outstanding horse, Keystone Model, who won 23 of 70 career starts and $278,029, and set a world record for 2-year-old fillies with Peter driving. But Joe and his wife, Sharon, also became close friends with Billy and Dotty. "Billy was a real close friend," Joe said. "My wife and I would go out with him after the races, eat and have a couple of drinks. He could keep going all night and get up the next morning at 6. I wouldn't get up until 9:30. I couldn't keep up with him, even though he was older than me. He'd also ride my four daughters in the sulky with him. He was very good with them."

He was very good for his sport. "When he died, I think harness racing died," Joe said. "He was like a magnet. Wherever he went, he drew people to him. His name was synonymous with Ted Williams or Joe DiMaggio."

Twenty-eight other horses in the Haughton Stable earned at least $23,500 that year: 2-year-old pacing filly Glasgow ($127,885), Keystone Pioneer ($110,791), Keystone Smartie ($100,794), Starral Hanover ($97,757), Peridot Pride ($85,834), Windshield Wiper ($79,362), Trooper Chip ($71,313), Keystone Model ($67,118), Boehm's Eagle ($53,671), Quick Pay ($51,760), Bret's Star ($49,500), Just Mine ($43,750), Superchick ($42,450), Earl's Blue Chip ($41,307), Victor Hill ($39,402), Funny Donut ($36,935), Puppet ($36,534), Racing Marvel ($35,880), Speedy Romeo ($35,116), Classic Lady ($34,198), Nardin's Express ($30,410), Tempered ($29,737), Jorge Hanover ($28,702),

Spearmint ($28,549), Call Back ($27,330), Meadow Roy ($26,550), Boehm's Dauntless ($26,000), Steve Lobell ($24,686), Quilla Donut ($23,928) and Scarlet Almahurst ($23,568).

Handle With Care finished her career with 53 wins, 10 seconds and 11 thirds in 99 starts, bankrolling $809,609.

When The Meadowlands opened in 1976, quickly becoming the site of America's premier harness racing, Billy was there. He didn't need to adapt to driving on the mile-track there, since it was no different than the mile tracks at many Grand Circuit stops such as Lexington and Springfield, Illinois. The depth and quality of the night after night competition at The Meadowlands, however, had never been seen before in harness racing history. Well-matched fields of 10 forced all drivers to adjust. And Billy did. "They do an awful lot of not hustling for the lead," he said. "They just sit outside and keep moving, trying to pick up cover. We used to leave out of there pretty good, try to find a hole and just sit back and wait awhile."

Billy learned, too, of The Meadowlands shuffle, where making the lead early in the race can be the worst mistake a driver makes. "One of the worst places to be there is in front and letting somebody go past at the quarter pole," he said. "By the three-quarters pole, 90 percent of the time you're going to be last and locked in. They just keep going around. It's a tough place to race unless you learn to follow their patterns."

That wasn't a problem for him. He was more concerned about the impact such demanding racing had on his horses. "It's tough on horses," he said. "You wear horses out there awful fast."

Billy finished as the third leading trainer in the initial 1976 Meadowlands meet with 28 wins from only 65 starts. Greg Wright finished first with 45 wins from 256 starts, while Buddy Gilmour was second with 46 wins from 281 starts. Ray Remmen was fourth (26 wins), but needed 183 starts to do it, nearly three times as many as Billy.

Billy didn't break the top five in The Meadowlands 1977 trainer standings, but he got a good performance from Crash in the inaugural running of The Meadowlands Pace for 3-year-olds. The first two runnings of the Meadowlands Pace consisted of eliminations and a final on the same night. Crash, a son of Good Time owned by the Oak Hill Farms in Clarkston, Michigan, had a successful if unspectacular 2-year-old season, winning seven of 21 starts with four seconds and five thirds and earnings of $85,279. He went into his $106,250 Meadowlands Pace elimination a decided longshot at 15–1 from the 2 post with Billy driving. Crash crushed the opposition by 3¼ lengths. Escort was second and Goose Filter third. In the $212,500 Final later that night, Crash was third behind Escort and Nat Lobell.

Back in New York, Green Speed won the $239,000 Yonkers Trot in 1:59 before taking the Hambletonian. He won 16 of 21 starts in 1977 with a record $584,405 in earnings. Billy's stable made over $3.8 million, led by Cold Comfort ($323,959), Crash ($317,513), Keystone Pioneer ($235,683), Wellwood Hanover ($160,000) and Future Fame ($132,899). Other major winners were Keystone Model, Seedling Herbert, Classic Lady, Luannes Jewel, Battling Brad, Keystone Banchee, Chappaqua Hanover, Doublemint, Ziggy The Pianist, Worthy Blue Chip, Cher Hanover and Haygood.

Billy came back to win the $560,000 Meadowlands Pace the next year with Falcon Almahurst, who defeated Abercrombie and Flight Director. Falcon Almahurst, a son of the immortal Meadow Skipper, had a modest 2-year-old campaign, notching three wins and two seconds in six starts, good for $12,380 in purses. As a 3-year-old, though, he had eight wins, six seconds and two thirds in 22 starts, earning $388,396. Besides The Meadowlands Pace, he won the Tattersalls, the Jug Preview and a heat of the Little Brown Jug before finishing third in the final. He retired as the fastest pacer ever over a half mile track, 1:55⅗, and as the fastest 3-year-old pacer of all time when he time trialed in 1:52⅖.

Billy finished second in the trainer standings at The Meadowlands in 1978 and '79. In '78, he had 63 wins from 315 starts, second only to Greg Wright, who had 65 wins from 436 starts. It was a long way back to third to Lew Williams with 39 wins from 192 starts.

Rosemary, a trotting daughter of World Champion Nevele Pride, helped Billy's 1978 numbers with 14 wins, eight seconds and a third in 28 starts and earnings of $168,115.

In '79, Billy had 59 wins from 347 starts, five less than Wright, who won his fourth straight Meadowlands title with 64 wins from 369 starts.

Billy drove Storm Damage in the $1,011,000 Meadowlands Pace, July 16, 1980, finishing second to Niatross, the first million dollar purse in racing history.

One of Billy's great trotters was Doublemint, a son of Speedster who won 12 of 20 starts as a 3-year-old. One of his wins came in the 1978 Kentucky Futurity as he bankrolled $350,160. Soreness delayed the beginning of his 4-year-old season, but he went on to post seven wins and three seconds in 11 starts, the highlight being his victory in the $200,000 Roosevelt International Trot for owner Em Ar El Stable.

McKinzie Almahurst won nine of 11 starts and $936,418 to be named 2-Year-Old Pacer of the Year in 1981. Owned by the 5 Guys & Me Stable of Westbury, N.Y., the son of BGs Bunny won the $1,760,000 Woodrow Wilson Pace, August 3, 1981, at The Meadowlands in 1:56⅕. "It was the first time we really saw Dad have a smile on his face in a long time," Tommy said. "Maybe that clicked a switch with him. It really helped him move on after Peter's death. I think it lightened him up. He was more himself."

Billy finished second behind Ticket To Ride in the Woodrow Wilson the following year with Fortune Teller. At Yonkers in '81, Billy made $298,242 with 18 wins from 42 starts. He took the LaPaloma Pace with Nut House and the Waterville Lakes Hotel Pace with Stretch Pants.

As a 3-year-old in 1982, McKinzie Almahurst made breaks in both the Battle of Brandywine and the Cane Pace. "He acts like his feet are a little tender," Billy said at the time. "We've been putting pads on his feet when he trains and just cut them out to race. He doesn't have any quarter cracks. He just acts like the soles of his feet are sore from sliding on stone dust."

McKinzie Almahurst seemed better on The Meadowlands' mile track. He finished second to Pitt Boy in the $519,000 New Jersey Classic, July 2nd, then on July 9th, won one of three eliminations to qualify for the $1 million Meadowlands Pace a week later in 1:54⅖. No Nukes and Hilarion won the other eliminations. In The Meadowlands Pace, Billy drew the nine post, and McKinzie Almahurst was 11th at the half. He was flying late, finishing third by a length and three-quarters behind Hilarion, driven by John Campbell, and No Nukes in 1:54⅕. McKinzie Almahurst came back to win the $150,000 Oliver Wendell Holmes at The Meadowlands in 1:56, August 5th. He finished his final year of racing with 10 wins, four seconds and two thirds in 24 starts and earnings of $596,452.

The Breeders Crown began in 1984. As a trainer, Billy sent out 14 horses in the two years before his death, with three wins, two seconds and one third. He only had two drives, finishing sixth with Wholly Arnie in the $558,000 3-Year-Old Colt and Gelding Trot at Pompano Park, November 16, 1984; then second behind Valentina in the $632,803 2-Year-Old Filly Pace at Yonkers, Oct. 11, 1985. The second wasn't hard to take—Billy also trained the winner, Caressable, who won by a length and a half with Herve Filion driving.

Back in 1971, the same year he finished second to Germany's Adolph Ubleis in the second annual World Driving Championships held at various tracks in North America, Billy was presented the Grand Circuit Gold Medallion for outstanding service to harness racing.

Fifteen years before his career was ended in a fatal accident at Yonkers Raceway, he'd already earned it.

Peter and Billy after Peter won the Columbus Touchdown Club's Outstanding Youth Award. Billy won the Columbus Touchdown Club's Horseman of the Year Award that same year.

15

Peter

By the time Peter Haughton was 3 years old, he was riding horses. At 4, he knew what his life would be. By 11, he was jogging horses. Five weeks before his 13th birthday, he was mentioned in a syndicated column by Red Smith for an extraordinary gesture of love for a horse. Peter became a groom for his dad soon afterwards, and then, after serving a four-year apprenticeship any other groom would have had to endure, was given the golden opportunity of driving horses in the world's best stable: his dad's. He won his first race at the age of 16 and didn't stop winning them until his life was stolen by a patch of icy road outside The Meadowlands on a hellish winter night in New Jersey. He was 25 years old, a handsome, blond-haired awesome talent well on his way to writing his own legacy.

"He was a natural," Dottie said.

There's a home movie of 3-year-old Peter riding a horse by himself in an enclosed paddock at Ben White Raceway in Orlando, Florida, where his dad wintered his immense stable. Peter was obviously loving the ride and in complete control. "We bought an old Army horse and he would gallop around the track," Billy said. "He always handled the horse well, although I know his mother was scared to death."

It didn't take Peter long to figure out his future would include horses. "I've been convinced since I was about 4-years-old," he said in a TV interview. "I never knew how good I'd be. I just wanted to be as good as my ability would allow me. Myself, I would rather be considered a good all-around horseman than a good race driver."

Ironically, some people believed that by the time he was 25, Peter was already as good a driver or better than his famous father, but that he still had much to learn about training. "He wasn't a finished horseman because he was too young, but he would have made a heck of a horseman," driver George Sholty said. "Peter and I were very good friends. We used to take him—my wife and I—to the races, when he was five or six until he was a teen-ager. Apples or somebody would drop him off, and he'd go to the racetrack with Myrna and me. We'd sit him up with Myrna and some other kids, and we'd bring him home. We didn't do it all the time, but he was a damn good kid. He had a lot of personality. All the traits he had were the good traits from his mother and from his father. He had a lot of his father's traits."

Peter's father was 100 percent all boy growing up, and Peter was, too. "When he was a kid, he was a real pain in the ass around the barns," Tommy Haughton laughed. "Grooms just hated to have him there. When he was a little guy, he would aggravate those grooms, messing up their work, dumping their buckets. Stupid things. Playing tricks. Messing their equipment up. He was a little devil."

And he was always around the barn. "Peter was around the horses all the time when he was 10 years old," Billy Jr. said. "I remember Peter went into a stall with a bad acting horse, and nobody knew where he was. Somebody asked:

'Where's Peter?'

'Oh, no, he's not by THAT horse!'

"That horse would bite and kick everybody and maim people. You never wanted a kid to go around there. And there's Peter in between his legs in the stall. He'd pet him and go out. The horse would never bother Peter, but he would kill anybody else."

Peter entered the world on Sept. 22, 1954, a month past his due date. "I weighed 194 pounds," Dottie said. "The neighbors used to call me King Farouk because we'd sit and play cards at night and you couldn't see my knees, and I won all the time."

Her obstetrician thought walking might induce Dottie's labor, so he ordered her to A & S (Abraham and Straus in Hempstead, Long Island), to walk around the store, floor by floor.

On a night Billy left for Delaware, Ohio, to catch drive Wilmington's Star in the Little Brown Jug for trainer Harry Fitzpatrick, Dottie went into labor. Her feet were so swollen that she had to wear Billy's loafers to the hospital. After enduring another difficult delivery, Dottie wanted to name her son Peter Campbell Haughton, the middle name in honor of Dottie's favorite trotter, Peter Campbell. "I just adored him, but Bill said you can't name this baby after a horse. So we named him Peter Delvin after Delvin Miller."

That kindled a remarkable relationship between Peter and Delvin and his wife, Mary Lib. Beginning when he was 9 years old, Peter spent four whole summers at the Millers' farm in Meadow Lands, Pa., near the racetrack Miller helped build, The Meadows.

"Mary Lib and I helped raise him," Delvin once said. "I always have thought a lot of him. He used to come to our farm. And he got a lot of the fundamentals around the stables at our farm when he was a kid. He's like his dad. He's a good horseman. He's always shown that. He drives a horse real well."

Mary Lib, who lost Delvin in 1997, cherishes the memories. "Peter would spend the summers here with us," she said. "He and Delvin were good buddies."

The Millers re-constructed a village from the 1800s, and it's become very popular. "We get 10,000 school children a year," she said. "We get three or four busloads some days, showing how we lived in the old days. Peter enjoyed the village. He stayed in an A-frame by himself. I'd say, 'Peter, what do you do out there?' He said, 'I like to listen to the katydids.'"

Mary Lib got a vision of Peter others did not. "He was a very lone person, a real loner," she said. "No one really knew that. You could look at him in a room and he'd be off somewhere. He was never a little boy. He always thought grown up. Things that a small child would like didn't interest him. He liked to spend time with adults."

Delvin agreed: "Peter was never a kid," he said. "He was always, to me and Mary Lib, a man."

A sensitive man.

Red Smith wrote about it in his column about the Adios Stakes, named after Miller's great pacer, Adios, Aug. 15, 1967.

"In the first heat, Bill's [Haughton] Romulus Hanover, who had won the Messenger Stakes and nine of 10 starts, was parked most of the way and finished a close fourth to Best Of All with Nardins Byrd second and Nevele Dancer third. 'I went to sleep,' Haughton said. 'It was my fault. They got out of there quicker than I thought and I had too much ground to make up.'

"In the second heat, Bill went out second behind Nevele Dancer, moved to the lead at the half and won in

1:57⅗, just one-fifth off the track record held by Adios' world champion son Bret Hanover.

"In the race-off of the two heat winners, Romulus went wire to wire off a :28⅗ first quarter and a half in 1:01⅖. When Romulus came back, the applause was spontaneous and real. They hung a blanket of orchids over his withers. Later, back at Meadow Lands, small Peter Delvin Haughton had an orchid for every lady. 'Mary Lib,' he told his hostess, 'I put one on Adios' grave.'"

More than 30 years later, Mary Lib is still amazed at Peter's gesture. "The Adios is a place for the orchids," she said. "They were flown in. And they had a blanket of them. They'd present each owner's lady an orchid. Peter said, 'Gee, we've got to take an orchid for Adios.'

"We brought back the orchid and Peter went down and put in on the bronze plaque. So we do it every year, but it was his idea. To even that think of that . . . None of us did."

It was no surprise that Peter developed deep feelings for his own horses. "Peter was out riding horseback all the time," Dottie said. "We had a thoroughbred that we brought home to rest in Oyster Bay. He bowed a tendon. In February, Peter said, 'Mom, I'm going to take Vale Blue, and I'm going to get ready for that point to point (race over hurdles). He was 14. And I said all right. And he didn't come back, didn't come back. Finally he came back in tears. The horse had gone over a jump and had a heart attack and dropped dead. Peter was beside himself. He came home and we all went there. We had a collie that Holley had brought home, Trusty, that had been with us for years and years. We could not drag the dog away from the horse. We finally got the saddle off the horse. And that dog stayed with the horse until the wagon came to get the horse's body. Would not leave that horse. Unbelievable. What love."

Peter had even more trouble handling another accident on Long Island six months later. "Peter was riding with his father, and they were riding across Berry Hill Road," Dottie said. "Peter was riding a gray horse called Trader Nardin. He came up to the road, and he was ready to stop to see if there were cars coming. And a rabbit jumped before him and scared the horse. His horse started across the street. A car hit the horse. Peter went flying. Peter was okay. But we had to destroy the horse. Broke his shoulder. The woman was all right, but her car was dented all up. It was terrible. The horse hobbled up the road a little bit and he just laid down at the estate next door in the rhododendrons and pachysandras. I had to get a vet from Roosevelt Raceway to come out to give him a shot."

Billy had taken Peter home, which was fortunate. "While we were waiting for the vet, there was a policeman there with a gun and he shot the horse in the shoulder," Dottie said. "I screamed that we had already called the vet, and there was no reason that he had to do that, and not to shoot another bullet. The police chief came right about then, and he was a good friend of ours, so I had no problem. But that first policeman was some rookie who thought that's what you do with horses: shoot them. And then the vet came and just put the horse to sleep. Oh my God, it was horrible. But, thank God, Peter didn't see any of that."

Peter was home, literally banging his head against his bedroom wall because he was so distraught. "That wasn't his fault, but for a young child like that, it's traumatic," Dottie said. "We had to call the doctor."

The doctor they called was their neighbor and friend, Joe Bebry. They called him so frequently for their five active children that the Haughtons named one of their horses Call Joe. The nurse in the emergency room at the Syosset Hospital, Miss Delaney, also got used to seeing the Haughtons. "She'd say, 'Here come those Haughtons again,'" Dottie said. "It was non-stop. Cammie blew his finger tip off with a firecracker one July. Part of his thumb was buried in his head. Joe operated on him for four hours. Holley, she cut her arm and broke her arm. Tommy skid with his motorcycle and sliced his whole chin open and had to have I-don't-know-how-many stitches. Then Holley ran over Cammie with a tractor, and he had to be rushed to the emergency room. That's part of growing up when you have five children."

Dr. Bebry perceived Peter as reserved. "Peter was very quiet, he said. "Bill was the talkative one."

Cammie sensed that his brother was more comfortable with adults. "If you asked me who was his best friend," he said. "I can't tell you. He spent his time with Delvin Miller, and he spent his time with my father. He spent a lot of time with Max Hempt and the Grants."

Peter was also close to Stanley Dancer. "When he was a little kid, he used to cheer for Stanley when we were in the same race," Billy Haughton said. "And when Stanley and Albatross got beat in the Little Brown Jug, Peter had tears in his eyes."

Holley, six years younger than Peter, saw her brother differently. "He was not a loner," she said. "He had so many friends that he was never really alone. He was very quiet onto himself, but when he let his hair hang down, he was a ball of fun. You never really saw him in bad moods. He was so easy going. One thing I really admired was that he treated every woman like a princess, elderly women right down to his girlfriend. He idolized my mother, like she was a queen. He had respect for everybody. I idolized him more than anybody. He was a doll, a very special person. I loved him so much. I couldn't have asked for a better brother. My oldest son is named after him."

Holley saw Peter develop interests outside of racing, reading, cooking and gardening, but knew that he'd spend his life with horses and be very good at it. "He was just so kind," she said. "How could he not be successful? There were so many good things about him."

Peter started jogging horses for his dad when he was 11, down in Florida. "Pete would sit there like an old-timer, charging through traffic," Billy said. "I was never afraid he would get in trouble. A lot of the kids scared me. They just didn't seem to have the right feel. It always seemed like they had a loose horse, no control."

Billy and Peter, of course, knew where this was headed, though following a legend is a tough career path, even harder if he's you're father. "I never coaxed any of them," Billy said when Peter was a teenager. "Peter, from the time he was 3 years old, that's all he's ever wanted.

"If he wants to come with me, I would love to have him. He knows it will be tough following me, since so much will be expected of him.

"No matter how well he does there will be a lot of guys sitting around taking shots at him, just as they do unfairly to many young drivers. I sometimes wonder whether I should encourage him or not."

Peter didn't need much.

After he had made it in harness racing, Peter reflected on the road he traveled to get there: "It was a blessing is my way of looking at it. My dad's been my idol ever since I was a young boy. I always idolized him as other kids idolized Babe Ruth or Mickey Mantle. The only thing that ever affected me was that he was always a great inspiration as a father. And once I decided to go into the business, to have the opportunity to work with the quality of stock that we have had, nobody could ask for a better chance."

It's a chance he earned. There was no favoritism for Peter, nor for his two brothers who followed him. "They all started at the bottom and worked their way up," Stanley Dancer said. "They got no special treatment."

Holley, though she didn't go into the business, learned the same lesson her brothers did, a lesson she has passed on to her children. "Every summer, since my Peter was an infant, we've come up to the farm in New Hampshire," she said. "And I teach them the way my dad taught me around the barn. You start from the bottom. And you have to learn to work up like everyone else does. If you didn't clean the tack, you didn't get to ride the next weekend, because you're going to be cleaning all the tack. I try to instill the same type things in Peter and Jake, because those were all things that have worked for me even today."

Her mother is certain it worked for her sons, too. "They worked very hard," she said. "They had to start—all of them—right from the bottom. Spend three or four years as a groom. They were treated no differently. In fact, it was a little tougher on them. It was. They couldn't get away with slighting a horse a little bit like another groom might try to do. They'd really get it if they did. And they were being watched closely by the other trainers and everybody else."

Watching Peter, most people couldn't believe what they saw. "Everything came natural to him," said Ben Steall, who was a groom, catch driver and assistant trainer for the Haughtons from 1957 to 1983. "He would have been like his father. He could get along with any kind of horse. And he had a good personality. He could get along with people. Peter was just a great kid. He just loved life. He loved everybody. If you walked into a restaurant with him, if he knew one guy sitting at a table with 10 people, he'd pick up the tab for all 10 people. He was just like his father. He walked like him. He acted like him. He talked like him."

He even sat in a sulky like him. "Watch them on the track, and you will never be able to tell the difference," Dottie once said. "Pete sits just like his father in a sulky, and the only way you can tell them apart is by Peter's blond hair."

They were hard to separate in a lot of ways. "They were very close, more like brothers than father and son," Steall said. "They were good friends. Bill was proud. Every time Peter went on a racetrack, you'd see Bill's face light up."

Steall witnessed the fire in Peter at an early age: "Since he was a little kid, Peter wanted to be the best, to win more Hambletonians than Delvin Miller and more Little Brown Jugs than his dad."

Peter realized how high he was setting the bar. "I've tried to style my life and driving after my father, but I don't ever compare myself to him," Peter said. "I always thought he was the greatest. Just about everything I know about driving a horse was taught to me by my father, or I learned by watching him. He does everything well. I would like to become as much like him as a driver as I can."

To Peter, that meant never driving in colors other than the green and white with gold piping made famous by his dad. "I'm proud of those colors," he said. "I'll never wear any others."

He didn't waste any time putting them on.

"That's all he wanted to do," Dottie said. "From the time he was a little child, all he wanted for his birthday was to go to the Little Brown Jug. And he did every single year. That's what we did for his birthday. We took him out of school and he went to the Little Brown Jug.

He just wanted to be around horses and wanted to train horses since he was a little bitty child."

When he was 15, he was given the responsibility of taking care of a trotting filly named Real Cool, who had a real bad disposition. "I remember the morning Pete took over the grooming on Real Cool," Dottie said. "It was at Goshen, and the filly was to start in a stakes race that afternoon. She hadn't done a thing up until that time. During the race, she went five seconds faster than she had ever been in her life. Afterwards, my son grinned and said, 'Look at that. I've been taking care of her for three hours and already she's improved five seconds!'"

Waiting for his 16th birthday, when he could get his fair license, must have seemed like an eternity to Peter. But it was worth the wait.

Billy and Dottie showed incredible faith in their teen-age son and in their 17-year-old groom/assistant trainer Doug Miller, by allowing them to go on the road the very summer Pete was 16 on the Pennsylvania fair circuit. Alone.

"It was just us two," Miller laughed. "Peter's parents had a lot of confidence in him. He'd been on the racetrack pretty much his whole life. I guess they trusted us. Times were different then. You wouldn't send two young kids alone like that nowadays."

They weren't completely alone. Dottie would drive from Long Island to each fair in a different Pennsylvania town, helping them in every way possible. "I just wanted to go," Dottie said. "He was 16 years old and Bill couldn't be with him. It was a mothering thing. Mother hen. You just want to make sure they're all right, that their laundry's getting done, that they're eating and sleeping and clean. But I ended up going over there and helping harness the horses and helping them cool out after the races. At four o'clock in the morning,

I used to make fried chicken and pies and take a great big picnic to the boys, like they didn't have anything to eat." She laughed at the thought.

Most 16-year-olds would be horrified to see their mother show up anytime anywhere, but Peter wasn't your typical boy. "He loved it," Dottie said. "There was no embarrassment. Peter was never ever a typical teenager. Peter was always one who just loved his mother and father. He was always much older than his years."

Maybe smarter, too. Would you rather eat on the midway or have your mother's home-made fried chicken and apple pie?

Dottie smiled at the memory. "Those were the best days of my life," she said softly.

Peter and Doug left Long Island with four young horses: Holley By Golly, the 3-year-old pacing filly named for Peter's sister, 2-year-old pacers Angel's Vicar and Hello Tomorrow, and Dottie's unraced 2-year-old trotter, Dr. Dewars.

Peter's first stop was Hughesville June 21st, 1971. Here's how tough Peter's first race was: he had to drive Dr. Dewars, an unraced 2-year-old trotter who had never even trained on a half mile track from the six post in the second tier in the first heat. In the second, Dr. Dewars would throw a shoe while on the lead.

But the race was easier on Peter than it was on his family. "I was so nervous, I thought I was going to die," Dottie said. "I had gotten one of those old-fashioned movie cameras and run all the way from the backstretch to get to the grandstand so I could film his first post parade ever. It was Dr. Dewar's first race, too. And he didn't come out and didn't come out. And the post parade went on and I am like a wreck. Then, finally, here he comes down the track. There was some piece of equipment that he wanted to change."

Peter wasn't the only one a little late.

Billy and Cammie were driving to Hughesville from Pocono Downs, where Billy had raced the night before. "We were coming down the highway," Cammie said. "The road ran along the fairgrounds. My dad looked over and he saw Peter. So we pulled over on the side of the highway and watched the race."

It was the second heat. Peter had already won the first. Billy Haughton liked what he saw. A lot. Peter eased Dr. Dewars away, made the lead and maintained it despite his baby trotter losing a shoe. "When I saw the colt throw a shoe I was afraid Peter would lose him, or that he would begin pacing," Billy said. "The colt did make a slight break at the five-eighths, but Peter got him back on the trot. I was still certain that when the other horses started coming at him in the stretch, Pete would get excited and start driving his colt again, instead of just keeping him together."

Peter, however, never panicked and won in 2:12. "I thought to myself Pete has a pretty good pair of hands," Billy said. "It took quite a driving effort to keep that colt on the trot when those others were going at him."

Peter confessed that Dr. Dewars had warmed up terribly, but "went right on" once the race began.

The starter told Dottie after the race, "You should be proud of him. Behind the gate, he's watching everything and he's very careful."

There was no wild celebration in the winner's circle. "He was just as cool as could be with a big grin on his face," Dottie said. "Just a great big smile and that was it."

Dottie wasn't surprised by Peter's quick success. "What surprised me was how he handled himself, that his success and popularity didn't go to his head," she said. "Because I know young people when they climb that fast, sometimes they don't realize it, but they do change personalities. And he never did."

Two weeks later, in Troy, Pa., Billy and Peter drove against each other in a race for the first time. Peter won with Angel's Vicar; Billy was sixth behind Hello Tomorrow. "Since I knew I had the better pacer, it wasn't a big thrill to beat my father," Peter said. "Although it was great being in the same race with him."

Years later in a TV interview with both Haughtons, Billy said of Peter, "I think he'd rather beat me than anybody else."

Who doesn't want to beat the best?

It'd be a while before they squared off in major stakes. In his first summer of driving, Peter again impressed his father with more than his physical ability. It happened at Carlisle, Pa. "Pete was driving Dr. Dewars, but he figured to get a good test from Brownie Hanover, a top flight stakes winner," Billy said. "After losing the first heat, Pete got cut off at the start of the second mile, then was parked outside the whole second heat, finishing second to Brownie Hanover.

"I told him he got some bad breaks, being cut off and parked out the whole mile. He answered, 'No, Dad. You told me that when you park a guy and win, you did the right thing.'

"Heck, he wasn't even mad at the driver who cut him off."

In a story in *Hoof Beats* that year, Peter talked about his parents' influence: "My parents have been great," he said. "Mom is my No. 1 fan and Dad is the greatest. As long as I can stay with him, I will continue to learn, just by watching him and remembering what he does."

Who wouldn't want to learn from the best?

But, although both Peter and Doug Miller were devoted to their horses, they were also two teen-agers on their own. "We never got into trouble or anything like that," Miller said. "We'd go out to the movies or go driving around. Go out and hit a bucket of golf balls, maybe have an occasional beer, things which seem pretty innocent nowadays compared to what teenagers do. As I look back on it and compare what we did then to what I see young kids do today in the horse business . . . We were very dedicated. The only thing in our lives really were the horses.

"We had a very dedicated work ethic. Up early every morning, give the horses exercise, jog and train them. On that circuit, it's county fairs and they race in the afternoons. You work, and a lot of times you're not done racing until 4 or 5, and by the time you get done at the barn taking care of the horses, it's 6 or 7. You go get something to eat, and you're pretty well done by then on days you race. You just call it an early evening and get some sleep and get up and do it the next day. After you got done racing, you ship to another fair. Set up and get ready for that week. I look back and I'm even surprised myself about how serious we were about the horses. Peter had a blend of wild enthusiasm, and, at the same time, a lot of maturity and professionalism for a young kid."

Miller, who grew up near Syracuse, N.Y., caught on with the Haughton stable at nearby Vernon Downs. He worked for the Haughtons from 1968 to 1981, so he saw Peter blossom both as a horseman and as a man. "He was a terrific kid, a terrific person," Miller said. "He was very loyal, very dedicated to his friendships. He was very generous like his father was. He wanted to do well in his life, but he wanted everyone else around him to do well, too. It was like one big family back then. He wanted everybody that was in the organization to prosper: second trainers, grooms, the owners."

Ben Steall knows. "Peter was like a brother," he said. "In fact, when he was racing at The Meadowlands in the wintertime, when they closed, he'd ride over to

Roosevelt Raceway with me and watch me drive the horses that he owned. And I asked him. I said, 'Peter, these are your horses. You want to drive them?' He said, 'No, you have a family. I don't.'"

Just like his dad, Peter treated different people the same way. "He was just like his father," Miller said. "He could go up to some derelict bum that's been sleeping under a shed row his whole life and relate to him just as he could to someone like Lloyd Lloyds or John Froehlich or other high-powered, wealthy owners that were multi-millionaires. He was the same to everybody. And everybody really loved Peter as they did his father."

Miller also witnessed the incredibly strong bond between the two. "They both respected each other professionally," Miller said. "Billy thought the world of Peter, and Peter worshipped his father. One of the unique aspects of their relationship was that they were best of friends, too, which you rarely see between a parent and a child. But they were really great friends. And they were father and son."

Except when they raced against each other.

"When they lined up behind the gate, for two minutes they weren't father and son," Miller said. "To me, each one always wanted to win. That was really the hallmark of Bill and Peter. Peter hated to lose. When they got behind the gate, I certainly don't think they would try to hurt each other, but they wanted to win and they would do whatever they could to win."

Peter once explained it in a TV interview: "Most of the times we are driving for different owners in the same race. As soon as I go out on the racetrack, I become an employee of that owner. So I try to do the best I can for him. In that case, my father becomes just like all the rest of the drivers."

That didn't preclude sparks from occasionally flying.

"I saw Bill come off the track a lot of times and just chew Peter's butt off if he'd make a mistake driving," Miller said.

It happened one day at Goshen in 1976 in the $14,510 Debutante Stakes.

"Peter was driving a 2-year-old pacing filly," Miller said. "Billy was on the front and Peter was on the outside. And they had Stanley [Dancer] locked in the 2 hole. And Peter drifted out and let Stanley come out between them and Stanley won the race. And I remember Billy really giving him hell for that. I don't think Peter did it on purpose. I think Peter's horse started to get tired, and a lot of horses will bear out a little bit when they tire. Stanley's horse was the best and they had him locked in. Not that they ganged up on him, but they had him where they wanted strategically. And Billy thought Peter made a tactical error and let Stanley out and beat him."

Stanley remembers the race vividly: "I had a chestnut filly by Jenny's Star named Gravel Pit. Her heart wasn't very big, but she did have speed for a ways. So she could leave good. I went to the front and let Billy go [past me]. Peter maybe came out at the half and did the logical thing. He just rode there [on Stanley's outside keeping him pinned in].

"Coming around those short turns—they weren't too pleasant back then—I was lucky enough to get out without hitting anybody, including Peter's horse's legs, and I did win the race. I don't think Peter deliberately moved over so I could get out. I don't think that for a minute. I never will. But Billy wasn't very happy about it with Peter. I told him it just happened: she just bore out coming out of that short turn. To this day, I know darn well that filly just took Peter out."

Regardless, Peter heard about it. "Peter was still a young kid and learning," Miller said. "He had tremendous raw talent to make a horse go fast. He usually had a horse in the right place at the right time. He was great that way, but Bill would occasionally give him hell if he made a mistake.

"Sometimes, in the heat of the battle, they'd get mad at each other, but by the time they were getting ready to leave the racetrack, they were great friends again and father and son. I never saw any time that Billy might have scolded one of his children where it lingered for more than an hour or two or a day. It just wasn't that kind of deal."

No, it was the beginning of Team Haughton, the Great Green Wave about to stretch the Haughton legacy.

Peter won 11 of 13 races that summer with Dr. Dewars, but gave the lines to Ben Steall for Dr. Dewars' victory in the Pennsylvania Sire Stakes Final at The Meadows. Regardless, Peter finished his first year of driving with 11 wins from 35 drives. He was in the money an additional 14 times, giving him a gaudy Universal Driving Rating (UDR) of .486 and earnings of $11,511.

But Billy still brought his talented son along slowly, which they both concluded was the right thing to do.

"I've never felt overshadowed because I was brought along carefully," Peter said years later in a TV interview. "My dad hasn't pushed me onto our owners. More or less, I was asked to drive when they wanted me. Their feelings were never hard against me. If I got beat on a horse, the owners didn't have any recourse and say you pushed him on us. Most of the owners have been very, very happy and very kind to let me drive their horses."

Billy was content to let Peter learn as he go. "You

can't teach it," Billy said. "They've got to learn. I don't think Peter's ever asked me three or four times in his life how to drive in a race. I never told him, because I think the quickest way in the world you can get messed up is having somebody tell you."

In 1972, Dr. Dewars was switched to the pace and raced for the Haughton Stable in New York. Peter spent most of the year racing a 3-year-old filly, Melody Gal, who took a mark of 2:04⅖. Peter finished the year with 48 starts, 10 wins, a .368 UDR and earnings of $12,617.

In 1973, Peter won 16 of 95 starts with a .310 UDR and earnings of $83,046.

It wasn't until 1974 that Bill finally gave Peter a drive in his first $100,000 stakes race. And he had to be prodded to do so by Delvin Miller. "I played a little role in helping Billy get started, too," Delvin said. "I gave him the mount on Tar Heel years ago when Billy was just starting out."

When Billy qualified three horses for the final of the $150,000 Prix d'Eté Stakes at Blue Bonnets in Montreal, he asked Delvin to drive Armbro Omaha, while he handled his great filly taking on colts, Handle With Care. "I said, 'Let me tell you something,'" Delvin said. "'Your son's standing there. And he's got his colors on. You can't take that mount away from him.' And he let him drive.'"

And Peter won. "Since that [day], the owners don't worry about Pete," Delvin said. "That really helped him, I think."

It was only the beginning.

In four incredible months in 1974, the same year Peter graduated from Cobleskill Ag and Tech with a degree in animal husbandry, he and Billy won eight separate $100,000 stakes, prompting the U.S. Trotting Association to salute the accomplishment with a fine film entitled "The Great Green Wave," narrated by Stan

Bergstein. Billy won the $160,150 Hambletonian with Christopher T and the $133,000 Jug, $104,350 Adios, $151,043 Messenger and $100,000 Shapiro Pace with Armbro Omaha. Besides driving Armbro Omaha to the win in the Prix d'Eté, Peter won the $117,005 Colonial Trot at Liberty Bell in Philadelphia with Keystone Gabriel—who'd won just one of his 39 prior starts—and the $100,000 American Pacing Classic with Keystone Smartie.

Billy won 10 other major stakes in '74: the $13,202 Acorn with Wishmaker, a division of the $9,375 American National Stakes with Brets Champ; the $14,215 E.H. Harriman with Surefire Hanover, a division of the $9,881 Historic Dickerson with Journalist, a division of the $21,359 Hoosier Futurity with Master Bill, the $45,558 Jugette, $51,281 Lady Maud and $35,830 Adios Volo behind the immortal pacing mare Handle With Care, and divisions of the $12,050 W.N. Reynolds Memorial and $13,950 W.N. Reynolds Memorial Fillies with Spearmint and Broadcaster B., respectively. Peter also won a division of the $15,917 John Simpson Sr. Stakes with Good Knight Star and the $48,370 Tattersalls Pace with Keystone Presto.

Billy made an interesting decision with Handle With Care. After taking the first heat of the Lexington Filly Stakes in 1:58, Billy declared her out of the final, to time trial her instead. She went in 1:54 2/5, the fastest mile by a filly ever.

In the 1974 American Pacing Classic, Billy drove Handle With Care while Peter handled Keystone Smartie. Peter made a daring move at the top of the stretch, angling to the inside, waiting and finally shooting through a narrow opening to win at 13–1. "I saw Peter go to the rail, and I could only think he was blowing his opportunity," Billy said afterwards. "I remember thinking if I were driving that horse, I'd have gone to the outside." Handle With Care, who didn't lose many in her illustrious career, finished third behind Keystone Smartie and Otaro Hanover.

In 1975, Peter won one of three $50,000 divisions of the U.S. Pacing Championship with Handle With Care and then, in her final start, won an invitational at Hollywood Park in 1:54⅖, becoming only the second driver in history to win a race in under 1:55.

A year later, Peter denied his father the Trotting Triple Crown.

There have been only six trotters ever to win the Yonkers Trot, Hambletonian and Kentucky Futurity in the same year and none since Stanley Dancer's Super Bowl in 1972.

To win the Kentucky Futurity, first raced in 1893, a horse had to take two heats. Billy drove Steve Lobell, who had won the Yonkers Trot and the Hambletonian in a grueling four heats. Peter drove Quick Pay, a horse of which Billy owned 25 percent.

In the first heat, Delvin Miller's Soothsayer edged Steve Lobell by inches.

In the second, Quick Pay and Steve Lobell finished so close at the wire that nobody was certain who had won. "They held the photo for about 10 minutes, and we're parading out in front," Peter said. "The announcer tried to be very dramatic and said, 'The winner is Haughton.'

"Then the announcer delayed, and I was getting real upset because I didn't know. I thought he'd won. Then he said, 'Peter.' It was a very exciting moment for me."

But it still wasn't over. In the third heat, Quick Pay beat Steve Lobell by a neck in 1:59⅕ to win the Kentucky Futurity and end his dad's shot at the Triple Crown.

"It was a damned tough race," Billy said afterwards. "And he just beat me a whisker. If I had to get beat, I'd rather it was him."

Dottie, of course, was frequently asked what it was like to have a son and a husband competing against each other all the time. "It was great," she said. "People would ask, 'Who are you rooting for?' I'd say, 'Whoever was closest to the wire at the end. There was no issue to handle. I loved it. They were very competitive. They loved to beat each other."

She said that Billy handled defeat better than Peter. "Peter always wanted to win," Dottie said. "Second was never satisfying for him. I can remember one time saying, 'Pete, you finished third and got a check.' He said, 'Mom, that's not winning. There's nothing like winning.' Bill was that competitive, but he wasn't terribly depressed if a horse raced the best he could and was second, third or fourth and got a check. He was never upset."

Peter was still growing and learning, which was hard to tell by the $2.8 million the Haughton stable earned in '75 or the record $3.6 million in '76. In 1977, Bill and Peter became the first father and son to each win $1 million in purses.

Peter won his second $100,000 Kentucky Futurity in 1978 with Doublemint and his first $200,000 Roosevelt International Trot behind Cold Comfort. Doublemint came back to win the $200,000 International in 1979. Bill watched both those Internationals from the paddock, saying Peter "knew both horses better than I did."

Peter drove five winners in one night at Louisville Downs, April 2, 1975.

Among the slew of stakes Peter won were the $113,681 Fox Stake with Crackers in 1978, the $166,665 Dexter Cup and $126,000 Zweig Memorial with Cold Comfort in 1977, the $48,370 Tattersalls Pace with Keystone Presto in 1974, the $93,500 Gaines Memorial with Windshield Wiper in 1976 and the $13,500 Tompkins-Geers with Puppet in 1975.

"He had hands like his Dad or better," Haughton Stable trainer Clarence Martin said. "He was a horseman from Day One."

Stanley Dancer said, "God knows how great he could have been had he lived. He was just super." Stanley was instrumental in creating the Peter D. Haughton Library at the Harness Racing Museum and Hall of Fame in Goshen, N.Y. "It was incredible that he would do that for another driver's son," Dottie said.

Nationally renown harness racing writer Clyde Hirt remembers a conversation he had in 1977 with Jack Krumpe, then Executive Director of the New Jersey Sports Authority, which operates The Meadowlands. "You know what," I blurted after one performance, "I think he will be as good or better than his father in a short time." Krumpe shook his head: "He's better right now and he's only 22." Two years later, even Billy confided to Al Adams, manager of Almahurst Farms in Lexington, Kentucky, "The kid's getting better than his old man."

By the age of 25½, Peter had won 573 of 2,794 starts, with 420 seconds, 350 thirds, earnings of $6,445,946 and an excellent UDR of .330.

Two of the horsemen Peter got close to when The Meadowlands opened in 1976 were John Campbell and Eddie Lohmeyer.

"We were good friends," Campbell said. "I'd met Peter one year I came down for the Jug in '77 and just met him in passing. When I came to The Meadowlands in '78, he was stabled there. We just hit it off and got along very well. We played pool a lot. Peter loved country music.

"We had a different background. He went to college and I didn't. He had a great time in college. I used to get a little kick out of listening to his stories. I wasn't envious of the education, but of the social life. Peter related to the whole industry. It didn't matter if you were running a track or taking care of a horse. He could get along with anybody. We were always making fun of each other. We had a lot of laughs."

Eddie Lohmeyer, a trainer who was one of the Haughton catch-drivers at The Meadowlands, became Peter's roommate. "I was at The Meadowlands when they opened in '76," Lohmeyer said. "I started driving some of the trotters for the Haughtons and did very well. I started to buddy around with Peter. I had a place up at The Meadowlands. When Peter came up, he stayed there for the winter.

"I think he had a lot of class about him. He'd play a joke on you in a second. Little stuff. I think that's why we got along good. We were easy-going. I don't think anybody couldn't get along with him. Maybe he wouldn't care for someone, but he'd be very polite around him."

Lohmeyer shares the popular belief that Peter's best years were ahead of him. "Peter hadn't even come close to reaching his potential," Lohmeyer said. "At the time he died, he wasn't even coming close to the horseman he would have been. You have to train for 10 years before you're going to get to be something. He was better than average at the time. There was no telling. He was a young boy. He had so far to go."

In December, 1979, Peter, Cammie, Bill and Dottie were spectators, standing on the outside of the Turf Club at Pompano Park, nervously waiting for Tommy Haughton's first drive in Florida. Paul Moran wrote in a story in the *Fort Lauderdale News and Sun-Sentinel*: "Peter became silent that night as he watched his brother go to the post. He watched intently along with his father, mother and brother. Tommy Haughton and his mount moved into contention on the final turn. 'He's got it,' Peter said, breaking his silence. 'He's got it.'

"Tommy Haughton won his first race in Florida and Peter led the family out of the Turf Club to the winner's circle to pose for the traditional photograph. Later, he said, 'I can't wait to get back to The Meadowlands. I've got some nice horses to race there this year, and the money makes having to be cold all winter a lot easier to take.'"

Peter had a string of 22 horses from the Haughton Stable at The Meadowlands in January. On Thursday night, Jan. 24, 1980, he had a single drive, finishing ninth in a field of 12 behind Battling Brad in the seventh race, the $35,000 second leg of the Presidential Series.

John Campbell was with him after the races. "We went out for dinner after the races that night and we had fun, as always," he said. "I remember leaving him at 1 a.m., and waving as he hopped into his Mercedes."

He was the last person to see Peter alive.

Traveling along Route 20, which runs parallel to The Meadowlands backstretch, Peter lost control of his late model 1979 Mercedes Benz on an icy stretch, skidded 174 feet and hit a concrete road divider, careening off that and becoming airborne before severing a utility pole across the road. The car came to rest upside down on the bottom of the pole and was covered with live wires. He died instantly.

Norma Campbell, who is unrelated to John, was working at The Meadowlands in marketing and promotions in 1980. She is still working at The Meadowlands now as a secretary. That night, she was the first person to see Peter's crash. She had been with Peter and John Campbell at The Front Row, a popular late night restaurant. "Peter was staying at Eddie Lohmeyer's in Secaucus," she said. "Peter and I were very dear friends. He was an absolutely happy-go-lucky great guy, a sweet nice person and very generous. Peter and Billy were inseparable, and he had such a special relationship with his mother. He just worshipped her.

"That night he had on a yellow turtleneck and a brown houndstooth jacket. I actually had left the restaurant a few minutes before Peter, but he passed me when I got stopped at a light. It was a very cold night and there had been a lot of snow. On Patterson Plank Road, I thought I saw a lot of smoke. It was Peter's car. I knew something was wrong.

"I pulled up ahead and ran back. It was awful. The horn was blowing. The car was upside down. I remember his cowboy boots were in the back seat pressed against the window. I couldn't see him. And I could hear the radio."

Unable to open the doors, she climbed over a fence and ran into a maintenance building. "A maintenance worker was in the building," she said. "I was in shock. The ambulance came. We tried to call people."

East Rutherford Police Captain Gilbert Logatto said, "The curve is difficult to negotiate at times if it's dark. He could have hit some ice. We don't know."

He said Public Service & Gas Company workers had to cut the utility wires strung over the wreckage before rescuers could free Peter.

Dottie and Bill were at Pioneer Farm for a few days with Joe and Joan Bebry. "We talked to Peter that Thursday afternoon, probably around 5 p.m.," she said. "He sounded fine. He had just qualified a colt of mine. He was very happy. Everything was great."

The phone rang between 4:30 and 5 a.m. Dottie answered. "It was Bill Rosenberg," Dottie said. "I was a little nasty because owners had started calling us at all hours. I wasn't the most polite person when he called, and I've regretted that. Little did I know. He asked for Bill. And I woke Bill up."

Their 25-year-old, blond haired son was dead.

"Bill just went to pieces," Dottie said. "He started just walking circles in the bedroom, wringing his hands. He was just destroyed."

Dottie ran into the Bebry's room and told them that Peter was dead. She actually had the presence of mind at that incredible moment of pain to tell them it was her Peter, not one of their sons, who was also named Peter. "I thought right away to assure them that it was not their son," she said.

Dottie and Billy and the rest of their children were left to deal with Peter's loss. "It was like such a bad dream," Dottie said. "Not ever having any brothers or sisters or any cousins, I never really lost anybody. You don't know what to expect. The only person I think I can remember seeing dead was my grandfather when I was 11 years old, and only for a second. Shock takes over. Shock is a wonderful thing, because it does, sort of, help get you through...."

Doug Miller was helping run the Haughton Stable office at The Meadowlands and serving as second trainer behind Peter. "I made up all the training schedules," he said. "I coordinated all the horses at the racetrack and took care of the payroll. And I walked in really early that morning, like 5:30. I saw Cammie's car outside. Cammie was not an early riser as a rule. I walked in the office and there's Cammie sitting there on the couch. And I knew something, I just had a gut feeling that something . . . because that was really out of character for Cammie to be there at 5:30 in the morning. I couldn't figure out what happened. I just walked in there and said, 'Is everything all right Cammie?' And he said, 'Peter got in a car accident last night and got killed.' He said it just stone cold, matter of fact. I'm sure it hadn't even sunk in yet to him. He hadn't realized what happened. It was one of those things that you don't even realize for two or three days. It doesn't sink in. I still . . . it doesn't even seem possible that happened."

Billy Jr. was asked to go to the scene of the accident and go through any of Peter's belongings. "Seeing that car, I knew he didn't suffer," Billy Jr. said.

At a service attended by hundreds at St. Dominic's Church in Oyster Bay Cove, Delvin Miller read Peter's eulogy. In part, he said, "He accomplished more in a few short years than most young men dream of in a lifetime, and he gave us rich memories that assure him of a very special kind of immortality. Peter leaves us an imprint that will endure—in our sport and in all our lives. But an enormous amount of talent wasn't the only thing owned by Peter Haughton. He was a good person. He was likable, kind, with no arrogance, which surely his quick success could have prompted, and he was a person who respected the personal qualities and abilities of older men in his sport. He was a terrific young man."

And now he was gone.

Peter was laid to rest Jan. 28, 1980, in Holy Rood Cemetery near Roosevelt Raceway.

He'd won 571 races and $6,417,862 in his short career. "He had the world in his grasp, but he never let you know it," said trainer Bob Gordon.

The Meadowlands lowered its flags to half-mast, and fans and horsemen had a moment of silence. At Yonkers, horsemen and officials gathered in a gigantic ring on the track and paused for a moment of silence. At Pompano Park, nearly 200 owners, trainers, drivers and friends paraded down the stretch behind a driverless horse and sulky. Driver Mike Harding gave a eulogy.

Eddie Lohmeyer was asked by the Haughton family to drive Peter's horse, Cold Comfort, in the second leg of the Su Mac Lad Series the night they buried

Peter. "They asked me to drive him, and I couldn't say no," he said. "I had terrible mixed feelings. My dad passed away in 1997 and it didn't affect me nearly as much. He was 78 and he was failing in health. Peter was the first close person to me that I lost. It tore me up. I was terrible at the funeral, real bad. After the funeral, there was no emotion left in me. It's a day that I'll never forget. I didn't talk to anybody that night. I stayed by myself and drove the horse. I just wanted to win so bad. I snuck up the rail, split a couple of horses and won. In the winner's circle, I couldn't stay there. I hung the lines up and walked out. It was real tough, like you're numb. I'm glad I did that. I'm glad I raced the horse that night. I felt it was for Peter. There was something I could do for him that day. But I couldn't get my picture taken."

16

Burgomeister

Life went on without Peter.
It just wasn't as good.

Billy Haughton's zest for life was buried with his son. "It was like somebody cut a part out of Bill," Eddie Lohmeyer said. "He aged like seven years in a day. He never bounced back from it. Never. Before, he was naturally jubilant. Afterwards, he had to try to be happy."

Dottie said, "Bill's hair turned white overnight after Peter died. I don't think he ever got past it. I don't think he ever stopped missing Peter."

Stanley Dancer and other horsemen would stop by Billy's office to console him. "Stanley would sit with Bill and they'd both be crying," Dottie said. "I went to the training track every single morning and sat there all winter long with Bill so he wouldn't be by himself at all. It was very hard for him."

Dancer said, "Bill took Peter's death bad. I took it bad. Everybody in the sport did. He was too young. Somebody as young as Peter and that great? Oh my god, that's just terrible. Bill never got over it. I've never gotten over it. I tried to help Bill. I don't know how much I could help him. I don't know if anybody could really help him. It was a rough deal."

Working in the Haughton Stable, Doug Miller saw Peter's death's incredible impact on Bill. "It's almost difficult to describe," Miller said. "Bill was a very strong man. And the most optimistic person I ever knew. But that crushed him. You hear so many parents say that when they lose a child, you can never experience that kind of grief in any other facet of your life. But with Bill, I think it was even compounded by the fact that they worked together; that Peter had become an integral part of his stable, and that he was a great driver in his own right by then. Peter really added to the stable. People were starting to give horses to the stable because of Peter and not just because of his father. It crushed him. It ripped him apart, and I'm sure he was never the same man after that. I was only there with the Haughton Stable for another year and a half and I left. I could see it on his face the last time I ever talked to him. Still."

Miller was with Billy the first time he went to The Meadowlands after Peter's death. "Their lockers were next to each other, and they still had Peter's colors hanging in that locker," Miller said. "The valet in the locker room polished Peter's boots every night and always had his stuff there. For years after that.

"I happened to walk into the locker room with Billy that night. And he saw that and he just went to pieces. And I think of many other times when he would just sit down and cry like a baby."

Billy Haughton was no more adept at handing personal tragedy than any of us. When his mother passed away, Billy drove to Fultonville the next day, but couldn't bring himself to attend her funeral. "He couldn't handle that at all," Dottie said.

After Peter died, Dottie tried hard not to cry at

home. "It was very hard because Bill was so devastated," she said. "I don't think I really let myself mourn because I knew I had to hold him together. I didn't want any of the kids to see me cry. I was so afraid that they'd fall apart."

Her children realized that. "When Peter died, she was strong," Tommy said. "She wouldn't cry in front of us. But down the hallway, you could hear her at night."

Billy Jr. said, "I heard it too. That was devastating. That was the epitome of sadness."

The Haughtons were flooded with sympathy letters from friends and from complete strangers. Michael J. McCusker, a lawyer from Westwood, Mass., said, "I last saw Peter at the Old Glory Sale at Yonkers last fall and remember thinking at the time that he was a living advertisement for everything that was good and clean and wholesome in harness racing."

Grosso Maurizio of Turin, Italy, who'd met Peter when he raced in Trieste, Italy, wrote, "I met your son Peter when he came to Italy and I was fascinated by him and by his style."

Mike Nelson of Ozone Park, Long Island, wrote, "I am merely a harness racing fan who had the good fortune to meet Peter once a couple of years ago at Roosevelt Raceway's backstretch cafeteria. Peter was wonderful to me, taking time out to talk and have a cup of coffee. Obviously, he didn't have to interrupt his busy schedule . . . but he did. He touched me and many, many others and we will never forget him. I have lit a candle in my church for Peter."

Sandra Russell said, "I remember when I first talked with Peter, then in his teens. He was fired up over the fate of the wild mustangs and told me of his involvement with Wild Horse Annie's crusade. I was impressed by this lovely boy who cared deep enough about something outside himself to pursue a worthy but unglamorous cause."

Billy and Dottie took out an ad in the Feb. 6, 1980, issue of *The Horsemen and Fair World*, where, as in *Harness Horse*, page after page was filled with condolences from horsemen. The ad read:

"Bill and Dot Haughton and Family wish to thank all our many wonderful friends for being so kind and thoughtful at a time when our grief and sadness is so heavy in our hearts. The love and respect shown for our Peter has helped to ease the pain and comfort us.

"We would like to share this poem with you. It was sent to us by a caring groom from another stable:

> "Do not stand at my grave and weep,
> I am not there, I do not sleep.
> I am a thousand winds that blow
> I am the diamond glints on snow
> I am the sunlight on ripened grain
> I am a gentle autumn's rain.
> When you waken in the morning's hush
> I am the swift uplifting rush
> Of quiet birds in circled flight
> I am the soft stars that shine at night.
> Do not stand at my grave and cry,
> I am not there, I did not die."

Peter's horses had not died. And there was one he had deep confidence in. His name was Burgomeister.

"I went to the 1978 Harrisburg sale, and Billy and Peter were already there," Dottie said. "Pete came up to me and said, 'Mom, I want you to come look at a colt.'

"Here was this great big colt. He said, 'I want to buy that colt.' I don't know what it was about Burgomeister, but he loved him."

Peter bought Burgomeister, then sold 50 percent to a partner, Marcello Fiorentino, who owned Cappriccio, a popular Italian restaurant in Syosset with Joan Bebry. "We all ate there a lot," Dottie said. "It was a great restaurant."

Peter broke Burgomeister, and trained him that winter. Peter wanted to race Burgomeister lightly at 2, but Peter was out of town one day and Bill raced him in Buffalo. "Peter got mad at me," Billy said

Dottie said, "Peter was fit to be tied. He didn't want him raced. He had his own way that he wanted to bring his horse along. So he got upset with Bill and he turned the horse out."

Burgomeister, a son of Speedy Count, who was the first foal of the Lindy's Pride mare, Burger Queen, raced just six times as a 2-year-old, winning only a baby race at Vernon Downs in 2:05.4, a modest mark even for a 2-year-old on Vernon Downs' ¾ mile oval, and earning just $1,994.

Doug Miller remembers how preoccupied Peter was with Burgomeister's training: "The very last time I saw Peter, he made up a training schedule for that horse, which I still have at home. When he went to New Jersey that winter, he gave me that training schedule and told me that he wanted me to train the horse and not let anyone else train him except his father. I'm not taking the credit for Burgomeister, but I trained the horse all winter. I drove him a couple of times."

After Peter died, Dottie said, "Bill had a bad time going near the horse for a while. Peter had said when Burgomeister was a 2-year-old, 'This is my Hambletonian horse.' Bill just couldn't go near him. And then, all of a sudden, he became obsessed with doing everything, and nobody ever touched Burgomeister but Bill. He was obsessed with getting him to the Hambletonian.

"I thought it was good, because I don't think it's

good when you do the other thing, when you ignore it. Because it's there. You can't ignore it. And I think Bill felt he was doing this for Peter."

But Billy was not the only Haughton trying to win the Hambletonian, which was held at Du Quoin for the final time in 1980 before it re-located at The Meadowlands, where its purse was guaranteed to rise to $1 million by 1983.

If Peter had been alive, he would have driven Burgomeister with the opportunity of becoming the youngest driver to ever win the Hambletonian, or to even win a single heat of the Hambletonian.

Tommy Haughton would get that same opportunity with Final Score, a trotter by Super Bowl, Stanley Dancer's 1972 Hambletonian and Trotting Triple Crown winner. "Final Score was my big break," Tommy said. "He was making breaks the whole year as a 2-year-old, and they turned him out and brought him back as a 3-year-old. He always had a lot of speed. And my father drove him, got him qualified, drove him in a race and he made a break. Then he qualifies. Now he puts John Campbell up. He drives him in a race. Makes a break. So now, they can't race him at The Meadowlands because he's not qualified. So they send him out to Pennsylvania, to Pocono. And Hubert Rydell, the owner, said, 'Let Tommy drive him. Nobody else is getting along with him.'

"So I drove him in a Pennsylvania Sire Stakes and he won in 2:00 and set a track record. From that day on, that was my big break. I just stayed with that horse. He turned out to be 3-Year-Old of the Year then 4-Year-Old of the Year."

In the days preceding the Hambletonian, Billy acknowledged the immense pressure he placed on himself: "I have never let anything get to me the way this has, thinking about it, worrying about it," he said. "I don't know what I'll do if we don't win."

Final Score drew into the first elimination and Burgomeister got the outside nine post in the second. Two of the best 3-year-old trotters, Netted and Rodney's Best, missed the Hambletonian because of leg injuries, leaving 19 to contest the trotting classic.

Dottie, who had always dressed up for big races, wore a $14 sun dress to the Hambletonian. "And I didn't care," she said. "I didn't care if my hair was a mess. Things weren't as important to me as they had been before, that everything had to be just so. If someone said something about me, I wasn't going to worry about it."

The day was difficult enough for her and Billy anyway. "It was hard, very hard, the whole day with pressure," she said. "And it was the last time at Du Quoin. It was a very emotional day."

Tommy drove Final Score like he was the best, moving up from third on the outside to gain the lead by the quarter and dare anyone to take it away. Nobody did. Final Score won in 1:56⅗, making 23-year-old Tommy the youngest winner of a Hambletonian heat ever. John Simpson Jr. had held the record when he won a heat in 1970 at the age of 27.

In the second elimination, Billy left with Burgomeister and wound up getting parked on the outside. But at least he had cover from Demon Renvach, driven by Jack Leonard. Billy sent Burgomeister three-wide, collared front-running Thor Viking and won in 1:58, the equivalent of seven lengths off Final Score's winning time, by a length and a half in front of late-closing Yonkers Trot winner Nevele Impulse.

Tommy loved his brother Peter dearly, but he fully intended to win the Hambletonian himself. "I really had the feeling that the owner thought maybe I wanted Burgomeister to win, which was crazy," Tommy said.

Final Score got the rail and Burgomeister the two post for the third heat. If any of the other trotters won, there would have been a three-horse race-off.

Tommy settled Final Score in fourth on the rail with Billy right behind him in fifth. A horse who had been parked on the outside broke, leaving them third and fourth. Tommy pulled Final Score out second over and Bill followed third over with Burgomeister.

Tommy said. "I actually thought I was going to win. It was unbelievable. He was so strong."

Maybe too strong. "We were going into the last turn, and he just ducked sideways and made a break," Tommy said.

That left Burgomeister without cover, but he stormed to the lead and won easily in 1:56⅗. When Billy brought him back, Cammie ran out and hugged Burgomeister's neck.

There were a lot of emotions in the winner's circle. One was anger. "I was totally mad because I made a break," Tommy said. "I wanted to win that race. I didn't have my head into where they were with Burgomeister."

Dottie said, "It was a great relief when it was over for Bill and the whole family. It was so incredible that this horse won the Hambletonian. He wasn't a horse people talked about all year. He was just a good horse. But that day, he was a great horse. It was very bittersweet. It was. Tears of happiness; tears of sadness."

Billy was handed the microphone to address the crowd of 18,000. Half-crying, he said, "I just wish Peter would have been here, because I wouldn't have been doing the driving."

Peter couldn't have driven him any better.

17

Cammie

At 15, Cammie Haughton knew what he wanted out of life: to be on the track with his father. Seven years later, despite spectacular early success, he would leave harness racing completely disillusioned, a feeling compounded by the deaths of his brother and father. Ten years after that, he would return to the sport as a racing official. It hasn't been a smooth ride, but he is now a presiding judge at Monticello and Yonkers Raceways for the New York State Racing and Wagering Board. He seems settled. Maybe even comfortable.

"Now, I'm trying to make my mother and everybody proud of me," Cammie said.

He didn't when he left high school early. "I didn't want to sit in my classes," he said. "I wanted to be with the horses."

Dottie and Billy reluctantly gave in, but Billy certainly gave his son no more an advantage than he had given Peter. "We were taught the right way," Cammie said. "Muck out stalls. Be a groom. Take care of the animals. Horsemanship. I enjoyed being a groom. You drive up to the barn in your car, and the horses come over the stable door and look at you. They knew you would take care of them every day. I loved that part of it. That was the best part: raising colts."

Having the world's greatest trainer/driver for a father wasn't exactly a downer. "Back then, the Grand Circuit was going," Cammie said. "We went to Goshen, and I watched my father fly in on a helicopter. It was unbelievable."

Robert Cameron got his middle name from Billy's uncle Cameron, the priest.

Cammie's apprenticeship went well. He began driving in the summer of 1979 at Brandywine under the tutelage of Dick Dudley, who handled a string of the Haughton Stable at the Delaware track, and Doug Miller, who eventually would move on to The Meadows with another Haughton string.

Cammie won eight of 16 qualifiers before finishing out of the money in his first pari-mutuel start. Cammie then won three straight, including a double on Friday night, July 12, with a pair of 2-year-olds, Flying Wings, a Bye Bye Byrd colt, and Fulla Thunder, a Fulla Napoleon colt owned by Don Mitchell of Wilmington.

Cammie upped his record to four-for-five, taking a stake at Pocono Downs with Flying Wings. He also finished second with Trenton Time to the brilliant, undefeated Niatross in 1979. Trenton Time and Niatross would meet again several times, and Billy Haughton would train Niatross' son Nihilator to be Horse of the Year.

At the time, Cammie credited most of his early success to his older brother: "I think a lot of Peter. He's helped me a lot. I don't see too much of my father."

His father, though, had seen him enough to be impressed. "Cammie has never been an athlete, but he has a great touch, a natural pair of hands," Billy said in Paul Moran's story in the *Fort Lauderdale News and Sun-*

Sentinel, Sunday, Dec. 2, 1979. In that story, which documented Tommy getting the first win of his career at Pompano Park, Billy talked about the development of all three of his driving sons:

"Sure, when I watch them starting out, I think back to when I was that age. I just hope they don't make the same mistakes I did.

"I never pushed them. I let them decide for themselves whether or not they wanted to get into racing. I wouldn't have been happy doing what my father did, and I've seen too many other fathers push their sons into something they really didn't want to do.

"Other than demanding a little discipline, I've let all of them learn on their own. I've never said, 'Do this or that.' Peter and I have driven in a lot of $100,000 races together, and only once has he ever asked for my opinion before a race. They've got to learn from experience.

"They learned the basics by being there, by grooming horses and being around the barn every day. If I see them doing something wrong, I'll tell them, and if one has a question, he'll come to me with it.

"Tommy is a natural athlete, but he's also a perfectionist. He's come to me with questions more than Peter or Cammie ever have."

Cammie seemed to have a lot of the answers, especially with Trenton Time, who would finish second in the Cane Pace and third in both the Little Brown Jug and the Messenger Stakes chasing Niatross.

"I was his trainer," Cammie said. "I had driven Trenton Time in Florida, starting him out early in his 3-year-old season. I drove him down there in a couple of qualifying races, then I drove him in a couple overnights. And I won four of them. Then he was eligible to the Florida Breeders Stakes down there, and my father let me keep driving him. I guess the purse was

$35,000. I won the Florida Breeders as the youngest driver ever and set a track record (1:57⅗) for 3-year-olds. The horse got exceptionally good. He had some big races coming up. And my father took over, which was fine with me. I got to train the horse. The horse was in my care. So I just kept right on rolling with him."

At that point in his budding career, Cammie confessed to no misgivings about his father or his brother taking over the driving. "No problem whatsoever for me to hand over the lines to my father or Peter," Cammie said. "They were so talented. Peter was a better driver, I think, than my dad was when he was 25. My dad was an all around horseman. But Peter as far as driving a horse? I tell you, I've never seen anything like him."

Trenton Time's glaring weakness was his timing. He was born the same year as Niatross, who won 37 of his 39 lifetime starts. "We were awful close to him in ability," Cammie said. "It seemed like we couldn't pass him, like Niatross would hang in there. He was a great horse, no doubt about it, a great horse. Trenton Time was like a kid of mine. I loved that horse. He knew exactly who I was and I knew who he was."

And on one unseemly cold July afternoon in Saratoga Springs, right across the street from the thoroughbred race course known as "the Graveyard of Favorites," another monumental upset was about to happen in 1980. At the time, Niatross was undefeated.

The cold rain had turned the track into a mess, and management delayed the feature event, the Battle of Saratoga, nearly 45 minutes to work on the track. Cammie saw something unusual: "All the horses were standing in the paddock waiting to go on the track, and I noticed that Niatross had a lot of blankets on him for some reason. Now it's good to keep a horse warm, especially if there's a delay, for their muscles not to tighten up. But they had three coolers on him. I thought that it was rather peculiar. So did my dad."

That was only the beginning to perhaps the strangest day in modern harness racing history.

Heading to the three-quarters on Saratoga's half-mile track, Niatross was on the lead and Trenton Time was on his outside trying to keep pace. Only this time, Trenton Time kept coming.

"My father pulled up right alongside of Niatross at the top of the stretch," said Cammie, who watched the race from the paddock. "Pulled up right alongside him eye to eye. And Niatross went right over the hub rail. I was amazed. I couldn't believe it. My father just kept looking back. He wanted to see what happened to Clint [Galbraith]. Trenton Time had a lot of pace. He just drew off."

Miraculously, both Niatross and his driver/trainer, Clint Galbraith, escaped injury.

"I ran to the winner's circle," Cammie said. "I was thrilled to death. I wasn't thrilled to death that a horse went over the fence like that, but I was thrilled to death with the race. It's a personal thing. I take care of these horses and see them every day and every morning. You break them when they're yearlings. It's amazing how you feel for these horses. From the start, from when you put a harness on him, you take care of them every single day. You watch them progress. You watch them jog slow. Then you train them."

By the time Cammie reached the winner's circle, Niatross and Galbraith had both gotten to their feet. "Dad asked, 'What happened? What happened?'" Cammie said.

What likely happened was that Niatross, who had never been beaten, was being passed by Trenton Time when Galbraith used his whip on the sulky to try to rally his champion. Niatross bore to the inside away from the noise of the whip, a noise he had never heard before, and went over the rail.

After the race, Billy saw his friend, Clint Galbraith, sitting alone on the steps of the racing office and went to console him. They talked quietly for several minutes.

Cammie had settled into his own niche in the Haughton family stable. In doing so, he became even closer to his dad.

"My dad was my best friend," Cammie said. "I miss my father so much it's unbelievable. You can't imagine how much I miss that guy."

His favorite time together with his dad was after morning training sessions at Pompano Park in Florida, when he and his dad would head out on their boat and pursue another of his dad's passions: fishing.

The first family boat was a 31-foot Bertram Sportfish, and Billy would frequently take out owners, his assistant trainers and friends. "Then we got a 45-foot boat with a big cabin, salon, color TV, kitchen, two state rooms and a big deck in the back for fishing," Cammie said. "It was a $200,000 boat, and he'd allow me to take it out. He'd be downstairs either rigging the fishing poles or doing something else and say, 'Take it out.'"

To Billy, the ocean was a sanctuary. "It allowed him to get away from the phones," Cammie said. "We'd be out on the racetrack training colts, and he'd say, 'You ready to hit the 1:45 bridge?' Because we had to catch a drawbridge. We'd go out five, six days a week right after training horses. We had so much fun, where he could unwind. We'd be out there for hours and hours just fishing. That's where I really got close to my father. Just him and me and whomever would go along. My brothers didn't like it."

On one fishing excursion, Billy lost a piece of his ear.

"We'd just gotten back from fishing," Dottie said.

"We were at the dock, and I was cleaning up the boat. He went to tie some rope and must have slipped and hit his head on the side of the boat. I heard a splash and didn't turn around. I thought he was emptying a bucket. I said something, but I didn't hear anything back. Then I looked, and he was hanging over the rope in the water unconscious. Then a man and his son came from the next dock, swam over and got him up on the deck and he was okay. He had a gash over his ear, and a bit of his ear lobe had been severed, and I flicked it in the water. But he was okay. He was training horses the next morning all bandaged up."

Dottie could have snipped part of Cammie's ear back when he was 13. "He had long hair, and I thought that gave him an attitude," Dottie said. "He'd done something that was real smart ass. I just took him in the powder room downstairs and gave him a haircut. He didn't have a choice. No way. It was a wonder I didn't cut his ears off. When you think about it, Bill wasn't home a lot, and I had five kids. I had to show them that they couldn't walk all over me."

It was a sentiment Cammie himself would echo when he took himself out of harness racing. Ironically, the horse involved was named Laughs.

In the spring of 1985, Cammie went to Roosevelt Raceway with a string of 22 horses while Billy and Tommy raced about 80 at The Meadowlands. "I stumbled across a good one," Cammie said. "This 2-year-old, he could fly, absolutely fly."

Laughs trained so well that Cammie entered and drove him in a baby race at The Meadowlands, where the competition could have been tougher than at Roosevelt. "He absolutely went off and hid," Cammie said. "I won in 1:58 and two [2/5]. We went back to Roosevelt and celebrated. We went back the following week and won in 1:56 and four [4/5]. Then I drove him at Yonkers and won with him in a baby race. The following week, he won again at Yonkers."

And then, just as he was ready to begin his career in pari-mutuel races, he was gone, taken out of the stable by Laughs' owner, Irving Liverman of Montreal, who'd owned and raced Handle With Care with Billy and Peter. "They gave him to [Meadowlands trainer] Charlie Sylvester," Cammie said. "The owners thought my father was spending too much time on Nihilator. That's the excuse they gave my father. I showed up one morning and the horse was gone. The groom said they came and got the horse."

Dottie said she can only remember Billy getting extremely mad twice, once when a groom named Courtland Johnny had one too many to drink. He forgot to put a sulky and jog cart underneath the shed row, and it rained that night. The other time was when Liverman took Laughs out of Cammie's care.

It still irks Dottie: "Irving Liverman decided that Cammie wasn't good enough to drive Laughs after Cammie had won all his baby races, taking that little horse under his wing all winter long. He was just so proud of that horse. And then they wanted Cammie off the horse for his first real [pari-mutuel] race. The owner called him. Bill just flipped. Bill was yelling on the phone, which was not like him at all. Irving had been a very good owner for us, but that really bothered Bill because Cammie had just done so great with this little horse."

Cammie said, "I never saw my father that mad in my entire life. He went nuts. He went ballistic."

Cammie just went away. "I stopped training," he said. "I needed a break. It really hurt me; it hurt me a lot. I told my father I didn't want to do it anymore, because I worked my ass off for Laughs. It was like he was my child." Cammie retired, having won 109 of 561 starts with 76 seconds and 67 thirds, a UDR of .309 and earnings of $538,492.

Laughs went on to win the $1,025,500 1986 Meadowlands Pace with Buddy Gilmour driving.

For a while, Cammie worked at La Serina, an Italian restaurant in West Palm Beach owned by Peter's former racing partner, Marcello Fiorentino, Joan Bebry and Dottie. Cammie then opened a seafood market in Boca Raton, a business venture which didn't pan out.

After Pompano Park General Manager Harold Duris recommended to Cammie that he go to judges' school, Cammie returned to racing in 1987 as an assistant race secretary at Saratoga Harness. "Then the Racing and Wagering Board noticed me there, and asked me if I would come on," he said. "It was a great opportunity for me. I like what I'm doing now. But I miss being hands-on with horses."

Peter and Tommy, wearing the Haughton colors, take a good long look at one of their father's horses at Ben White Raceway in Orlando, FL, in 1962. Tommy is five and Peter is eight.

18

Tommy

Change is inevitable in any harness or thoroughbred stable. The Billy Haughton Stable was not an exception.

A look at Apples Thomas' meticulous books showed that just six drivers who catch drove for the Haughton Stable in June 1970 were doing the same in 1980: Jack Bailey, Stanley Dancer, Herve Filion, Charles Fitzpatrick, Del Insko and Ben Steall.

In the '70s, Billy used Carmine Abbatiello, Jimmy Arthur, D. Blasdell, Jack Bailey, "Tug" Boyd, Don Bromley, Johnny Chapman, Benoit Cote, Eddie Dunnigan, Stanley Dancer, Jay Edmunds, Lucien Fontaine, Gillies Filion, Herve Filion, Charles Fitzpatrick, Eldon Harner, Del Insko, C. James, Jack Kopas, Clarence Martin, Joe Marsh, Delvin Miller, Joe O'Brien, John Patterson Sr., George Sholty, Ben Steall, Harold Story, Jim Tallman, Al Thomas, Billy Vaughn, Russ White and Tom Wilburn.

In the '80s, he used Joe Adamsky, Jack Bailey, Del Cameron, John Campbell, Stanley Dancer, Dick DeSantis, Bucky Day, Jim Doherty, Merrit Dokey, Herve Filion, Charles Fitzpatrick, Mike Gagliardi, Glen Garnsey, Gary Gibson, Buddy Gilmour, Shelly Goudreau, Jim Grundy, Bill Herman, Jacquie Ingrassia, Del Insko, Jimmy Larente, Jr., Ed Lohmeyer, Jim Marohn, Ed McKnight, Doug Miller, J. Murray Neilson, Sam Noble III, Bill O'Donnell, Kelly O'Donnell, Jim Parkinson, Pawlik, John Patterson Jr., Dave Rankin, Ray Remmen, Patsy Rapone, Dan Ross, Ben Steall, Ron Waples, Ben Webster, Dick Williams, Ted Wing and Mike Zeller.

Of course, all of Billy's sons drove for the stable, too. Peter's untimely death accelerated both Tommy and Cammie's development, one Tommy could never have envisioned when he graduated Oyster Bay High School as an All-American quarterback in football, though he was only 5-foot-10 and 155 pounds.

Unlike Peter and Cammie, Tommy was not smitten with harness racing.

That changed in the summer of 1977 after his freshman season at East Stroudsburg State in Pennsylvania, where he played little filling in as a punter and defensive back. "I went and groomed horses that summer at Roosevelt Raceway," Tommy said.

He never left. "I really liked it," he said. "It's like people tell you: once you start doing it, you can't get away from it."

Instead of returning to college that fall, Tommy accompanied the Haughton string shipped to Florida and began working as a groom, helping Bernie Peck, an assistant trainer and groom, take care of Dottie's outstanding trotting mare Keystone Pioneer. The first horse Tommy groomed on his own was Wellwood Hanover, a top 3-year-old pacer in 1977.

Tommy spent two years grooming before Billy gave him a string of horses to train in Lexington and Delaware, Ohio, home of the Little Brown Jug. Tommy tried learning as much as he could. "I always used to stick around the blacksmith's shop all day trying to learn," Tommy said. "I always wanted to know 'why' which my dad said Peter didn't. Peter already knew what he was going to do."

But Billy took the same approach with both. "Dad was great, because you couldn't start an argument with him," Tommy said. "If you wanted to argue over something, he'd say, 'Go and try it.' Always. He was never a guy to say, 'Just do it this way.' Which is probably the best way in life anyway. He was perfect to work for in that way."

Not so perfect in every way. "He would call you at 3 o'clock in the morning thinking of some horse," Tommy said. "I didn't like it. I'd get all pissed off: I'd say 'Jesus Christ, tell me in the morning.'" Tommy laughed. "He would say, 'I was just thinking about this. I want to try this on this horse tomorrow. And I want to make sure it gets done.' He thought he might forget his idea. That's the way he was."

Tommy began driving in the summer of 1979 with a provisional license, first at Lexington then at Vernon Downs. Tommy won his first race at Lexington with Teddy Hanover. Ideal Valentine gave him his first win at Pompano Park, Dec. 1, 1979, going off the 4–5 favorite from the rail in the sixth race.

Paul Moran chronicled that night in a story the next morning in the *Fort Lauderdale News and Sun-Sentinel*:

"Billy, Peter and Dottie watched the race from the Turf Club Terrace. Dottie sat between Billy and Peter.

Tommy got away second behind Temples Taurus, driven by George Harp, Jr. He sat in the pocket until past the ¾'s and coasted home in a :29⅕ final quarter to win in a 'touch over 2:00,' a lifetime mark."

Later in the story, Moran wrote:

"Afterwards, Tommy says 'She was never that good at Vernon.'

"Billy: 'What you did was right. Remember what you did. Remember how you trained her.'

"Tommy smiled. 'Before the race, there was a big fat man at the rail. He yelled, 'You better win this race or you're in trouble.'

"Peter looked over his shoulder at his younger brother and said, 'Just wait until you drive a horse at Yonkers.'"

Tommy finished 1979 with 15 wins, 14 seconds and 10 thirds in 72 drives, a UDR of .363 and $46,969 in earnings.

With Final Score leading the way, Tommy's numbers jumped dramatically in 1980, the year his brother died. Tommy won a phenomenal 47 of 158 starts with 29 seconds and 22 thirds, posting a career best UDR of .446 and earning $602,543 in purses. Besides winning a heat in the Hambletonian, Final Score gave Tommy his first two major stakes wins: the $120,000 Zweig Memorial at the Syracuse Fairgrounds in upstate New York and the $100,000 Kentucky Futurity at the Lexington Red Mile.

Final Score won two other major stakes for Tommy in 1981, taking the initial running of the $80,000 Nat Ray and the $103,000 Final of the Hiram Woodruff Series at The Meadowlands. Billy was second in the Nat Ray and third in the Hiram Woodruff behind his 1980 Hambletonian winner Burgomeister. The year before, Billy was second in the Hiram Woodruff with Keystone Pioneer behind Pride of Carlisle.

Final Score also won the Hambletonian Maturity and the Marquis de Lafayette, and would finish his career with 20 wins, 14 seconds and six thirds in 64 starts and earnings of $625,989. Tommy upped his victories in 1981 to 58 from 292 starts and his earnings to $747,738. One of Tommy's wins came in one of three $75,000 divisions of the inaugural Peter Haughton Memorial 2-

Year-Old Colt Trot at The Meadowlands behind Triplement. Billy was second in another division behind Speed Bowl.

Tommy and Speed Bowl made harness racing history in 1982.

At the Harrisburg Sales in 1980, Billy bought Sebastian Hanover, a yearling by 1972 Hambletonian winner Super Bowl, for $58,000 for the Pony Stable, a partnership of Dr. Paul Soldner, Max Hempt, Bowman Brown, Dale and Floyd Miller and himself, then renamed the horse Speed Bowl. In a 1982 story by Mike DelNagro in *Sports Illustrated* entitled "Call it the Haughtontonian," Billy said, "We had about $60,000 to spend and there were several horses we liked better, but they all went by us on price. Speed Bowl was the last one left."

Speed Bowl showed two tendencies early in his career. He liked to trot from far back and, many times, he didn't like to trot at all, making a break. When Billy drove Speed Bowl, he repeatedly made breaks. When Tommy drove him six times, he didn't make a break once. "Whatever I do is wrong," Billy said. "Tommy doesn't do it. It's hard to explain. I think it's just the way he handles the colt. He goes better for Tommy than he does for me."

Regardless, Speed Bowl, who'd won eight of 16 starts as a 2-year-old, had won just one of seven starts in 1982 before the Hambletonian, prompting Tommy to suggest to Billy, "Dad, maybe you better do the driving?"

Billy said, "No way. Son, this fella is yours."

Just two nights earlier, Billy had won the $150,000 Oliver Wendell Holmes Pace behind McKinzie Almahurst. Afterwards, he said, "This one was for the money. But the Hambletonian is for pride."

Tommy knew, which didn't make his decision to

change Speed Bowl's equipment the day before the Hambletonian any easier. "It's stupid to shoe a horse on the day before a race, but I didn't like him last week in the Beacon Course [Stakes]," Tommy told Paul Moran in the *Fort Lauderdale News and Sun-Sentinel.* "He didn't trot a bit. We had changed to an open shoe when he'd been racing good all along with a bar shoe (which offers the foot more support). I decided to put him back the way he had been."

Tommy didn't stop there. "We also changed his bridle," he said. "He'd been wearing a blind bridle and been getting beat heads and necks. We thought the change would help, but I put the blind bridle back on him for the Hambletonian. They (the rest of the stable) thought I was crazy, but I took the responsibility."

Dottie talked Billy into watching the Hambletonian from the stands. "I said to Bill, 'Let's go to the clubhouse like normal people.' So we went to the clubhouse and had lunch. That was the first time Bill was ever in the stands with one of the boys driving. He was an absolute nervous wreck. He said he would never do that again."

Twenty-two 3-year-old trotters contested the 57th running of the Hambletonian with a record purse of $875,000 in its second year at The Meadowlands. Jazz Cosmos won the first 11-horse division by 3¼ lengths in 1:57⅗ as Delvin Miller's odds-on favorite, Arndon, broke on the lead turning for home.

In the second division, Speed Bowl faced Mystic Park, who'd won 10 of 13 previous starts in '82. Mystic Park also went to the lead, and also broke, allowing Speed Bowl to rally from a distant 10th at the half to win by 5¾ lengths in 1:56⅖.

The top five finishers in each division raced in a third heat. With a chance to win it all, Jazz Cosmos went for the lead from the two post with Mickey McNichol, and Tommy hustled Speed Bowl up to make him earn the front before settling in the pocket behind him.

"Tommy forced me to the lead and I had to use my horse to get there," McNichol said. "Once I got him going, he was pretty excited. He heard those other horses and it was pretty hard to slow him down and try to save something for the end. I heard Speed Bowl breathing down my back. I didn't expect him to be that close."

Neither did Billy. "I was surprised Tommy left like he did," Billy said. "I was nervous when I saw him sitting in the two-hole the way he was. I thought Mickey was going to be able to back him right off and keep him trapped."

McNichol did until the middle of the stretch when Tommy tipped Speed Bowl outside. Speed Bowl bobbled for a second, but Tommy kept him on gait, and he won by a neck in 1:57, making 25-year-old Tommy the youngest winner in Hambletonian history and giving Billy his fifth Hambletonian as a trainer. "Tommy did a hell of a job," Billy said.

Tommy finished 1982 18th in the country in earnings, winning $1,785,829, a number he would bump up to $1,952,022 in '83 (15th nationally) and then $2,717,264 in 1984, when he finished ninth nationally thanks to his outstanding 3-year-old filly pacer Naughty But Nice, who won the $465,000 Breeders Crown, the $158,353 Jugette, a $58,615 division of the Lady Maud, the $590,750 Mistletoe Shalee and a $76,278 division of the Helen Dancer Memorial. He had improved his win total every year he drove, from 15 to 47, 58, 75, 82 and, in 1984, 125 from 605 starts. His 95 seconds and 83 thirds produced a UDR of .340. Billy couldn't have been any prouder.

19

Nihilator— Like Father, Like Son

By any standard, Stanley Dancer's Albatross was a magnificent pacer, winning 59 of 71 career starts with eight seconds, three thirds and earnings of $1,201,470, and he became an even better stallion. But his son, Niatross, was a better race horse, winning 37 of 39 lifetime starts. Whether Niatross' son, Nihilator, was better than his old man is open to conjecture.

Nihilator won 35 of 38 lifetime starts, and the man who trained him, Billy Haughton, said he was the best horse he ever raced, quite a compliment coming 40 years into Billy's Hall of Fame career.

Nihilator was also a source of considerable controversy, much of it centering on his principal owner, Lou Guida, the head of the Wall Street-Nihilator Syndication. Guida went out of his way telling people he owned "the greatest horse of all time" and playing games with his engagements, at one point threatening to pull the horse out of the Little Brown Jug at the last minute, then entering three other 3-year-olds with Nihilator and scratching the other three.

Billy Haughton tried to steer clear of Guida's theatrics, but he apparently got tired of it, too, and, Dottie said, that was the main reason Billy shocked the harness racing world in 1984 by handing the reins for Nihilator over to top catch driver Bill O'Donnell for the $2,161,000 Woodrow Wilson Pace. O'Donnell would drive Nihilator for the final five of his 13 starts as a 2-year-old and his entire 3-year-old campaign.

First, though, Billy Haughton offered the horse to Tommy, who declined, sticking with another top Haughton colt by Niatross named Pershing Square.

Publicly, Billy Haughton said at the time, "I'm a split second slower than I used to be, but if O'Donnell hadn't been available I probably would have driven Nihilator myself."

Regardless, many of those closest to Billy knew better. "He'd lost nothing," Stanley Dancer said. "That's why it hurt a lot of us to hear that he wouldn't drive Nihilator. He could drive one as good then as he ever could."

But even Billy Haughton didn't know how good a horse he had when he began training the son of Niatross out of the Bret Hanover mare Margie's Melody, who was bred by Robert Gangloff.

"I didn't know he was a top colt real early," Billy told Dean Hoffman in a story in *Hoof Beats* in April 1985. "Before he hit 2:40, he was racky-going [not smooth] and even today he has a racky gait going slow. It wasn't until we started beating 2:40 that I could get him pacing good."

That April of his 2-year-old season, Billy asked his pacing colts to start going quarters regularly in 30 seconds, and Nihilator's immense ability began to surface. Yet Billy didn't have him ranked any higher than two other 2-year-olds in the Haughton Stable, Pollinator and Pershing Square. "It took a while to separate those three," Billy said.

Not once they started racing, though it seemed that Pershing Square, who would give Billy his eighth training win in the Messenger Stakes the following year, kept drawing into the tougher divisions of the stakes in which he and Nihilator both entered. "Then again, maybe Nihilator just made his divisions look easy because he won so handily," Billy said.

But three weeks before the eliminations for the Woodrow Wilson Stakes at The Meadowlands, Nihilator came up with a quarter crack on his right front foot.

Nihilator had some bleeding, but didn't appear to be lame. Billy, however, wanted to be sure he was all right and shipped him to the New Bolton Center at the University of Pennsylvania, where Dr. William Moyer treated the crack by suturing it rather than the standard method of patching it. "He just drilled holes in the hoof wall and used a number nine suture thread to lace the crack together," Billy said. "It turned out just super."

Billy then put a window bar shoe on Nihilator's right front foot, and Nihilator won his elimination heat in the Wilson to advance to the final the following week.

Nihilator had a second quarter crack on his left front foot, but Billy didn't think it was serious. He did, though, make one change: he took himself off as driver, offering Tommy the choice between Pershing Square and Nihilator in the Wilson. Tommy elected to stick with Pershing Square and O'Donnell got the catch drive of a lifetime.

"That was quite a compliment from him, getting to drive that horse," O'Donnell said. "He called me the night before. Me and Tommy were together at Springfield. He said, 'I put you down to drive that colt tomorrow night.'

"I said, 'Are you crazy?'"

He said it was supposed to rain and that he wasn't

fond of driving in the mud. When you get older, it's an aggravation. He just said, 'You go ahead with him.'"

O'Donnell had never driven Nihilator. "Billy told me how to warm up and how he was. Billy was exactly right. And he jogged that night, and the rest was history."

Nihilator won the Wilson in a world record 1:52⅖. "When I tipped him out, he accelerated so fast he almost dumped me right out of the sulky," O'Donnell told Billy.

In the winner's circle, Nihilator's groom, Chuck Robard, asked Billy why he didn't drive Nihilator. Billy said, "Geez, if I knew he was that good, I would have, Chuck."

Billy told *Hoof Beats'* Hoffman that the Wilson was not Nihilator's best race that year, but rather at Lexington in the first heat of the Blue Grass Stakes when Nihilator sat outside another son of Niatross, Niafirst, and won in 1:53 2/5 on a dull track.

Billy scratched Nihilator out of the second heat, and instead trained him up to the $772,500 Breeders Crown 2-year-old pace at The Meadows, Oct. 12, 1984. Nihilator brought in a perfect 11-for-11 record, but anyone who'd seen hometown favorite Dragons Lair, a son of Tyler B trained and driven by Jeff Mallet, knew this wasn't a gimme for Nihilator. Dragons Lair had prepped for the Breeders Crown by setting a world record on a five-eighths track at The Meadows.

Nihilator broke the record in the first elimination, edging pacesetting Dragons Lair by a neck in 1:54⅗. But afterwards, O'Donnell told Billy that, despite the world record, Nihilator "wasn't interested tonight."

Billy said, "Then Nihilator expelled a big gob of mucous from his left nostril between heats. I'll never forget it." But he didn't scratch Nihilator from the Final.

None other than Pershing Square won the second

elim, as Tommy set a leisurely pace and came home in :28⅖ to beat Broadway Express.

The top four from each elimination qualified for the $579,375 Final and it was as dramatic a race as anyone could have imagined with Nihilator, seeking to complete an undefeated season and lock up Horse of the Year honors, leaving from the rail, Pershing Square from the 2 post and Dragons Lair from the 3.

Mallet wanted Dragons Lair on the lead, but so did Tommy behind Pershing Square. They hooked up in an incredible speed duel, with Dragons Lair finally making the front after pacing his first quarter in :26⅗, an amazing display of speed for 2-year-olds in a second heat on a five-eighths track. What was even more amazing is that Dragons Lair survived it.

Mallet bought Dragons Lair a breather, sneaking in a second quarter in :30 flat. When O'Donnell left the three hole and went after Dragons Lair, Dragons Lair gamely held him off, winning by a length in a new world record 1:54⅕. Broadway Express, a 49–1 longshot, got up at the wire to nose out Nihilator for second.

It was a startling defeat for Nihilator, allowing the 3-year-old filly trotter Fancy Crown to be named 1984 Horse of the Year. "I guess it cost him Horse of the Year honors," Billy said.

Then why had he raced him? And why did he send out his champion for the Final? "Maybe we shouldn't have raced, but I wanted to race him for Delvin [Miller], Joe Hardy, Ed Ryan and all the other good people at the track [The Meadows]."

After the Final, Billy and Dottie went to congratulate Mallet. Nihilator had to settle for 2-Year-Old Pacer of the Year honors off 12 wins and a third in 13 starts and earnings of $1,361,357. He would get his Horse of the Year title in '85. The Breeders Crown battles between Dragons Lair and Nihilator energized the sport, but Guida took the edge off that when he bought a 25 percent interest in Dragons Lair before his 3-year-old season.

"I'd have to say that Nihilator is the best horse I've ever trained," Billy said before Nihilator began his 3-year-old season. "I don't like to make that kind of statement, but of all the great ones I've had, Nihilator stands out."

Nihilator would be nearly as dominant as a 3-year-old as he was at 2, winning 23 of 25 starts and becoming harness racing's all-time leading earner, $3,225,653, a record he still held through 1998. His win in 1:49⅗ at The Meadowlands was the first sub-1:50 race mile ever.

In each of his two losses at 3, it took a world record to beat him. He was fourth by 2¼ lengths to Marauder in the Adios Stakes at The Meadows in 1:52⅕. His second defeat at 3 came when he drew the outside 10 post in the Pilgrim Stakes at Garden State Park, was parked the entire mile and lost by a neck to Armbro Dallas in 1:52⅗ on a brutally cold and windy night, Nov. 22.

"Yes, sure he had a rough trip, a brutal trip," Haughton Stable trainer Ernie Gaskin told Bill Lyon in his column in *The Philadelphia Inquirer*. "But the point is, I've seen him overcome that sort of thing before and win anyway. Maybe we're just asking too much of him at this point of his career. This year has been a long, tough campaign. I think he's tired." In Lyons' delightful column, readers learned that Nihilator was fond of apple-filled doughnuts—which were only offered to him on non-race days—and that Nihilator had a 24-hour security guard. Gaskin told Lyons that a veterinarian in Kentucky had done an ultra-sound of Nihilator's heart, and that it was the second largest he'd ever seen to two time thoroughbred Horse of the Year John Henry. Gaskin told Lyons that the vet did ultra-sounds on as many as 1,500 horses each year.

On Nov. 29, 1985, a week after his defeat at Garden State, Nihilator went to post there for the final time of his brilliant career in the $565,053 Breeders Crown 3-year-old Colt And Gelding Pace. Only six others, including Armbro Dallas, were entered, meaning that this Breeders Crown race would be a single heat, giving Nihilator one last chance to display his awesome talent before heading off to make good on the $19.2 million stallion syndication formed by Guida and Bob Boni. Forty shares at $480,000 each were sold, and the people that bought them were deeply concerned that Nihilator would smudge his career by losing his final two races.

Nihilator drew the five post, and O'Donnell sent him right to the lead, making it after being parked three-wide in a quick :27⅘ first quarter. O'Donnell backed off the half to :57⅕ and the three-quarters to 1:27, and Nihilator flew home in a final quarter of :26 flat, to beat Chairmanoftheboard by 2¼ lengths in 1:53.

O'Donnell offered this anecdote of Billy's dealings with Nihilator: "When Nihilator was 3, he had another quarter crack, and, a week after, I jogged him and he was only fair. I came in and said to Bill, 'He's as good as he's ever going to be.'

"'And Bill said, 'No, he's not. There's one more thing I can do.'

"Bill had put aluminum shoes on him just once as a 2-year-old. He had saved it. He never forgot anything a horse wore. This was his ace in the hole. If they had used the aluminum shoes all the time it would have bothered Nihilator's feet. So we used them just that one time and it worked. Bill had his own computer in his mind. He was a genius."

20

Last Drive

One of Billy Haughton's last stakes wins was behind Traveling Salesman in the Canadian Trotting Classic at Greenwood Raceway in Toronto in the summer of 1986. Billy and Dottie owned the rough-gaited trotter with Harry and Robert Vallery, Dr. Paul Soldner, Glenn E. Deling and Jeanne M. Thomson. Dottie was there for that win, and the trophy presentation was made by Jake Howard, a Trustee of the Ontario Jockey Club.

Billy had been named to drive a horse earlier in the card at Greenwood, but someone forgot to tell him. He didn't arrive in time and was replaced by a local driver. When Billy found out, he sought out the trainer to apologize anyway.

In an article by Dave Perkins in the *Toronto Star*, a Canadian racing official, who was an old friend of Billy's, remarked that Billy seemed to be "back to his old, fun-loving self (which he hadn't been after Peter died). He bounced around the paddock, shaking hands and joking with the horsemen, signed autographs for fans, pulled pictures of his new twin grandsons out of his wallet and proudly showed them off."

Two nights before his final drive, Billy was racing at The Meadows in the Pennsylvania Sire Stakes, driving a 10–1 longshot named Good Day Luv. Delvin Miller was there that night. "I saw him drive his last winning race, and I'll never forget it," Delvin said. "Two-year-old trotters were racing and they went to the quarter in :28 and four, and that is just too fast for such young horses. Billy just waited with his horse and let him go. He won it by a nose. It was a drive that I'll remember forever." Good Day Luv paid $23.80, a heck of a price for any horse Billy drove in a stakes. It was Billy's 4,910th win from 22,884 starts and upped his career earnings to $40,160,336. He had 3,638 seconds, 3,238 thirds and a phenomenal career UDR of .344.

At that time, Billy knew he'd already been selected as the 1986 Honoree at the Little Brown Jug Festival Mayor's Breakfast in mid-September. He never made it.

* * *

Bill O'Donnell had been bugging Billy Haughton. "The new helmets, Grattan Helmets, had just come out, and he wouldn't buy one," O'Donnell said. "I said to him, 'Are you going to get one of those new helmets?' He said, 'I can't find one that fits.' I called the guy that made them in Ontario, and he sent me one.

"The week he got killed, Bill asked me to drive at Yonkers, but I had to be in Freestate [Maryland] to drive Laag [a top gray stakes colt]. He said, 'I'll go get those horses qualified in the Sheppard [Pace for 2-year-olds].'

"The helmet came the next Tuesday. I gave it to Tommy. He wore it a long time. It would've made a difference. There isn't a person who's died from head injury wearing one." O'Donnell said in 1998.

* * *

Dottie really wasn't planning on going to Yonkers July 5, 1986. "Bill must have asked me four or five times that day, 'Are you sure you're going tonight?'" Dottie said. "Why did he want me to go so badly that night? The night before, I didn't go because I wanted to stay home and watch the fireworks on TV and out back at the Meadowbrook Club. The next night, I was really planning on going to a friend's house for a party. But he wanted me to go badly. So, we popped in the car and away we went."

Billy was driving a 2-year-old, Sonny Key, in the second race, the first elimination for the Lawrence B. Sheppard Pace.

After another horse made a break directly in front of him, Crimson, driven by Jody Stafford, stumbled and fell. Sonny Key, moving behind Crimson, jumped, throwing Billy onto the track. He was thrown backward from the sulky and his head hit the track with such impact that his helmet split. A third horse fell, too. The two other drivers were not seriously injured.

Dottie was watching the race from the drivers' stand in the paddock. "We always said that it was so terrible when there was an accident, that the drivers' wives ran out onto the track," Dottie said. "What could they do? They couldn't do anything but get in the way. I always said that I would never to that."

So she didn't. She ran down the stairs while her husband lay prone on the track. She remained on the apron, until a driver took Dottie's hand and led her onto the track to her unconscious husband.

"I just stood there," Dottie said. "I was dumbfounded. I thought he had broken his back. I didn't know he had damaged his brain stem."

Billy was placed in the ambulance. Dottie jumped in. What ensued was hard to comprehend. "I can't believe it, but we had to go to the front entrance of the racetrack and wait until the track doctor came down," Dottie said. "And we waited, and we waited and we waited until the track doctor came down and said that he was hurt bad enough to go to the hospital."

On the way to Lawrence Hospital in Bronxville, Billy stopped breathing. "He died in the ambulance," Dottie said. "Stopped breathing. Everything was gone. And one of the paramedics in the ambulance got him breathing again. Then we got to Lawrence. I must have walked a hundred miles that night. I never stopped. I could not stop walking. Up and down, up and down."

After doctors evaluated Billy's condition, he was transferred at 4:45 a.m. to the Westchester County Medical Center in Valhalla, where neurosurgeons confirmed severe brain injury.

Billy Haughton was in a coma.

Dottie's first phone call had been to Holley, who notified the rest of the family and Joe and Joan Bebry.

Dottie will never forget how people helped her family attempt to deal with what had happened. "Steve Starr [Yonkers Race Secretary] was so wonderful," Dottie said. "He found us a house to rent near the hospital. We only needed it for a short time, but it was really great because we could all stay together.

"And Billy O'Donnell and John Campbell and Jackie Parker and everybody came to the hospital all the time with big trays of food for us. It is so wonderful to know that people are there to try to help you when you're standing alone with so much hopelessness and sadness."

New York Yankees owner George Steinbrenner, who owns both thoroughbreds and harness horses, reached out to the Haughton family. Billy had shown him how to drive before he competed in an amateur race. "He had been an owner for about eight years with Bill," Dottie said. "He and Bill were quite close. They were real good friends. He called every single day. When I couldn't find out as much as I needed to know from the doctors, he had the top neurosurgeon from New York Hospital explain things to me and answer questions I had. I put him in touch with Bill's surgeons. George was wonderful, absolutely wonderful when Bill was in the hospital."

It didn't make it any easier. Billy would hang on for ten days, but never regain consciousness, though his family kept talking to him day after day praying for a response.

"Boy, I'll tell you, it was a tough 10 days," Dottie said. "You're up and down. All the emotions. The pressure would build so high in his head, and then they'd operate and the pressure went down. They operated on his brain four or five times. It was horrible."

The city of Vallhalla takes it name from the great hall in Norse mythology where the souls of brave heroes were honored. In general usage, Valhalla is the final resting place of great men of a nation.

"At the hospital, everybody went up to say good-bye to him," Cammie Haughton said. "I didn't go. I didn't go. Not me. When my mother starts putting old tapes on a VCR, I can't sit there. I can't do it. I miss him. I don't want to say good-bye. I don't want to ever say good-bye."

Tommy said, "I never saw my father's accident. I never will."

Billy Jr. said, "I did only once. It was on the news. I couldn't help it. It was right there."

Billy Haughton died at 8:30 a.m., Tuesday, July 15, 1986,

The funeral was held at 11 a.m., Friday, July 18, 1986, at St. Paul the Apostle Roman Catholic Church in Brookville, Long Island. Billy was laid to rest at the Holy Rood Cemetery on Old Country Road in Westbury. Instead of flowers, the family suggested that contributions be made to the Harness Racing Museum and Hall of Fame in Goshen, N.Y., the University of Pennsylvania New Bolton Center Large Animal Clinic or the Cornell University Large Animal Clinic, where a college scholarship was set up in Billy's name.

Stan Bergstein, Executive Vice-President of Harness Tracks of America and a family friend of the Haughtons for decades, delivered Billy's eulogy, concluding:

"In my lifetime, I have never seen a bond closer, stronger, more ennobling and more uplifting, more inspiring than that which tied Bill and Peter Haughton. The terrible separation of six years ago, which left its heavy hand on Bill Haughton's heart, has now been lifted. They are together again. And for that, the angels surely must be singing. In our moment of dark despair, let that be our consolation, too. Shalom."

At Billy's funeral, Dottie unburdened a load of pain she'd been carrying silently for 6½ years after Peter's death. "The priest came to the house after Peter's death and announced that this was the happiest day of Peter's life," Dottie said. "I'll never forget this as long as I live. I've never been so angry in my whole life at anyone. I just couldn't see how a priest, and he's a monsignor now, could say to someone who had lost a 25-year-old boy that the whole world just loved, the best kid in the world with so much talent and so much to live for, could say that this is the happiest day in his life? To me, if it had been someone like my mother, when she died at 98 in a nursing home, saying 'This is the happiest day of her life,' I would say, 'Yes, absolutely.' But not ... At our home after Bill's funeral, I did tell the monsignor what was on my mind, that it had bothered me for all those years, and he understood. And he said that he would really think about what I said and that he'd be very careful consoling parents who have lost children."

Seven years later, Dottie was aghast when she learned of another unfinished matter. In 1993, she discovered that stacks of thank-you letters she'd written to people following Billy's death had never made it to the post office. Instead, they'd been placed in a closet in the house and forgotten.

A couple months after Billy died, Dottie and Holley went to Roosevelt to see Traveling Salesman race. He broke down and had to be destroyed. Dottie said, "It's almost like he went up there to be with Bill."

21

Carrying On

Harness racing had lost its brightest hero. Tommy, Cammie, Billy Jr. and Holley lost their father. Dottie lost her husband and her best friend. "He was definitely my best friend," Dottie said. "And I was his best friend. I was his buddy. For a while, I went fishing with him almost every day. Everything he did, he wanted me to be with him, just like a guy, like a buddy."

Once again, Dottie subjugated her feelings for the good of the family.

"She felt she couldn't cry," her dear friend, Joan Bebry, said. "I kept telling her, 'You've got to mourn. You've got to cry.'"

But she wouldn't. "If it wasn't for Mom, we all would have been in the crapper," Billy Jr. said. "Cuz' it was bad, really bad. Here was a guy that employed hundreds of people, and, in effect, indirectly, thousands of people, and all of a sudden he was gone. The sport and the people had to get by without him. And everything fell on my mom's shoulders. She had to take care of all of us and all the homes and the owners and worry about

Tommy and everything else. And she made it. God bless her for being so strong."

Cammie isn't quite sure how she did it: "I have no idea. That lady is so strong. You got me on that one. First her son and then her husband. It's an awful thing. She's quite a lady, quite a lady."

Cammie's voice softened. "She's tough."

To a point. Billy's death wasn't the only concern weighing heavily on Dottie's mind. Her own mother's deteriorating health had Dottie agonizing whether or not to place her in a nursing home. Cammie had invested in a seafood market which was losing money. Tommy's wife, Lynn, and Dottie—now very close—were not getting along. "Dottie was having trouble and not feeling right," Joan Bebry said. "I told her to see somebody."

She had to. "After Bill died, four or five months afterwards, I was getting to the point where I couldn't function," Dottie said. "I could hardly walk. I couldn't think. I couldn't concentrate on even a headline in the newspaper. I was in Florida, and I called Doctor Bebry, and I told him that I was feeling really, really down, and he said, 'You be on an airplane in the morning. I'll pick you up at La Guardia.'"

Dr. Bebry matched Dottie up with Frank Santagata, a social worker who had helped the Bebrys when their son, Scott, had been paralyzed after a motorcycle accident a year earlier.

"I saw the social worker," Dottie said, "And it was the first time that I just cried and cried and cried and cried. And he asked me questions about what was going on in my life. And I told him all the problems. And he just told me how to handle everything, what to do first. I went to see him three times that week. I flew back to Florida and landed on my feet. It certainly helped."

Tommy needed all the help he could find.

The Haughton harness empire was placed on his shoulders. Where once there had been four Haughtons, there was now just one. An amazing one, really.

In the two years before his dad died, Tommy's life had been marked by changes.

Lynn Hitchcock, a vivacious hairdresser from Belle Vernon, Pennsylvania, some 20 minutes from The Meadows, was visiting friends in Florida, and one of them had another friend who trained horses in the Haughton Stable. "And she had this picture on her table of Tommy in the winner's circle," Lynn said. Lynn looked at the picture and said, "Who's that guy? He's cute. I want to meet him."

The friend was supposed to arrange a meeting but it never happened, and Lynn, then 22, went back to her life in Pennsylvania. She sold radio advertising before getting hired by Peoples Express, a no-frills airline based in Newark, N.J., which grew quite popular in the early '80s.

Then 25, Lynn found herself with nothing to do on a rainy, Memorial Day afternoon. So she went to The Meadowlands. This time, she met Tommy. They went out that evening, became engaged after three months and married after six, on November 24, 1984. Lynn became pregnant the next month and, on the following August 15th, gave birth to identical twins, Tommy and Billy, four months after Tommy broke his leg in an accident at The Meadowlands.

"It was a bad year to get hurt," Tommy said. "Nihilator and Pershing Square were 3-year-olds. It really killed my driving career."

He's lucky he wasn't killed. He still has six screws in his knee as souvenirs of his first, but not his last, bad spill. The filly he drove, Romantic Fling, was a full sister to Laughs, who had already been entered in a race at The Meadowlands when her Canadian owner, Irving

Liverman, called the Haughton Stable and said, "Send her to Canada. We don't want to race her any more."

Apples told Tommy, however, "Well, she's in. Go ahead and race her."

Herve Filion was driving a filly on the front end when she took a bad step, stumbled and caused horses behind her to fall.

"I was about eighth, and we all started to pile up," Tommy said. "And it was the first accident I was ever in. I stayed inside and tried getting through it. The experienced guys, like Carmine Abbatiello, the second they saw something happen, they grabbed their horses to avoid the accident. They didn't care. They took their horses right out of the race. And I'm young. I'm looking to get through the accident and win the race. I had to learn the hard way."

It was a painful lesson. Tommy's filly stumbled over the fallen horses, catapulting Tommy high into the air and onto the track. "I piled right over the top," he said. "I landed with my knee locked." Tommy had fractured his upper leg.

There were other casualties. Cat Manzi, one of the top drivers in the country, suffered a broken collarbone. The timing for Tommy couldn't have been worse. The injury reduced his starts in '85 to 361, compared to 605 the year before. His wins plummeted from 125 to 60 and his earnings from a career high $2,717,264 to $1,156,983.

"She (his filly) ended up being a great broodmare, but she ruined me," Tommy said.

If being newly-married wasn't enough on Tommy's mind, he had the added worries of what the accident would do to his career. Then he was faced with bringing up two children, not one, when Lynn gave birth.

"Everything had changed in his life so drastically," Lynn said. "Really, he and I had known each other for 14 months and we had two children already. I was always very independent, and Tommy had been single. At that time, there was much on our plate. So we were sort of just getting acclimated to being a family . . ."

Then Billy Haughton died.

Tommy said, "The ball gets put in your hands and you run with it. It was very strange how I took my father getting killed as I did my brother. My brother, to me, was a lot worse. I think it just hardened me up. How much more of this shit can you take? So you just harden up and go. I had a lot of good people around me when that happened. I really didn't have time to think about it. I was already so hard-assed from what happened to my brother. We were pretty close. So that like destroyed me. And then, that happened to my father. I said, 'What's going on here?' That was just crazy. And I just worked. That's all. Just go, go, go."

Even on the night his father died.

The Haughton Stable had a pair of 2-year-old trotters, Hillmint and Super Speedy, entered that night in New York Sire Stakes races at Saratoga Harness. Tommy drove both. "That would be his father's wishes," Apples Thomas said. "His father lived and died these horses. He wouldn't want anything to stop."

Tommy said, "I cried on the way to the races, but I had to keep doing things. I had to do what needed to be done." He finished sixth with Hillmint, who broke as the favorite, and fourth with Super Speedy. Still, in an interview that night, he said, "Driving makes it a little easier. My father impressed on us to keep our chins up and go forward. I'll just try and do that."

It's an impression of Billy Haughton that Holley shared with her brother: "It was more or less the way we were raised," she said. "You've got to do it. Never say never. Never say you can't do anything. You can always do whatever you want to do if you try hard enough. And that was always drilled into us. Tommy had no choice. He had to go on."

At the age of 29, Tommy was asked to replace the greatest driver and trainer the sport had ever known. And he did.

"It was very hard for Tommy," Doug Miller, then an assistant trainer in the Haughton Stable, said. "He had a huge stable (some 80 horses). He was a competent trainer and he was a good driver. But to inherit a stable that size, especially following in the footsteps of someone like his father, was nearly impossible for a young kid to handle. And he did it. He had the highest echelon of owners who paid a lot of money for horses and demanded a lot. It was a position I wouldn't want myself to be in."

Tommy did it without the inherent ease his father had for dealing with owners. "I'm so proud of Tommy," Dottie said. "Tommy was always a very shy boy. It was very hard for him to communicate a lot with the owners like Bill could do, but he overcame it. He works so hard."

Paul Brezinski, a groom for the Haughtons, said, "Billy had more energy than anyone I've ever seen, but Tommy seems to be going in that direction."

Hard work was never a problem for Tommy.

Losing owners was. Tommy's 1998 stable numbered just 23.

"Most of them stayed initially," Doug Miller said. "And I think over the years, some of the owners got out of the business. Some of them passed away. Some of them left for other reasons like owners do. He has a much smaller stable now then when he started, but that really is just representative of how the whole business has shrunk. He did a remarkable job. He's had some great horses."

That didn't make it any easier seeing horses leave his stable.

"Not only was he grieving for his father, but he was the last Haughton left in the stable, and he saw his horses being pulled out of the barn two weeks later," Lynn said. "But he just kept on going. He said, 'You can lay down and die, or you can keep on going.' That was his attitude then. That's what his father would have wanted him to. And he had his own responsibility because he had his own family, and he did it. I'm not so sure how."

Not everyone left the Stable. Joe Caico did not. "When Billy died, I stayed with Tommy," he said. "I felt loyalty to the family. For all the money and the happiness Billy brought me, I thought it was only fair to give Tommy a shot." Max Hempt is another owner who still has horses with Tommy.

You'd think there'd be some correlation between Tommy's dwindling stable and his lack of success. But it's been the exact opposite.

Tommy developed one of the greatest trotting mares of all time, Peace Corps, who won both the $459,219 Breeders Crown Two-Year-Old Filly Trot by 4½ lengths at Pompano Park and the $474,500 Merrie Annabelle at The Meadowlands in 1988. She did even better at 3, and was named the 1989 Trotter of the Year after defeating colts in both the $600,000 World Trotting Derby—setting a world record for 3-year-old fillies by taking the second heat in 1:52⅖—and the $177,230 Kentucky Futurity on the way to winning 16 of 19 starts and just over $1 million in earnings. She equaled Mack Lobell's all-age half mile record of 1:56 for trotters on a half-mile track taking The Buckette Stakes at Delaware, and finished her outstanding career with $5,506,443 in earnings, more than $1.5 million ahead of any pacer or trotter in the history of the sport.

Tommy also set world records driving Trenton, T.V. Yankee, and Leverage Buyout.

Tommy dubbed Somatic, who won the $700,000 World Trotting Derby in 1991, "The Little Rat." Somatic also won a heat of the Kentucky Futurity, a heat of the Alexander Memorial at Springfield and the Arden Downs.

Two years later, Tommy's Magical Mike, a son of Tyler B, won 13 of 16 starts with one second and $769,408 in earnings, as he became the first horse to win both the $747,700 Woodrow Wilson and the $550,000 Governor's Cup. In the Wilson Final, he won by a nose in 1:51⅗, equaling a world record. Magical Mike was named the 1993 Champion 2-year-old Pacer, and, the following summer, won the $512,830 Little Brown Jug, the $259,000 Oliver Wendell Holmes and the $400,000 Cadillac Breeders Crown. At 3, he had nine wins, three seconds and four thirds in 18 starts, making $912,677.

"After Magical Mike won the Little Brown Jug, Tom Walsh and Dave McDuffee (Magical Mike's owners) said, 'Let's go out and buy the best pacer and trotter we can find at the sales this fall,'" Tommy said. "I was partial to Cam Fella, so I looked at every son of Cam Fella there was. For the trotter, it was a no-brainer: Valley Victory."

The trotter they bought for $150,000, Southwind Pinnacle, won $232,275 as a 2-year-old and then, Tommy said, was sold as a 3-year-old overseas for $300,000.

The pacer they settled on, Armbro Operative, cost $175,000. "He wasn't very big or strong, but he moved super at the farm and was very racy and classy," Tommy said. "He raced as a 2-year-old and was timed in 1:53⅗ on a mile track and 1:56 on a half-mile track. He made some $30,000 and was turned out, thank God. He just wasn't strong enough. Early in his 3-year-old season, I was still taking it easy on his training, thinking he'd be fresh for the Jug and the rest of the year."

But Armbro Operative suffered a breathing problem which required minor surgery. "I had already heard that Tom and Dave were saying they might move the horse to another barn if he didn't start winning," Tommy said.

Well, the surgery worked. "In his first race back, he paced in 1:50⅖ with a last quarter in :26⅖," Tommy said. "I was so relieved."

It was temporary. After finishing second in his next start, his owners moved the horse to top Meadowlands trainer Brett Pelling's barn.

Armbro Operative went on to win the 1996 $400,000 Breeders Crown 3-Year-Old Pace.

Tommy went on to lose another top pacer to Pelling in 1998, Armbro Romance, an Artsplace filly owned by Armstrong Farm. "She was a beautiful filly," Tommy said. "I was told from the start to take my time with her and race her later in the season because all her siblings raced late. And she demanded to come along late anyway. As a 2-year-old, she won three races, including a heat of the Three Diamonds at The Meadowlands. A few days after her last start as a 2-year-old, I was told to deliver her to the Pelling Stable. Another sad story."

It wasn't as if Tommy had never trained an outstanding pacing filly. Back in 1984, he drove Naughty But Nice to win the Breeders Crown 3-Year-Old Filly Pace, the Jugette, Mistletoe Shalee and Helen Dancer Memorial. "That filly was a great mare," Tommy said. "She was the first 3-year-old filly to ever make a million dollars, and I drove her all the time."

Naughty But Nice, though, had more than one personality quirk. She stopped eating regularly until Billy put a goat in her stall. "Some fillies need a companion," Tommy said.

Tommy learned a couple things about her on the track, too, from his dad.

Tommy thought Naughty But Nice should be racing better than she was at one point and spoke to Billy about it. Billy asked how he was training her. Tommy told him he was training his filly in 2:10 between races. "My Dad said, 'It sounds like too much,'" Tommy said. "He said, 'Don't train her at all and race her.'"

Tommy tried it. "And she won," he said. "So we sent her out to the house in Long Island (the Haughtons had moved to a smaller house in Jericho in 1983, which was next to the Meadowbrook Golf Club), jogged her along the grass by the golf course at 4 or 5 in the morning and really didn't do much else with her. And she won again. He said, 'Don't train her until she gets beat. And she won seven straight.'"

Another time, Tommy sought his father's advice on the filly.

"We sent her out to the American National Stakes, and I drove her," Tommy said. "I hit her really hard there finishing and she kind of backed up. And then I didn't hit her any more in the stretch and she went on. And I told my father about it, and he said, 'Don't sting hit her there (on her right side) with the whip ever again. Do something different, whatever you have to do.'"

"From that day on, if you ever see tapes of her, you'll see me switch the whip over and hit her on the other side through the stretch. I knew if I hit her on that side, she'd just get pissed off and stop. That's how temperamental a horse can be. My dad is a guy that understood a horse. Any kind of horse. He could communicate with them."

Ten years later, Tommy let Mike LaChance drive

Magical Mike in the Breeders Crown. Each year, Tommy drives less and less. In 1998, he had just 52 starts with four wins, five seconds and nine thirds and earnings of $61,348. That brought his career totals to 6,944 starts, 1,012 wins, 944 seconds, 916 thirds, earnings of $17,776,197 and a UDR of .270.

"In this day and age, those guys are great drivers," Tommy said. "You give a horse to Campbell and O'-Donnell and they're going to drive any horse good. But I feel that I can drive with them. I always have. I beat them when I had the best horse and set records and all that. But in this business . . ."

In this business, there are owners who demand that trainers use top catch drivers. "My father told me it's my mistake if I wanted to drive," Tommy said. "Because if you want to drive, you have to stay up there and do it every night. You're not going to just come up from Florida to The Meadowlands and jump right in. So he was right again." Tommy laughed.

Despite everything, Tommy's love of his sport still lives. "It's what I know," he said. "It's what I do. It's a great thing to do. Sometimes you drive horses at the track on a beautiful morning, in the spring with the babies, when you're breaking them and training them, and you say, 'I can't believe we're getting paid to do this.' There's no pressure then. The pressure all comes when you have to actually make a living in the summertime."

A dozen years after Billy died, Tommy thinks of him often: "Every time I'm training, when I see a horse do something wrong, I wonder, 'Well, what do you think he would say about this? Then I try it."

Dottie has never walked away from harness racing. "I just made up my mind: that this is what Bill and Peter would want me to do: to pick up my life and go on," she said. "You've got two choices, either go on or give up." In maintaining her strong presence in the sport, she has grown as a person. "I was always a very shy person, because I think that Bill was so gregarious, and everybody loved him so much," she said. "I was just terrified that we'd get with a group of people and everybody would be grabbing Bill to talk and I'd be standing there by myself. It was like a nightmare I had. I was scared to death. I don't know why. Out of being an only child maybe. I really don't know. But I do know that's the way I felt. I used to dread going to parties, just dread it, unless I was the hostess. I was just terrified."

It changed. She changed. "It started out right away when John Cashman and Ebby Gerry Sr. came to see me separately and asked me if I would be the chairman of the first Breeders Crown Ball at the Boca Raton Hotel and Resort," Dottie said. "So I said I would be delighted. I never did anything like that before. It was scary, but it was a great success. It was a beautiful ball. I think we had 500 people."

She remains an owner and breeder. She has been a member of the Harness Racing Museum and Hall of Fame Board of Trustees since 1981. She supports the United States Harness Writers Association and regularly attends its annual dinner awards as well as the annual Hall of Fame inductions in Goshen, just as her husband did. "I tried to do as much as I could for harness racing because he wasn't here to do it and because I felt like I needed to do it," Dottie said. "He would want me to do it. I can remember the first time I drove over to Pompano Park all by myself. I thought in the car, 'Bill, you'd be so proud of me.' I made myself do all that stuff. I made myself."

Her first trip back to Yonkers was a nightmare. After getting lost in a bad section of the city, she made it to the drivers' lounge at the track, where Tommy was driving a 2-year-old in the Sheppard Pace, the race Billy went down in. Tommy got into an accident and went down, too. "I was in such shock," Dottie said. "And I started to cry like crazy." But Tommy was all right. And Dottie, remarkable person that she is, was all right, too.

More than a dozen years after his death, Billy and Peter Haughton still have a presence in harness racing. It's not just the Peter Haughton Room of the Immortals or the Peter D. Haughton Library or the William Haughton Hall at the Harness Racing Museum and Hall of Fame. It's The Meadowlands deciding in 1998 to rename the Driscoll Stakes the William Haughton. It's a feature story about highly successful owner Robert J. Key, written in the March 1998, issue of *Hoof Beats* by Jeff Zidek. Key, who owned Sonny Key (the horse Billy drove on the night of his accident at Yonkers Raceway), was a successful lawyer and had his own successful manufacturing company. He was introduced to Billy through a friend.

Zidek quoted Key: "I had my own plane, and this gave me an excuse to go to Florida. I met Billy and he was just super. I would have never, never stayed in this sport had I not had Billy Haughton as my original trainer. He had time for you. He made it interesting. He really worked at it, and could have been the greatest politician that ever lived. He met my son for 10 minutes one time, and six months later he remembered everything they talked about. That's what kind of ambassador he was.'"

It's a story in the January 1999, issue of *Hoof Beats*, when Canadian horseman John G. Hayes Sr. is quoted saying, "If they were all Haughtons in this game, I'd have a tough time making a living. But they're not."

Many of Billy's records have fallen, especially ones related to earnings. Others have endured a long time. When trainer Brett Pelling won both the 1998 Little Brown Jug with Shady Character and the Jugette with Armbro Romance, he was the first trainer to do so since

1974 when Billy won the Jug with Armbro Omaha and the Jugette with Handle With Care.

It's the eve of the 21st Century and there are hints of optimism with all the Haughtons. Billy Jr., freshly remarried to Cathy Calligan, has his first child, a one-year-old daughter named Mary Kate, and continues to prosper selling horseman's insurance. Tommy has found a new owner, Stefon Balazsi of Sweden, who backed his faith in Tommy in 1998 by buying a $270,000 Valley Victor yearling colt and a $97,000 Pine Chip yearling filly. "It's a great group of 2-year-olds," Tommy said. Cammie has been promoted to presiding judge. Dottie just moved into a new house in southern Florida, a mile and a half from Lynn and Tommy's house. Lynn and Tommy's twins, 13-year-old Tommy and Billy, inherited Tommy's athletic ability, winning numerous championships in baseball, soccer and football. "They've got a room full of trophies," Tommy said. They also do well in school. Tommy once bet them they couldn't bring home straight A's on their report cards. When they did, Tommy had to shave his head. "They are my best friends on earth," Tommy said of his sons.

Holley and her two boys, Peter, 10, and Jake, 6, have relocated from Florida to the Haughtons' Pioneer Farm in New Hampshire, Holley's haven as a young girl. Before they left Florida, Holley got a call from Jake's pre-school teacher. "It's a feeling where your heart drops," Holley said. Her heart was soon lifted. Jake's teacher told Holley that there was a girl in Jake's class who was very sad that her parents were getting divorced. The girl was sitting and crying on her teacher's lap, and Jake went over to her and said, "Don't worry. My mom and dad are divorced, too. But now I have two places to go visit. And you know what? After a while, they get along much better."

Peter and Jake, who both love horses and enjoy

horseback riding, never got to meet their grandfather, Billy Haughton. But they know about him. There are two oil paintings of Billy done by Bill Orr and Bill Orr, Jr., at the farm.

"Peter and Jake have been brought up knowing who their grandfather is and how proud we all are of him," Holley said. "Jake never met him. Peter never met him. But they know who he is and they're so proud of him. And Jake sometimes will get very emotional and cry:

'I want my Grandpa! I miss my Grandpa!'"

We all do, Jake. We all do.

Billy Haughton's Driving Record

Year	Starts	1sts		2nds	3rds	UDRs	Money Won	
*(a)	—	132		—	—	.000	—	
1949	414	77	(10)	59	57	.324	114,606	(7)
1950	501	86	(7)	80	76	.311	181,881	(3)
1951	694	97	(3)	133	91	.290	220,816	(2)
1952	559	110	(2)	100	96	.283	311,728	(1)
1953	703	116	(1)	126	98	.310	374,527	(1)
1954	775	153	(1)	112	130	.334	415,577	(1)
1955	775	168	(1)	139	118	.367	599,445	(1)
1956	787	167	(1)	123	91	.338	572,945	(1)
1957	743	156	(1)	127	100	.350	586,950	(1)
1958	833	176	(1)	109	133	.337	816,659	(1)
1959	925	157	(2)	146	127	.315	711,435	(1)
1960	749	116	(6)	110	114	.295	537,500	(3)
1961	733	98	(10)	137	132	.298	508,944	(2)
1962	691	151	(3)	114	85	.353	677,531	(2)
1963	629	144	(4)	119	90	.382	790,086	(1)
1964	780	152	(5)	135	105	.336	844,558	(2)
1965	910	222	(2)	149	106	.374	889,943	(1)
1966	754	194	(5)	141	109	.409	1,062,588	(2)
1967	575	142	(18)	91	88	.386	1,305,773	(1)

Year								
1968	676	180	(10)	116	111	1,654,172	.416	(1)
1969	738	161	(18)	117	129	1,238,390	.364	(3)
1970	647	156	(17)	119	83	1,317,195	.386	(3)
1971	708	139		115	112	944,022	.339	(6)
1972	672	140		112	105	1,199,630	.353	(5)
1973	686	179		126	68	1,260,908	.396	(7)
1974	680	151		114	89	1,596,475	.359	(2)
1975	513	136		82	60	1,359,394	.393	(7)
1976	475	107		70	62	1,726,660	.351	(6)
1977	362	94		64	43	1,617,949	.397	(10)
1978	402	95		67	55	1,718,105	.375	(8)
1979	387	73		47	61	1,082,339	.309	
1980	457	89		70	58	1,966,201	.322	(9)
1981	411	90		46	52	2,276,515	.323	(10)
1982	400	91		63	52	2,534,181	.358	(8)
1983	361	53		43	64	1,408,154	.272	
1984	323	72		49	37	1,290,758	.345	
1985	373	73		53	49	1,858,261	.318	
1986	84	14		15	12	460,981	.313	
Life	22,885	4,910		6,638	,236	40,160,336	.344	

*Prior to 1949.
Numbers in parentheses are his national ranking.

Index

-A-
Abbatiello, Carmine, 89, 203, 230
Abercrombie, 150
A.C.'s Orion, 142, 145, 146
Acorn Stakes, 174
Adams, Al, 177
Adamsky, Joe, 203
Adios, 11, 158
Adios Boy, 75
Adios Butler, 117
Adios Stakes, 71, 144, 147, 158–159, 174, 216
Adios Volo, 174
Aiken (SC), 38, 67
Albatross, 114, 161, 211
Alexander Memorial, 234
Allen, Rusty, 29
Allyson, June, 41
Almahurst Farms, 177
Altamont (NY), 18
American National Stakes, 72, 174, 236
American Pacing Classic, 174
American Trotting Championship, 40
Anderson, Bert, 120
Anderson, Meg, 120
Andrews, Edward, 147–148
Andrews, Rodney, 147–148
Angel's Flight, 142
Angel's Vicar, 166, 168
Ankaway, 36, 37, 40, 49, 55, 58, 72
Anvil, 134–135
Aqueduct, 118
Arcaro, Eddie, 117
Arden Downs Stakes, 71, 106, 234
Arica, 142
Armbro Dallas, 216, 217
Armbro Lament, 146
Armbro Norma, 142
Armbro Omaha, 141, 147, 173, 174, 240
Armbro Operative, 234–235
Armbro Regina, 137
Armbro Romance, 235, 239

Armstrong, Elgin, 127
Armstrong Farm, 235
Arndon, 208
Arthur, Jimmy, 203
Artsplace, 235
Arvilla Hanover, 61, 142
Ash Grove Pace, 50
Astaire, Fred, 41
Ata Connie, 142
Audobon Hanover, 143
Autocrat, 58
Autumn Pace, 75
Avery, Earl, 98
Ayres, 133

-B-
Bachelor Hanover, 74–76, 142
Bachner, Arnold, 106
Bailey, Jack, 203
Balazsi, Stefon, 240
Baldwin, Ralph, 67
Batavia Trot, 40
Batter, Mr. and Mrs. Carl, 58
Battle of Brandywine, 152
Battle of Saratoga, 1, 196
Battling Brad, 150, 179
Beacon Course Stakes, 208
Bebry, Dr. Joe, 6, 122, 160–161, 180, 222, 228
Bebry, Joan, 180, 189, 201, 222, 227, 228
Bell, Hugh, 59
Bell, Mrs. Jan, 111
Belle Acton, 3, 53, 62, 73–76, 141, 146
Belle Pointer, 58
Belle Vernon (PA), 229
Belmont, 118
Ben White Raceway, 26, 52, 111, 112,155
Benner, Wilmer "Bud,", 116
Bergen Hanover, 142

Bergstein, Stanley, xiii-xvi, 98–99, 173, 224
Berry Hill, 142
Berry, Tom, 58
Bertram Hanover, 58
Best Of All, 158
Best Of Donut, 142
Better Heather, 143
Betty, 15–16
BGs Bunny, 151
Big Band Sound, 143
"Billy Haughton Good Guy Award", 2
Bischoff, Esther Linder, 25, 26, 27, 28, 29, 30, 33, 77, 122
Bischoff, Whitney, 25, 26, 27, 30, 33, 50, 60
Bit O' Sugar, 142
Blasdell, D., 203
Blauvelt, Abe, 28
Bloomsburg Fair, 56, 75
Blue Bonnets, 173
Blue Grass Stakes, 214
Blue Nile, 145
Bluett Hanover, 61
Boca Raton (FL), 201, 238
Boehm's Dauntless, 149
Boehm's Eagle, 148
Boni, Bob, 217
Bostwick, Dunbar, Mr. and Mrs., 40, 41
Bower, Ned, 58
Boyd, "Tug,", 203
Boyden Hanover, 147
Braim, Albert K., 36
Brandywine, 112, 120, 194
Breeders Crown, 95, 152–153, 209, 214, 215–216, 217, 233, 234, 235, 237
Breeders Crown Ball, 238
Brennan, Dr. Bernard, 38–39, 58, 115

INDEX 247

Bret Hanover, 58, 146, 159, 212
Bret's Champ, 142, 147, 174
Bret's Star, 109, 142, 147, 148
Brewster (NY), 30
Brezinski, Paul, 232
Bright, 127–129
Broadcaster B., 142, 174
Broadway Express, 215
Bromley, Don, 203
Bronxville (NY), 222
Brookville (N.Y.), 78, 224
Brown, Bowman, 207
Brown, Murray, 67, 68, 114
Brownie Hanover, 168
Buckette Stakes, 233
Buffalo Raceway, 189
Buffalo Street, 61
Burger Queen, 189
Burgomeister, 9, 143, 188–192, 206
Burroughs, Mal, 40
Buxton Hanover, 56, 142
Bye Bye Byrd, 194

-C-

Cadillac Breeders Crown, see Breeders Crown
Caico, Joe, 147, 148, 233
Caico, Sharon, 148
Call Back, 149
Cam Fella, 234
Cameron, Del, 133, 203
Cameron, Warren, 23
Campbell, John, xiii, 3, 95, 152, 177–178, 179, 190, 203, 222, 237
Campbell, Norma, 179–180
Canadian Trotting Classic, 219
Cane Pace, 70, 142, 146, 152, 195
Cap d'Antibes, 146
Cappriccio, 189
Captain Carefree, 58, 78

Caputo, John, 39
Caramel Boy, 39, 49, 58
Carbine Hanover, 145, 146
"Care and Training of the Pacer and Trotter, The", 2, 35, 37, 48–49, 65–67, 69–70
Caressable, 143, 153
Carlisle, 71–72, 142
Carlisle (PA), 168
Cary, Ted, 60
Cashman, John, 119, 238
Cassaro, Mr. and Mrs. Bill, 41
Cassaco, W., 22
Castleton Farm, 67, 119
Ceywey, 58
Chairmanoftheboard, 143, 217
Chapel Chief, 142
Chapman, Johnny, 59, 203
Chappaqua (NY), 25, 26, 51
Chappaqua Hanover, 142, 150
Charlie, 105
Charlottetown Driving Park, 98
Charlottetown, Prince Edward Island Guardian, 98
Charming Barbara, 142
Chase, Raymond, 41
Cheerful Hanover, 58
Cher Hanover, 142, 150
Cherry Valley (NY), 14
Chief Abbedale, 61
Chris Spencer, 40, 41, 49, 58, 59
Christie Hanover, 58
Christine, Bill, 66
Christopher T, 91, 133–135, 141, 174
Circo, 133
Classic Lady, 148, 150
Clukey, Henry, 57
Cobb, Bob, 41
Cobb, Eddie, 74, 75
Cobleskill (NY), 21

Cobleskill State Agricultural
　College, 20, 173
Cochran, George, 60
Coconut Grove, 41
Colby's Match, 58, 78
Cold Comfort, 139, 142, 150,
　176, 182
Coleman Lobell, 143
Colonial Trot, 174
Columbia Presbyterian
　Hospital, 127
Connie's Pride, 23, 24
Cornell University Large
　Animal Clinic, 224
Cory, 146
Cote, Benoit, 203
Counsel Pick, 61
Count's Pride, 142
Cox, Walter, 27
Crackers, 176
Cramer, Ludwig, 26
Crash, 142, 150
Crawford, Alan, 60
Crimson, 221
Crossbow, 40, 133
Cruise, Jimmy, 127
Cupid's Arrow, 142
Cyril Hanover, 36

-D-
Dalton (MA), 25
Dan Patch Pace, 36
Dancer Hanover, 70, 71, 114
Dancer, Stanley, 2, 3, 43, 44, 45,
　46, 50, 59, 62, 64, 74, 75, 76,
　93–94, 95–96, 114, 116, 120,
　129, 134–135, 136, 146, 161,
　163, 171, 177, 185–186, 190,
　203, 212
Dancer, Vernon, 136
Dark Sun, 56
Darn Flashy, 58

David Caudle, 58, 61
David H. McConnell Memorial
　Mile and a Half Trot, 40
David Stone, 39
Day, Bucky, 203
Dear One, 26
DeBakey, Dr. Michael
Debutante Stakes, 171
Deling, Glenn E., 219
Delmonica Haover, 66
DelNagro, Mike, 207
Delvin Hanover, 142
Demon Hanover, 40
Demon Renvach, 191
DeSantis, Dick, 106, 203
DeSantis, Joe, 23
Desperado, 22
Dewey Abbe, 38
Dewey, Thomas E., 58
Dexter Cup, 72, 176
Diane Scot, 73
Diller Hanover, 133
DiManvro, Marino, 108
Direct Vix, 36
Doherty, Jim, 203
Dokey, Merrit, 203
Donadio, Jospeh, 39
Dondarski, Mary Lou, 7
Dottie's Pick, 61
Doublemint, 141, 150, 151, 176
Doxsee, Charkes, 39
Dr. Dewars, 109, 110, 166–167,
　168, 172, 173
Dragon's Lair, 214, 215–216
Driscoll Stakes, 239
Dudley, Dick, 194
Du Quoin (IL), 89, 91, 92, 190,
　191
Duke Rodney, 141, 144
Duane Hanover, 62
Duenna, 45
Duke Rodney, 56, 143

INDEX

Duncan, 119
Dundee Lassie, 73
Dunkin, Dr. Tom, 138
Dunnigan, Eddie, 203
Dunnigan Lobell, 142
Duris, Harold, 201
"Dusty Old Jacket of Black, The" 10–11
Dutton, Bradford, 119
Dynamic Hal, 58

-E-

Earl's Blue Chip, 148
Earl's Ensign, 61
East Rutherford (NJ), 180
East Stroudsburg University, 89, 204
Edmunds, Jay, 203
Effrat, Louism 118
Egan, Fred, 23, 58
E.H. Harriman Trophy, 72, 174
Em Ar El Stable, 151
Empire State Pacing Classic, 62
Enright, Malcomb "Pally", 30, 32
Ensign Melburn, 58
Ervin, Frank, 58, 92, 133
Escort, 150

-F-

Faber Hanover, 60
Falcon Almahurst, 142, 150–151
Fall Brook, 37
Fancy Crown, 215
Fanny Hall, 142, 145
Farmstead Acres, 60, 71, 74
Farmstead's Fame, 142
Farrington, Bob, 142
Father Hanover, 61
Federal Hanover, 58
Filion, Gilles, 203

Filion, Herve, 43, 94, 153, 203, 230
Final Score, 141, 190–192, 206
Fingo, 61
Finn, Anthony, 39
Fiorentino, Marcello, 189, 201
First Attraction, 143
Fitzpatrick, Charles, 203, 204
Fitzpatrick, Harry, 59, 157
Fitzsimmons, Sunny Jim, 69
5 Guys & Me Stable, 151
Flamboyant, 141, 144
Flemig, Vic, 19, 21, 36
Flicka Frost, 91, 92, 93, 133
Flight Director, 150
Flo Napoleon, 50, 58
Flora Temple Stakes, 62
Florida Breeders Stakes, 195–196
Florida Livestock Exposition, 112
Florita, 60
Flush, 146
Flying Wings, 194
Fonda (NY), 17, 23
Fonda Fairgrounds/Fonda Fair, 14, 15, 16, 17, 18, 23
Fontaine, Lucien, 203
Fort Lauderdale News and Sun-Sentinel, 178, 194–195, 205–206, 208
Fort Miami, 49
Fortune Teller, 152
Fox Stakes, 70, 176
Foxboro Raceway, 97
Freestate, 220
Froehlich, John, 60. 61, 66,70, 71, 114, 170
Fulla Napoleon, 194
Fulla Thunder, 194
Fultonville (NY), 13, 40–41, 51, 186

Fultonville Community Club, 40, 41
"Fultonville Flash, The," 40
Funny Donut, 148
Future Fame, 142, 150

-G-
Gagliardi, Mike, 204
Gaines Memorial, 177
Galbraith, Clint, 1–2, 72, 197–198
Galophone, 142
Gangloff, Robert, 212
Garden State Park, 216, 217
Garnsey, Glen, 204
Garnsey, Glen and Paula, 97
Gaskin, Ernie, 216–217
Gay Frost, 142
Geers Stakes, 50
Gerry, Sr., Ebby, 238
Gert Barmin, 146
Gibbons, Walter, 60
Gibson, Gary, 204
Gil Hanover, 142, 145
Gilmour, Buddy, 62, 64, 150, 201, 204
Glasgow, 142, 148
Gloversville (NY), 14
"Gold Dust Twins, The", 44, 46
Golden Sovereign, 134–135
Golden West Trot, 41
Good Day Luv, 220
Good Knight Star, 174
Good Note, 72
Good Time, 150
Goose Filter, 150
Gordon, Bob, 182
Goshen (NY), 26, 27, 50, 74, 96, 165, 171, 177, 194, 224, 238
Goshen Cup, 71, 144
Gotham Trot, 49
Goudreau, Shelly, 204

Gouvernor's Cup, 234
Grand Circuit, 9, 21, 44, 60, 62, 89, 138, 142, 149, 194
Grand Circuit Gold Medallion, 153
Grattan helmets, 220
Gravel Pit, 171
"Great Green Wave, The, " 8, 172, 173
Green Bay Packers, 88
Green Speed, 36, 138–139, 141, 150
Greene, Joe, 111
Greenwood Raceway, 219
Greers, Edward F. "Pop,", 10–11
Greyhound, 27, 58
Griffith, Dodger, 23, 41
Grundy, Jim, 204
Guida, Lou, 211, 212, 217
Gypsy, 16
Gypsy Flyer, 106

-H-
Hackett, Bob, 138
Hal Mix, 22
Hall, Wilbur, 19
Hall of Fame Day, 96
Hambletonian, 3, 9, 26, 40, 46, 50, 91, 92, 133–139, 150, 164, 173, 175, 189–192, 206, 207–209
Hambletonian Maturity, 206
Hambletonian Oaks, 106
Handle With Care, 141, 146–147, 149, 173, 174–175, 200, 240
Hanover Colt Stakes, 71, 72
Hanover Shoe Farms, 67, 114
Harding, Mike, 182
Hardy, Joe, 215
Harner, Eldon, 203
Harner, Levi, 57, 61

INDEX   251

Harness Horse Magazine, 21, 22
Harness Racing Museum and
  Hall of Fame, 26, 50, 106,
  142, 177, 224, 238, 239
Harness Tracks of America, xvi,
  98, 116, 224
Harold Abbe, 39, 49, 55, 58
Harp, Jr., George, 205
Harp, Joan, 110
Harp, Warren, 109, 110
Harris, Col. William C., 39, 49
Harris, Mrs. William C., 116
Harrisburg Evening News, 40
Harrisburg (PA) Sale, 36, 37, 66,
  68, 70, 138, 188, 207
Harrison, Jim, 2, 9–11, 14, 50
Hasty Pete, 50
Haughton, Father Cameron, 13
Haughton, Cathy Calligan, 240
Haughton, Dorothy "Dottie"
  Bischoff, 2–3, 4, 5, 7, 14–15,
  25–33, 45–46, 50–53, 55,
  60–61, 63, 69, 77–79, 80–81,
  85–89, 91–93, 94–95, 96–97,
  101–102, 105, 106–109, 110,
  112–113, 116–117, 118, 119,
  120, 121–129, 131, 133, 138,
  144, 146, 155, 157, 159–161,
  163, 164–167, 176, 177, 178,
  180–181, 185, 186–192, 193,
  198–199, 200, 201, 204, 205,
  208, 212, 215, 219, 221–223,
  224–225, 227–228, 232,
  237–239
Haughton, Edith Greene, 14, 19,
  40, 123–124, 186
Haughton, Holley, 78, 88,
  101–106, 117, 122–123,
  124–126, 159, 161–162, 163,
  222, 225, 227, 231–232,
  240–241

Haughton, Lynn Hitchcock, 228,
  229, 230, 233, 240
Haughton, Peter Delvin, xv, 4, 9,
  11, 61, 78, 80, 84, 94–95, 97,
  103, 104, 106, 107, 108, 109.
  113. 116, 117, 133, 134,
  136–139, 144, 148, 152,
  155–183, 185–190, 191, 192,
  193, 194, 195, 196, 205, 206,
  219, 224, 237, 239
Haughton, Robert Cameron
  "Cammie", 1, 3, 9, 78, 87, 88,
  89. 116, 161, 167, 178, 181,
  192–201, 204, 223, 227, 228,
  240
Haughton, Tommy, 3, 5, 23, 57,
  66, 78, 86–89, 123, 148, 152,
  156, 161, 178–179, 187,
  190–192, 195, 199, 204–209,
  212, 223, 227, 228–237,
  238–239, 240
Haughton, William Francis, 13,
  14, 15, 40
Haughton, William Harris
  "Billy" Jr., 3, 5, 6, 44–45,
  78–87, 116, 156–157, 182, 187,
  223, 227–228, 240
Hayes, Bill, 138
Hayes, Sr., John G., 239
Haygood, 150
Haygood Hazel Hanover, 142
Herman, Bill, 204
Herman, Dick, 136
Houghton (sic), Billy, 21
Hel Hague, 58
Helen C., 19
Helen Dancer Memorial, 209,
  235
Hello Tomorrow, 166, 167
Hempt Farms, 6
Hempt, Max, 6, 65, 66, 114, 161,
  207, 233

Henry T. Adios, 146
Henson Hanover, 142
Herman, Mrs. Billy, 6–7
Hesek, William "Doc", 23
Hickory Hill, 142
Hickory Pride, 72, 138
High Score, 142
High Sir, 32
Highland Scot, 18
Hilarion, 152
Hillmint, 231
Hillsota, 61, 147
Hiram Woodruff Series, 206
Hirt, Clyde, 177
Historian, 50, 58
Historic Dickerson, 174
Hodge, Seeley, 41
Hoffman, Dean, 212, 214
Hogan, John, 97
Holley By Golly, 104, 166
Hollywood Classic, 144
Hollywood Park, 41, 68, 145, 146, 175
Holmes, Sonny, 52
Holy Rood Cemetary, 182, 224
Honest Jimmie, 75
Hoof Beats, 10, 14, 56–57, 64, 73, 102, 111–112, 114, 116, 168, 212, 239
Hoosier Futurity, 174
Horace Greeley High School, 29
Horseman and Fair World, The, 138, 188
Horseman Futurity, 134
Howard, Jake, 219
Hoyt, Harrison, 40
Huff, Dutch, 23
Huff, Willian, 39
Hughesville (PA), 166, 167
Hutchins, Kay, 63

-I-
Ideal Rodney, 142
Ilo Kid, 60
In The Light, 102, 103, 104
Inaugural Pace, 49
Incorporator, 142
Ideal Valentine, 205
Indianapolis (IN), 89
Ingrassia, Jacquie, 204
Inside Joke, 143
Insko, Del, 203, 204
International Pace, 147

-J-
James, C., 203
Jan Hanover, 142
Jazz Cosmos, 208
Jenny's Star, 171
Jericho (NY), 236
Jetsam, 58
JJ's Metro, 142
Joaniss, Harold, 41
Joe C. Abbe, 36
Johammes, Harold, 21
John Henry, 216
John Simpson Sr. Stakes, 174
Johnson, Dr. Howard C., 39
Jordan, James, 57
Jordan, Michael, 16
Jorge Hanover, 148
Journalist, 134, 142, 174
Josedale Arrow, 21
Josedale Lynn, 22
Jug Preview, 151
Jugette, 174, 209, 235, 239, 240
Just Mine, 148

-K-
Kading, 143
Kenniworth Farms, 144–145
Kent & Sussex Fair, 63, 64

Kentucky Futurity, 139, 151, 175, 176, 206, 233, 234
Kentucky Futurity Filly Division, 106
Key, Robert J., 239
Keystone Aaron, 145
Keystone Banchee, 150
Keystone Brian, 142
Keystone Gabriel, 134, 142, 174
Keystone Flamingo, 143
Keystone Model, 141, 148, 150
Keystone Pioneer, 106, 107, 141, 148, 150, 204, 206
Keystone Presto, 174, 176–177
Keystone Pride, 133
Keystone Signal, 142, 143
Keystone Smartie, 142, 148, 174–175
King, Jr., Henry, 73, 75
Kings Park, 116
Knight Boy, 58
Kopas, Jack, 203
Kram, Mark, 117–118
Krumpe, Jack, 177

-L-

La Serina, 201
Laag, 220
LaChance, Mike, 236
Lady DeGrasse, 118
Lady Emily, 147
Lady Maud Stakes, 174, 209
Lady Suffolk Trot, 145
Lana Hill, 145
Landers, George B., 53, 73, 74
LaPaloma Pace, 152
Larente, Jimmy, 204
Larkin, Mr. and Mrs. R.C., 144
Larsen, Carl, 51
Laughs, 199–201, 229
Laurel Racetrack, 74
Laverne Hanover, 141, 144, 145

Lawrence B. Sheppard Pace, 70, 220, 221, 238
Lawrence Farms, 29
Lawrence Hospital, 222
Leonard, Jack, 191
Lepp, Barry, 61
Leverage Buyout, 234
Levy, George Morton, 52
Lexington (KY), 149, 177, 204, 205, 214
Lexington Filly Stakes, 174
Lexington Horse Sales, 71, 127
Lexington Red Mile, 206
Liberty Bell, 141–142, 174
Liberty Bell Sale, 148
Lightning Strikes, 142
Lime, 127–129
Linder, Bessie, 25
Linder, Theodore, 25
Lindy's Pride, 189
List, Dick "Listy", 23
Little Brown Jug, 3, 36, 37, 40, 45, 59, 61, 63, 70, 144, 147, 151, 157, 161, 164, 174, 177, 195, 204, 211, 220, 234, 235, 239, 240
Liverman, Irving, 146, 147, 200, 229–230
L. K. Shapiro, 146
Lloyds, Beverly, 138
Lloyds, Lloyd, 72, 138, 144–145, 170
Lloyds, Mrs. Margaret, 72
Logatto, Gilbert, 180
Lohmeyer, Eddie, 4, 177, 178, 179, 182–183, 185, 204
Lonway, 58
Lord Hanover, 142, 146
Lord Rip, 118
Los Angeles Times, 66
Losee, Pete, 18
Louisville Downs, 176

Lowe, Fred, 40
Luabbes Jewel, 150
Luro, Horatio, 119
Lyon, Bill, 216–217

-M-
MacGregor, James "Roach,", 98
Mack Lobell, 233
Macklin, Joyce, 28, 51
Madison Square Garden, 30
Magical Mike, 234, 237
Magnus Apollo, 146
Malabar Man, 40
Mallet, Jeff, 214, 215
Mamaroneck (NY), 30
Mamscot, 58
Mancuso, Louis and Connie, 145
Maneros Pride, 142
Manhattan Medical School, 30
Manzi, Cat, 230
Marauder, 216
Margie's Melody, 212
Marohn, Jim, 204
Marquis de Lafayette, 206
Marsh, Joe, 203
Marshmallow, 146
Martin, Clarence, 22, 46–48, 55, 60, 73, 177
Martin Tannabaum International, 145
Martin Vic, 40
Mary Duke, 80
Maryland Hilly, 58
Massapequa (N.Y.), 77, 78
Master Bill, 174
Maurizio, Grosso, 187
McCarthy, Mike, 7–9
McCusker, Michael J., 187
McDuffee, Dave, 234
McGregor, Mary Louise, 56–57, 111, 114, 116
McKay, Marshall, 41

McKinzie Almahurst, 141, 151, 152, 207
McKnight, Ed, 204
McMillen, William N., 55
McNichol, Mickey, 208–209
Meadow Abbe, 58
Meadow Elva, 141, 144
Meadow Grant, 142
Meadow Lands (PA), 157, 159
Meadow Leo, 61
Meadow Paige, 142
Meadow Roy, 149
Meadow Skipper, 146–147, 150
Meadow Wilma, 142
Meadowbrook Golf Club, 221, 236
Meadowcroft Farm, 128–129
Melody, see High Sir
Melody Gal, 173
Mercy Hill Hospital, 77
Merrie Annabelle, 233
Messenger Stakes, 70, 71, 76, 144, 146, 147, 158, 174, 195, 213
Mickey Mantle Sport Festival, 97
Mighty Grattan, 58
Mighty Jet, 60
Mighty Worthy, 21, 22
Mill Island Stable, 136
Millar, Don, 133
Miller, Dale, 207
Miller, Delvin, 9, 41, 45, 50, 59, 66, 72, 96, 97, 113, 128–129, 157–158, 161, 164, 173, 175, 182, 203, 208, 215, 220
Miller, Doug, 165–166, 168–172, 181–182, 186, 189, 194, 204, 232
Miller, Floyd, 207
Miller, George, 97
Miller, Mary Lib, 72, 157–159

Miss Bobby Sox, 58
Miss Mamie, 58
Mistletoe Shalee Stakes, 209, 235
Mitchell, Don, 194
Modest Yankee, 142
Moiseyev, Jack, 43
Montgomery County Fair
Monticello Raceway, 94, 121–122, 126, 193
Moore, Bill, 16–17, 23
Moran, Paul, 178, 194–195, 205–206, 208
Morril, Charlie, 17, 18
Mount Kisco, 26, 28, 29, 30
Moyer, Dr. William, 213
Mr. Pride, 142
Muckle, Billy, 20, 41–42,
Murphy, "Thin Dime," 85
Murphy, Thomas W., 36
Murphy, Tom, 36, 144
My Opinion, 142
Mynah Hanover, 58
Mystic Park, 208

-N-
Nailor, 18, 19, 20
Nardins Byrd, 158
Nardin's Express, 148
Nardins Gayblade, 142
Nassau (NY), 21
Nassau Pace, 61
Nat Lobell, 150
Nat Ray Stakes, 206
National Byrd, 142
Native Straight, 139
Naughty But Nice, 141, 209, 235–236
Navy Hal, 39, 49, 58
Neal, Pat, 119
Neilson, J. Murray, 204
Neloy, Ed, 119

Nelson, Mike, 187
Nero, 147
Netted, 191
Nerud, John, 119
Nevele Dancer, 158
Nevele Diamond, 134–135
Nevele Impulse, 191
Nevele Pride, 136, 151
Nevele Thunder, 136–137
New Bolton Center, University of PA., 213, 224
New Hampshire State Fair, 108
New Jersey Classic, 152
New Jersey Sports Authority, 177
New York Institute of Technology, 83
New York Sire Stakes, 231
New York State fair circuit, 18
New York State Racing and Wagering Board, 193, 201
New York Times, 118
Next Knight, 142
Niafirst, 214
Niatross, 1, 191, 194, 195–198, 212, 214
Nihilator, 3, 141, 194, 200, 211–217, 229
No Nukes, 152
Noble, Sam, 204
Norlander, Anders, 138
Northern, William E., 7
Northern Westchester Hospital, 30
Nut House, 143, 152

-O-
O'Brien, Joe, 62, 93, 98, 137, 203
O'Brien, Virginia, 97
Oak Hill Farms, 150
O'Donnell, Bill, 44, 57, 66,

95–96, 204, 212, 213–215, 217, 220, 222, 237
O'Donnell, Kelly, 204
O.K. Spur, 38
Old County Trotting Association, 38
Old Glory Sale, 187
Old Westbury (NY), 52, 78
Oliver Wendell Holmes Pace, 152, 207, 234
Olmstead, Betty, 31
Ontario Jockey Club, 219
Orangeburg (NY), 26
Orlando (FL), 25, 38, 52, 67, 73, 111, 112, 155
Orr, Bill, 241
Orr, Jr., Bill, 241
O'Shea, Paul, 130–131
Otaro Hanover, 175
Owen, Bill, 118
Oyster Bay (N.Y.), 78, 103, 107, 118, 121, 126, 127, 129, 159, 182, 204

-P-
Pacing Triple Crown, 70, 144, 147
Pagan Princess, 142
Palin, Sep, 58
Palmer, Walter, 10–11
Pammy Lobell, 142, 146
Parker, Jackie, 222
Parkinson, Jim, 204
Passing Speed, 106
Pat Dillon, 23
Patterson, Jr., John, 204
Patterson, Sr., John, 23, 203
Peace Corps, 233
Peck, Bernie, 204
Pelling, Brett, 235, 239–240
Pennsylvania Sire Stakes, 172, 190, 220

Peoples Express, 229
Peridot, 138
Peridot Pride, 138, 148
Perkins, Dave, 219
Pershing Square, 212, 213, 215, 229
Peter Campbell, 157
Peter Campbell II, 119
Peter D. Haughton Library, 177, 239
Peter Haughton Memorial 2–Year-Old Colt Trot, 206–207
Peter Haughton Room of the Immortals, 239
Peter Voletta, 18
Philadelphia Inquirer, The, 216–217
Phonograph, 72
Pierce, Mark and Joy, 7
Pilgrim Stakes, 216
Pimlico, 118
Pine Chip, 240
Piney Fingo, 60
Pioneer Farm, 105–106, 107–109, 110, 120, 163, 180, 240–241
Pitt Boy, 152
Pleasantville (NY), 28
Pluso, Anthony, 23
Pocano Downs, 167, 190, 194
Pollinator, 212
Pompano Park, 2, 9, 52, 96, 112, 129, 153, 178, 182, 195, 198, 201, 205, 233
Pony Stable, 207
Powers, Jimmy, 4, 57, 59
Presidential Series, 179
Pride of Carlisle, 206
Pridewood, 145
Prince Edward Island
Prix d'Eté Stakes, 173, 174
Prologue Mac, 21, 22, 23–24

Propaganda, 50
Proximity, 40
Puppet, 142, 148, 177

-Q-
Quick Chief, 61–62, 63, 75,
Quick Pay, 136–138, 143, 148, 175
Quilla Donut, 149
Quiri, George, 37, 39

-R-
Race Time, 67
Race Time Boy, 142, 143
Racing Bretta, 143
Racing Marvel, 148
Racing Sailor, 146
Rankin, Dave, 204
Rapid Gallon, 58
Rapone, Patsy, 204
Reach Up, 39, 49, 58
Reading Futurity, 74, 76
Real Cool, 145, 146, 165
Realization Trot, 145
Redmond Land, 146
Remmen, Ray, 150, 204
Reprise, 139
Rhinebeck (NY), 26
Ringmaster, 22
Ritter, Johnny, 82
Robard, Chuck, 214
Roberts, Irvin, 22, 111
Robin Almahurst, 143
Robinet, Rudy, 111
Rochester Fair, 109
Rockingham County Gazette and Bordertown News, 119
Rockingham Park, 7, 109
Rodney, 41
Rodney, Aubrey, 36, 39
Rodney's Best, 191
Romantic Fling, 229

Romeo Hanover, 70, 71
Romola Hanoverm 70,
Romulus Hanover, 70, 71, 141, 144, 158–159
Roosevelt International Trot, 66, 151, 176
Roosevelt Raceway, 5, 37, 38,39, 40, 44, 45, 49, 52, 57, 59, 60, 61, 64, 74, 76, 83, 89, 91, 103, 107, 116, 117, 120, 126, 131, 145, 146, 160, 170, 182, 187, 199, 204, 225
Roosevelt Two Mile Trot, 59
Rosecroft Raceway, 7, 50, 73, 74, 95
Rosemary, 72, 143, 151
Rosenberg, Bill, 107, 180
Ross, Dan, 204
Rossi, Peter, 40
Roy S. Mamscot, 50
Royal Value, 58
Ruben, Dr. I. Ben "Doc", 36, 41
Rubin, Mrs. Hazel L., 74, 75
Rum Customer, 141, 144–145, 146
Russell, Sandra, 187–188
Ryan, Jr., Bill, 23
Ryan, Ed, 215
Rydell, Hubert, 190

-S-
Safford, Frank, 35
St. Dominic's Church, 182
St. Francis Prep, 82, 83
St. Paul the Apostle Roman Catholic Church, 223
Santagata, Frank, 228
Saratoga Harness, 1, 2, 20, 21, 22, 23, 24, 36, 37, 38, 39, 40, 41, 47, 49, 50, 55, 97, 196–197, 201, 231

Saratoga Harness Hall of Fame, 97
Saratoga Stable, 39
Scandalize, 142
Scarborough Downs, 110
Scarlett Almahurst, 149
Schaub, Roy, 28
Scotland, 73
Scotland Trot Classic, 145
Scott Frost, 76
Season Champion, 143
Seatrain, 147
Sebastian Hanover, 207
Secretariat, 103, 119
Seedling Herbert, 143, 150
Seton Hanover, 114, 145
Shady Character, 239
Shady Hanover, 49
Shapiro Pace, 174
Sharp, Dwight, 119
Sheppard Pace, see Lawrence B. Sheppard Pace
Shivley, Bi, 58
Sholty, George, 5, 116, 127, 156, 203
Sholty, Myrna, 156
Shudt, Roy, 41, 97
Siegel, Murray, 136
Silent Majority, 143, 146
Silk Stockings, 147
Silky Cedar, 143
Simpson, Sr., John, xiii, 50, 55, 62, 75, 133
Simpson, Jr., John, "Johnny," 22–23, 191
Sing Away Herbert, 134–135
Sir Dillon Volo, 17–18
Siver, Jim, 111
Smart Rodney, 142
Smith, Red, 155, 158–159
Somatic, 234
Sonata Hill, 143, 145, 146
Soothsayer, 175
Southern Style, 143
Soldner, Dr. Paul, 207, 219
Sonny Key, 221, 239
South Florida Training Center, 112
Southwind Pinnacle, 234
Spartan Almahurst, 143
Spartan Hanover, 66, 143, 146
Spearmint, 143, 149, 174
Speed Bowl, 207, 208–209
Speedster, 151
Speedy Count, 133, 136, 142, 189
Speedy Rodney, 138
Speedy Romeo, 148
Speedy Streak, 133
Sports Illustrated, 28, 62–64, 117–118, 120, 207
Sports Illustrated Award of Merit, 61
Spring Sun, 118
Springfield (Il.), 89, 149, 234
Stafford, Jody, 221
Stand By, 142
Standardbred Owners Association, 116
Stanton, Cliff, 23
Stanton Hal, 58
Star's Pride, 50
Starr, Steve, 222
Starral Hanover, 148
State Fairgrounds (Syracuse, NY), 58
Statesman, 39
Steall, Ben, 4, 44, 109, 163–164, 169–170, 172, 203, 205
Steele, John "Doc", 37, 45
Steinbrenner, George, 222
Steve Lobell, 136–138, 141, 149, 175
Stock Split, 134–135
Storm Damage, 143, 151

Story, Harold, 203
Stout Fellow, 103
Stretch Pants, 152
Strike Out, 146
Stubbs, Geneva, 102, 105, 124
Su Mac Lad Series, 182
Sun-Tattler (FL), 61
Sunshine Park, 118
Super Bowl, 137, 146, 190, 207
Super Speedy, 231
Superchick, 106, 148
Surefire Hanover, 143, 174
Surfer Scott, 143
Sweet Edie, 143
Swineboard, George, 71
Sylvester, Charlie, 200
Syosset Garden Club, 108
Syosset Hospital, 160
Syracuse Fairground, 206

-T-
Tallman, Jim, 203
Tammie Hill, 145
Tar Heel, 50, 70, 144, 173
Tarrytown (NY), 28
Tattersalls Pace, 151, 174, 176
Tatum, Mary, 102, 124
Tax, Jeremiah, 62–64
Teague, M., 73
Teddy Hanover, 205
Tempered, 148
Temples Taurus, 205
That's Great, 142
The Blood-Horse, xv
The Kiltie, 73
The Meadows, 157, 172, 194, 214, 215, 216, 220, 229
The Meadowlands, 91, 94, 149–150, 151–152, 155, 159, 170, 177, 178, 179, 182, 186, 190, 199, 200, 206, 207, 208, 213, 216. 229, 233, 235, 237, 239
The Meadowlands Pace, 150, 151, 152, 201
The Widower, 73
Thin Dime, 23, 24
Thomas, Alfred Wanstall "Apples", 3, 5, 22, 47, 55–58, 60, 74, 78, 91, 102, 105, 111, 114, 115, 116. 120, 124, 156, 203, 230, 231
Thomas, Billy, 111
Thomas, Dick, 27
Thomas, Henry, 27, 57
Thomson, Jeanne M., 219
Thor Viking, 191
Thorpe Marge, 142
Three Diamonds, 235
Thro, John K., 133, 134
Thruway Pace, 74
Ticket To Ride, 152
Timothy T, 133
Titan Cup, 106
Titanic, 58
Tokyo Express, 39
Toledo Raceway, 49
Tompkins-Geers Stakes, 72, 177
Toronto Star, 219
Torpedo, 142
Trader Horn, 141, 143
Trader Nardin, 160
Traveling Salesman, 143, 219, 225
Trenton Time, 1, 194, 195, 196–197, 234
Triplement, 207
Troll, Pat, 23
Trooper Chip, 148
Trotting Triple Crown, 136, 138, 139, 175, 190
Troy (PA), 168
Trusty, 159–160

Tryhussey, 50
Turcotte, Ron, 103, 119
Turf Club, 178. 179
T.V. Yankee, 234
Tyler, B, 214, 234
Tyler Hanover, 58, 59

-U-
Ubleis, Adolph, 153
Universal Drivers Rating System, (UDA), 59, 142, 172, 173, 177, 201, 206, 209, 220, 237
United States Harness Writers Association (USHWA), 2, 74, 96, 116, 238
United States Harness Writers Association, Saratoga Chapter, 97
U.S. Pacing Championship, 175
United States Trotting Association (USTA), 10, 35, 116, 173
United States Trotting Association Board of Directors, 61, 95
University of Pennsylvania New Bolton Large Animal Clinic, see New Bolton Center

-V-
Vale Blue, 159
Valentina, 143, 153
Valhalla (NY), 222. 223
Vallery, Harry and Robert, 219
Valley Victory, 234, 240
Vandeweght, Ernie, 63
Vaughan, Bill "Bones", 22, 47, 55, 60, 111, 203
Vernon Downs, 19, 62, 63, 64, 74, 85, 169, 189, 205

Vicar Hanover, 142
Victor Hill, 148
Vivace Song, 58

-W-
Wadkins, Lanny, 83
Wake Forest, 83
Walker, Dan, 137
Wall Street-Nihilator Syndication, 211
Walpes, Randy, 99
Walpes, Ron, 99, 204
Walsh, Tom, 234
Waterville Lakes Hotel Pace, 152
Webster, Ben, 204
Wellwood Hanover, 143, 150, 204
West Palm Beach (FL), 201
Westbury (NY), 224
Westchester County Medical Center, 222
White, Ben, 58
White, Russ, 203
Whitmore, Gil, 20
Whitney, Harry, 58
Wholly Arnie, 153
Widow's Mite, 23, 24
Wilburn, Tom, 203
Wild Horse Annie, 187–188
William Haughton Hall, 239
William Haughton Stakes, 239
Williams, Dick, 204
Williams, Lew, 151
Willglow Jr., 37
Wilmington's Star, 58, 59, 157
Wingfield, Jimmy, 27, 58
Windshield Wiper, 143, 148, 177
Wing, Ted, 204
Wishmaker, 143, 174
Wiswall, Betty, 41

Wiswall, Frank, 41
W.N. Reynolds Memorial, 174
W.N. Reynolds Memorial Fillies, 174
Woodrow Wilson Pace, 151–152, 212, 213–214, 234
Woods, Denny, 37
Woolworth, Norman, 60, 119
World Trotting Derby, 233, 234
Worthy Blue Chip, 150
Worthy Bowl, 143
Worthy Master, 143
Wright, Gordon, 30
Wright, Greg, 150, 151
Wyllie, Dr. William F, 18, 19, 20

-X-Y-Z-

Yonkers Raceway, 5, 25, 31, 32, 40, 42, 44, 45–46, 49, 51, 60, 66, 74, 77, 78, 83, 106, 112, 145, 147, 152, 153, 182, 187, 193, 199–200, 206, 220. 222, 238, 239
Yonkers Trot, 136, 138, 150, 17, 191
Zeller, Mike, 204
Zeyak, Jahn A., 39
Zidek, Jeff, 239
Ziggy The Pianist, 150
Zoot Suit, 136–137
Zweig Memorial, 176, 206